Thomas Muir of Huntershill
Essays for the Twenty First Century

Specially commissioned bust of Thomas Muir by celebrated Scottish artist Alexander Stoddart. On permanent exhibition at Bishopbriggs library. Replica made for the Museum of Australian Democracy on exhibition in Canberra.
Courtesy of East Dunbartonshire Leisure & Culture Trust

Thomas Muir of Huntershill
Essays for the Twenty First Century

Edited by Gerard Carruthers and Don Martin

humming earth

Published by
humming earth
an imprint of
Zeticula Ltd
Unit 13
196 Rose Street
Edinburgh
EH2 4AT
Scotland

http://www.hummingearth.com
admin@hummingearth.com

Friends of Thomas Muir, 102 Crowhill Road
Bishopbriggs, G64 1RP
info@thomasmuir.co.uk

Front Cover image:
Ken Currie, 'The Trials of Thomas Muir'
Oil on Linen (2015)
Collection of Lillie Art Gallery, Milngavie,
East Dunbartonshire Leisure & Culture Trust

Back Cover image: Gabrielle Joy Henderson, with Ken Macintosh, at the
unveiling of Gabrielle's Muir portrait on 20 September 2016.
Photograph by Andrew Cowan

ISBN 978-1-84622-051-7

This collection of essays is affectionately
dedicated to

John S L Watson

who has done so much to promote remembrance of
Thomas Muir of Huntershill
and to inspire many others
to find ways of honouring him.

Acknowledgements

The editors wish to thank the following people, who have helped in different ways with preparing this collection of essays:

Dr Carol Baraniuk
Mungo Bovey QC (Faculty of Advocates)
David Brown (National Archives of Scotland)
Dr Rhona Brown (University of Glasgow)
Ken Currie
Julie Gardham (Glasgow University Special Collections)
Martyn Jones
Dr Craig Lamont (University of Glasgow)
Andrea Longson (Faculty of Advocates)
Peter McCormack (East Dunbartonshire Leisure & Culture Trust)
Dr Colin McIlroy (National Library of Scotland).
Bob Mclean (Glasgow University Special Collections)
Dr Ralph McLean (National Library of Scotland)
Ian Marshall
Kenneth Martin
Janice Miller (East Dunbartonshire Leisure & Culture Trust)
Lesley Richmond (University of Glasgow Archives)
David Roberts
David Smith (East Dunbartonshire Leisure & Culture Trust)
Julie Watson

We are grateful to those who provided illustrations, credits for which appear in each appropriate caption.

We are particularly pleased to have permission to use as our cover image
Ken Currie 'The Trials of Thomas Muir'
Oil on Linen (2015)
Collection of Lillie Art Gallery, Milngavie, East Dunbartonshire Leisure & Culture Trust

Contents

Illustrations

Introduction

Many people in Scotland are at least vaguely aware of the name 'Thomas Muir of Huntershill' even if they are unsure of the man's significance or context. In recent years renewed Scottish interest in John Muir, the pioneer of national parks in the USA, has led to confusion between the two, not least because both now have a 'way' or 'trail' in their honour in Scotland and indeed these trails share a common route for a short distance in the Campsie/Kirkintilloch area. Also in recent years the Friends of Thomas Muir organisation has made a concerted effort to try to ensure that people in Scotland are fully aware of the part that Muir played in promoting some of the most basic of our democratic rights. During 2015 this effort was concentrated in a series of 'Thomas Muir 250' events to commemorate the 250th anniversary of Muir's birth.

Muir was born into a deeply religious family in the High Street of Glasgow, near the old University, on 24 August 1765. In due course Muir attended the University with the intention of qualifying as a Presbyterian minister and during this period the family moved home to the Bishopbriggs mansion of Huntershill House, a name with which he will be forever linked. At Glasgow University Muir changed his career plans and began to study Law, during which time he became aware of many injustices and inequalities in the way that Scottish society was organised. He was soon making his voice heard as a campaigner, both at University and as an elder at his local Cadder Church. In 1792 he became a leading organiser of the various Friends of the People organisations that were set up in that year to campaign for universal suffrage and shorter parliaments. He soon became a marked man and was arrested on a charge of 'sedition', for which he was put in trial at the High Court of Justiciary in Edinburgh. His pleading during the trial amounted to a campaign speech for the introduction of democratic rights. As such it attracted great attention in the press of the day and several editions of the trial proceedings were published and widely circulated. Many people have seen this as a significant event in

Scottish history, poignantly highlighted by Muir's harsh sentence of fourteen years transportation as a convict to Australia.

Over the years a number of biographies have been published, with Christina Bewley's *Muir of Huntershill* (1981) still probably the most useful. However, Muir awaits his definitive biographer. He certainly deserves painstaking and careful assessment, employing the wide range of primary resources that undoubtedly exists. The purpose of the present volume is to provide some suggestions for the direction of studies of this kind. It also includes an international dimension, with contributions from Australia and France on Muir's activities in these countries; and the texts of some high profile tributes to Muir that were paid during 'Thomas Muir 250' year.

Thomas Muir of Huntershill in Memory, Culture & Literature[1]

Gerard Carruthers

On several occasions in 2015 during the 250th anniversary celebrations of the birth of Thomas Muir (1765-1799), a story was reiterated. This was of how the Scottish folksinger, Adam McNaughtan, had sought songs about Muir, the 'father of Scottish democracy', one of the 'martyrs' of 1793, and had found very little. As a result McNaughtan penned his own tribute, which he recorded in 1996:

My name is Thomas Muir as a lawyer I was trained
Remember Thomas Muir of Huntershill
But you've branded me an outlaw, for sedition I'm arraigned
Remember Thomas Muir of Huntershill
But I never preached sedition in any shape or form
And against the constitution I have never raised a storm
It's the scoundrels who've corrupted it that I want to reform
Remember Thomas Muir of Huntershill

M'lord, you found me guilty before the trial began
Remember &c
And the jury that you've picked are Tory placemen to a man
Remember &c
Yet here I stand for judgement unafraid what may befall
Though your spies were in my parish Kirk and in my father's hall
Not one of them can testify I ever broke a law
Remember &c

Yes, I spoke to Paisley weavers and addressed the city's youth
For neither age nor class should be a barrier to the truth
M'lord, you may chastise them with your vitriolic tongue

Portrait of Joseph Hume by Charles Lucy.
Reproduced by kind permission of the V&A, London.

You say that books are dangerous to those I moved among
But the future of our land is with the workers and the young

Members of the jury, it's not me who's being tried
200 years in future they will mind what you decide
You may send me to Van Dieman's Land or clap me in the jail
Grant me death or grant me liberty my spirit will not fail
For my cause it is a just one and my cause it will prevail

With quiet words and dignity Muir led his own defence
He appeared completely blameless to those with common sense
When he had finished speaking the courtroom rang with cheers
Lord Braxfield said, 'This outburst just confirms our greatest fears'
And he sentenced Thomas Muir to be transported 14 years

Gerrald, Palmer, Skirving, Thomas Muir and Margarot
These are names that every Scottish man and woman
       ought to know
When you're called for jury service, when your name is
       drawn by lot
When you vote in an election when you freely voice your thought
Don't take these things for granted, for dearly were they bought[2]

Here, with good reason, Muir is seen as a pioneer of democracy, and citizenship, though the precise and direct impact that he has had on freedom of speech, extension of the franchise or the opening up of jury service is far from historically clear. Indeed, much has been said about Muir's legacy but now is the time to bring the claims, the history, into tighter focus, a project to which this present volume attempts to contribute. One of the things we must do on the way to such evaluation, however, is to bring into site the memorialised Muir, including as Don Martin argues elsewhere in this volume, the oral history. The expressive, retrospective, mythic iterations of Muir are also part of the reformer's legacy. These are part of his historic afterlife, even if sometimes, perhaps, they are things that might not always speak to an absolutely accurate version of Muir's life-time history. The present essay simply sets out, in a way that is far from exhaustive, some of the key materials that have spoken to the memorialisation of Thomas Muir.

Illustrious Martyr in the glorious cause
Of truth, of freedom, and of equal laws.

John Kay's 'Illustrious Martyr' etching of Thomas Muir, 1793. The phrase below perhaps suggests that Kay was a supporter of Muir, although equally well it might just indicate that he was keen to sell prints to supporters. Jimmy Watson Collection.

The most tangible memorialisation of Muir occurred in 1844 with the erection of the Political Martyrs' Monument on Calton Hill in Edinburgh. This commemorates also those tried in the same year as the young lawyer: Thomas Fyshe Palmer (1747-1802), William Skirving (c.1745-96), Maurice Margarot (1745-1815) and Joseph Gerrald (1763-96). The monument's sides are inscribed with its provenance, 'Erected by the Friends of Parliamentary Reform/In England and Scotland./1844'; with:

'I have devoted myself to the cause of The People. It is a good cause – it shall ultimately prevail – it shall finally triumph'. Speech of Thomas Muir in the Court of Judiciary on the 30th August, 1793.

and with:

'I know that what has been done these two days will be Re-Judged'. Speech of William Skirving in the Court of Judiciary on the 7th January, 1794.

The Political Martyrs' Monument was the brainchild of Joseph Hume (1777-1855), a Scottish politician who began his career by buying the seat for Weymouth and identifying as a Tory. His was a chequered biography of public service and eventually he became associated with the 'Radical' cause campaigning, for instance, for trade union freedoms. Not satisfied with one monument to Muir *et al*, Hume was the driving force behind a second one unveiled in 1852 at Nunhead Cemetery, in south London. If the Edinburgh monument is a familiar part of the capital's skyline, there are probably very few inhabitants of the city who could tell you to whom it is dedicated, or who would know anything about the names of those commemorated if told. Muir's commemoration in Joseph Hume's monuments seems not to have had continuous impact, and it is remarkable that neither of the two modern biographies of Hume think his efforts in memorialising Muir *et al* worthy of mention.[3]

The trials of Muir and the other martyrs certainly had an impact on the first generation of British Romantic writers. For Samuel Taylor Coleridge (1772-1834) waxing lyrical in a lecture in 1795, it was Joseph Gerrald particularly who caught the imagination:

Withering in the sickly and tainted gales of a prison,
his healthful soul looks down from the citadel of his
integrity on his impotent persecutors. I saw him in the
foul and naked room of a jail – his cheek was sallow with
confinement – his body was emaciated, yet his eye spoke
the invincible purposes of his soul, and his voice still
sounded with rapture the successes of freemen, forgetful of
his own lingering martyrdom![4]

Sharing Gerrald's qualities and fate was the 'illustrious triumverate',[5] Muir, Palmer and Margarot and in his lecture, Coleridge read a poem, 'To the Exiled Patriots' by Robert Southey (1774-1843). It begins:

Martyrs of Freedom — ye who firmly good
Stept forth the champions in her glorious cause,
Ye who against Corruption nobly stood
For Justice, Liberty, and equal Laws.[6]

These lines by Southey and Coleridge's pamphlet-lecture were echoed in the famous John Kay print of Muir: 'Illustrious Martyr in the glorious cause/Of truth, of freedom, and of equal laws'. From early on then Muir *et al* were couched in terms of secular martyrdom, even if perhaps Muir and also Palmer at least were imbued by religious as much as earthly conviction. Southey's 'To the Exiled Patriots' ends rousingly:

So shall your great examples fire each soul,
So in each free-born breast for ever dwell,
Till Man shall rise above the unjust controul—
Stand where ye stood, and triumph where ye fell.[7]

Muir and the martyrs, then, exemplify an interesting moment in the early romantic period as the French Revolution and fin de siècle moment of the 1790s optimistically reached for the idea of a transfiguration of the human lot. This meant quite precisely appropriating a language of sanctity for matters secular, and was a key component in the unfolding Romantic aesthetic of the transcendent.

In a melancholy, hopeful letter of 5 April 1794 to another poet Robert Lovell, Southey reflects on the Botany Bay-bound martyrs, and the circumstances that had given rise to 'To the Exiled Patriots', implicating Muir in the Romantic sense of newness:

> [...] poor Gerald cannot possibly survive his ~~trial~~ {voyage}. Muir's mother is actually dying of a broken heart. have you seen the very beautiful address from the Sheffield society to these virtuous exiles? Wyndham wished the same laws were established in England when William Penn was tried for speaking seditious words in Gracechurch Street the Recorder declared that it would never be well for England till the Inquisition was introduced. you know the memorable verdict of the jury, & you know the future fate of the founder of Pensylvania. who knows but Muir may prophecy when he says "my imagination sometimes whispers to me, that I shall not be a spectator of inanimate Nature merely, but that I may contemplate an infant empire, a new Europe in embryo".[8]

The life of Robert Burns (1759-1796), an early Romantic, certainly shares some interesting cultural space with Muir (see 'Thomas Muir and Kirk Politics' elsewhere in this volume), but his link with Muir has been factually overdriven. The poet's 'Scots Wha Hae' (1793) is about the reformist struggles in Britain of the 1790s as much as its ostensible theme, the medieval wars of independence in Scotland. However, the text's direct connection with Muir is a myth generated by the fact that, as reported by the *Northern Star* and detailed by the modern scholar James Epstein, 'Scots Wha Hae' was sung at a Chartist dinner in 1838 at which Thomas Muir and Thomas Fyshe Palmer were toasted along with Thomas Paine near Ashton-under-Lyne, Lancashire, and this 'tradition' had possibly been going on for some years.[9] It is in this contemporary context that the radical-leaning, and often unreliable Burns editor, 'Honest' Allan Cunningham (1784-1842) makes the over-driven claim that Burns wrote his song for Muir.[10] Burns's one certain poetic reference to Muir appears in his 'Fragment — Epistle from Esopus to Maria' (written in 1794 or 1795):

> The shrinking Bard adown an alley sculks,
> And dreads a meeting worse than Woolwich hulks —
> Tho' there his heresies in Church and State
> Might well award him Muir and Palmer's fate [11]

Although the poet hints at his own heterodox politics here, the overall strategy is a typical Burnsian poetic manoeuvre of the 1790s: relegating serious political reference within apparent comedy. 'Esopus to Maria' details Burns's embarrassment over a social faux pas (that Burns's biographers have never fully explained) which caused a breach with the family of his patron, Robert Riddell (including Riddell's sister-in-law, Maria).

However, the fate of Muir, Gerrald *et al*, likely did make Burns along with other Romantic writers, wish, indeed, for 'a new Europe' and see Muir as one of the leaders consciously looking towards this new age. It is in this mood generally that Burns pens 'Is there for honest poverty' ('A man's a man for a' that') in 1795.[12] After the general highpoint in the Romantic sensibility of the 1790s, Muir and his transported colleagues, if not exactly forgotten, seem to be names much less directly with which to conjure. In the Scottish literary imagination, particularly, we have only infrequent referencing of Muir. A most striking refraction occurs in the work of John Galt (1779-1839), in the novel *Annals of the Parish* (1821). Galt's main character is the Reverend Micah Balwhidder who fearfully dreams at the beginning of the year 1793 of an 'old popish kirk' from which the dead rise from their tombs and process towards a city where there is a tower on which Balwhidder reads the words 'Public Opinion'. Then a storm of fire destroys the processing revenants, and the wind blows them back to their tombs which again slam shut on their occupants. Balwhidder sees this dream as a prophecy, since shortly afterwards King Louis XVI of France is beheaded, on 21 January 1793. Forearmed by his prophetic dream, Balwhidder preaches against the revolution the next Sunday in his fictional Ayrshire parish of Dalmailing. However, some days later Mr Cayenne, the local magistrate who has made his money in the sugar plantations and who has arrived back in Scotland with a black servant in tow, has in front of him two weavers to be examined on suspicion of high treason. Cayenne arraigns the suspects in front of Balwhidder and other respectable worthies of the parish summoned for the occasion. Our clergyman relates what happens next:

> [He] began to ask them how they dared to think of dividing, with the liberty and equality of principles, his and every other man's property in the country. The men answered him in calm manner, and told him they sought no man's property, but only their own natural rights; upon which he called them traitors and reformers. They denied they were traitors, but confessed they were reformers, and said they knew not how that should be imputed to them as a fault, for that the greatest men of all times had been reformers, – "Was not," they said, "our Lord Jesus Christ a reformer?" "And what the devil did He make of it?" cried Mr. Cayenne bursting with passion; "was He not crucified?" I thought, when I heard these words, that the pillars of the earth sunk beneath me, and that the roof of the house was carried away in a whirlwind. The drums of my ears crackit, blue starns danced before my sight, and I was fain to leave the house and hie me home to the manse, where I sat down in my study, like a stupefied creature awaiting what would betide. Nothing, however, was found against the weaver lads; but I never from that day could look on Mr Cayenne as a Christian, though surely he was a true government man.[13]

Mr Cayenne's uttered words about Christ's failure mimic comments attributed to Lord Braxfield, the chief trial judge at Muir's trial. Variously, Braxfield's words are accounted for as uttered at Gerrald's trial, or, alternatively in Muir's mythic afterlife at the latter's court appearance.[14] The weaver-lads, clearly, represent a version of Muir in his Christian idealism, an importantly real aspect that ought not to be forgotten in the formation of his 'democratic' outlook. Muir's radically active, idealistic perspective is not the result of contemporary secular thinking only, the ideas of Thomas Paine, for instance (undoubtedly influential on Muir though these are), but as we'll see elsewhere in this volume pertain also to his Presbyterian sensibilities. In his historical sensitivity, Galt, a Tory registers in his fictional episode Muir's Christian conscience as well as the way in which Muir's trial was flagrantly, brutally unfair.

There seems to have been something in the zeitgeist in 1821, when Galt was completing *Annals of the Parish* as between this year and 1830, Henry (Lord) Cockburn (1779-1854) was compiling his *Memorials of His Time* a work which was posthumously published in 1856. Cockburn, a Whig, had become Solicitor General for Scotland in 1830 and a judge of the Court of Session in 1834. As a pillar of the Scottish legal establishment Cockburn looked back on the sedition trials of 1793-4 and saw scared, over-excitement where the high court of justiciary had not acquitted itself well:

> The madness of the people, if it existed, would have
> been best allayed by giving them reason to rely on the
> administration of justice. But I fear that no impartial censor
> can avoid detecting, throughout the whole course of the
> trials, not mere casual indications of bias, but absolute
> straining for convictions.[15]

In the early part of the nineteenth century British politics in general seemed more settled and – especially after the defeat of Napoleon – there was nothing like the sense of threat that had been perceived in the 1790s. Albeit not always smoothly, the causes of Reform and Chartism gradually found legally acceptable spaces in which to operate from the 1830s. The memory of Muir in printed popular culture, though scarce as Adam McNaughtan was to find in the twentieth century, was not altogether missing during this period. In the pamphlet collection, *The Altar of Liberty* (1842), we see a clear transmission of Muir's reputation through the movement of Chartism.[16] In this publication we are presented with 'A Song, Political Martyrdom of Thomas Muir, Esq written 1837':

> Immortal Patriotic Martyr,
> Robb'd and wrong'd in Freedom's cause;
> Tyrants have destroyed the charter
> Of our freedoms and our laws.
> We detest the Tory tyrants—
> Scourges fierce of former times;
> We abhor their legal murders,
> Massacres, and fiendish crimes.

CHORUS
Shade of Muir, immortal spirit,
Boast and glory of the free,
Bards shall sing his deeds of merit,
*   And their song shall deathless be.*

Tory tyrants we abhor them,
Foes to truth and human joy,
The guiltless daily fall before them,
And the virtuous they destroy.
    Muir, the virtuous Muir they murder'd,
By a sentence far from just;
Still his judges and his jury
Fill our bosoms with disgust.
Shade of Muir, immortal spirit, &c.

Much of human ill he suffered,
In his country's cause he fell—
Was on Freedom's altar offered
Much we in his virtues glory,
Human weal was all his aim,
And a Patriot which story
Has enrolled and deathless fame.
Shade of Muir, immortal spirit, &c.

Patriotic Muir, and daring,
Rous'd to tell the people's wrongs,
Like a meteor appearing,
Told what unto man belongs.
It was criminal, great martyr!
To say mankind should be free:
    They've destroyed our rightful charter,
They who wrong'd and murder'd thee!
Shade of Muir, &c.

We will sing thy deeds of glory,
We will fight in Freedom's cause;
We will curse the ruthless Tory,
Framer of Tyrannic Laws.

We will tread the paths of virtue,
We, as men, our rights will claim,
We, like thee, are foes to Tyrants,
Truth and Justice is our aim.
Shade of Muir, &c.[17]

Written in the same decade, 'Epitaph on Thomas Muir' appears in the collection, *Corn Law Rhymes* (1831) by the Yorkshire Chartist and poet, Ebenezer Elliott (1781-1849):

Thy earth, Chantilly, boasts the grave of Muir,
The wise, the lov'd, the murder'd, and the pure!
While in his native land the murderers sleep,
Where marble forms in mockery o'er them weep;—
His sad memorials, telling future times
How Scotchmen honour worth, and gibbet crimes.[18]

The conclusions drawn by these texts, that Muir was engaged in an important constitutional fight and that he was destroyed by the state are reasonable enough and clear-sighted historical positions. With both *The Altar of Liberty* and *Corn Law Rhymes*, we glimpse something of the cultural depiction of Muir that presumably also inspires Joseph Hume in his Muir memorialisation project of the 1840s and 1850s. These poetry publications prove that Hume was not unique in being imaginatively drawn to Muir, and, as mentioned earlier, Muir was toasted during at least one significant Chartist dinner in England in 1838 and likely more. A great deal more work remains to be done, however, on the precise strength and formulation of the nineteenth-century memory of Muir, including in the context of English and Scottish Chartism. This is something that in itself would make an excellent PhD topic for a resourceful postgraduate student.

Later in the nineteenth century, the 1793 martyrs and, indeed, their nemesis Lord Braxfield powerfully underwrite *Weir of Hermiston* (a novel unfinished at the time of its author's death in 1894) by Robert Louis Stevenson (1850-94). As David Angus has detailed from this text:

If we examine the professions of the five condemned
Radicals whose names appear on the Calton obelisk, we
find that they coincide remarkably with those of Archie
Weir and the four Black Brothers (i.e. young Kirstie's
brothers) in the novel:

Thomas Muir was an advocate, which is what Archie had
   aimed to be.
Thomas Fyshe Palmer was a preacher, like Gib Elliot.
William Skirving was a farmer, like Hob Elliot.
Maurice Margarot was a merchant, like Clem Elliot.
Joseph Gerrald was not, of course, a Burnsian poet,
   like Dand Elliot, but being an orator, he *was* a
   wordsmith, we may say.[19]

Stevenson was particularly fascinated by Braxfield, prompted by
the Henry Raeburn portrait about which he writes in his collection
of essays, *Virginibus Puerisque and Other Papers* (1881). It is
tempting to see the idealistic young Archie Weir who comes into
conflict with his father Adam Weir (the Braxfield figure) as a version
of Thomas Muir, Archie being treated with contempt by Adam as an
over-sensitive dilettante (though I think we can be certain that this
was not the view that Thomas Muir's father, James, entertained
of his son, even if it might have been Braxfield's perspective on
his younger legal colleague). However, along with the Raeburn
portrait, the most likely prompt to Stevenson's bringing Braxfield
so vividly to life in Adam Weir is again Cockburn's *Memorials*,
which Stevenson would have known well. The 'giant of the bench',
Weir senior, dominates Stevenson's novel, like Braxfield in
Cockburn's words 'without any taste for refined enjoyment, [and
his] strength of understanding, which gave him power without
cultivation, only encouraged him to a more contemptuous disdain
of all natures less coarse than his own'.[20] One wonders if this
version of Braxfield, channelled by Stevenson and before him
Cockburn (very much representing the Whig interest), is actually a
bit fictitious, the product of propaganda rather than being entirely
true to life. As we find in Gordon Pentland's essay elsewhere in this
volume, the various trial reports, each with its vested interest, gives
some doubt as to the veracity of all of Braxfield's brutal supposed

Etched glass window by Anita Pate memorialising Muir; installed at Cadder Church in November 2015.

pronouncements.[21] It must also be said, however, that even if all this is the case, it does little to exonerate Braxfield from his leading part in the sedition trials of the 1790s.

During the twentieth century, Muir and Braxfield and their entanglement during the 1790s have almost invariably been cast by creative writers of drama and novels as representing light and darkness. *A Prophet's Reward* (1908) by EH Strain (*d.* 1934) is perhaps the least political fictional treatment of Muir and it also dares to enter into a little nuanced psychology, something that usually tends to be missing from fictional treatments of our young protagonist. In Strain's novel, Colonel Charles Stirling of Balgray (the narrator) is witness to the events of Muir's downfall, and through his eyes we see a rather pious, naïve, impetuous, proud Muir whose naïve optimism is ultimately his signature quality. Stirling tries to warn Muir in advance of his trial that there are traps being set for him, that things will be managed and that the fight he is entering into is not a fair one. Colonel Stirling recommends that Muir should employ Henry Erskine an individual who has dangled before his young legal colleague the possibility that his skills might bring off a 'not proven' verdict. Muir though rebuffs the idea of Erskine representing him:

> 'I'll say to you what there was no use in saying to him,'
> said he, 'that it would be an ill return for his friendship
> to thrust him into danger! If half be true that comes to
> my ears (oh, I'm not wholly cut off from the world!) his
> popularity has suffered already, and very sorely, through
> his association with me. I will do him no more harm than I
> can help.'
> 'Maybe' (I tried the effect of a gibe,) 'maybe you covet the
> opportunity to exhibit your own powers?'
> He took it quite seriously. 'There's just the spice of truth
> in that which makes it sting,' said he. 'Not from vanity; God
> knows I would never compare myself with Harry Erskine!
> But it is a great opportunity; I do think it would be wrong
> to let it slip. The objects we aim at are our legal rights; a
> court of justice cannot but pronounce them so. And if they
> be, where's the crime in seeking to get them authoritatively
> reaffirmed?'

Cairn in memory of Thomas Muir, erected by John Watson at Huntershill Village, Bishopbriggs.

He rubbed his hands together, like a man contemplating
an enticing prospect. 'Man,' said he, 'think of the
satisfaction of getting the claim upheld by my very judges!'
  'You're infinitely more likely to fail!'
  'Yes. I don't close my eyes to that probability. But it's my
opportunity as it's no-one else's, and I think myself bound
to take it.'[22]

It is in the later twentieth century, however, that Muir's currency
has markedly quickened. In 1984, Muir played by the excellent Bill
Paterson, appeared prominently in Scottish Television's 24-part
series, *Scotland's Story*, a series in its left and nationalist leaning
tendencies that owed much to the political and cultural outlook
of the 7:84 theatre company, founded by John McGrath (1935-
2002) and others in 1971. Muir also features in McGrath's *Border
Warfare* (1989), his trial staged replete with stirring Burnsian
music, and a narrative that is as black and white as they come. If
McGrath's agit-prop wears its heart on the sleeve, the most recent
fictional rendition of Muir is generically odd. Murray Armstrong's
The Liberty Tree (2014) is often a rattling good read but is caught
somewhere between a novel and a biography and it ends up being
neither. Cheer-leader rather than scholar, Armstrong presents an
unproblematic leftist nationalist version of Muir (soaked in the
atmosphere of the 2014 Scottish Referendum). It concentrates
almost entirely on the 'sexy' 1790s and incorporates a large amount
of dubious interpretation and 'fact'. Its principle value, perhaps, is
in highlighting the urgent need in the early twenty-first century for
an academic biography of Muir.
  Literature, however, has not been alone in the recent
commemorations of Thomas Muir. The remarkable bust of
Thomas Muir by Alexander Stoddart (2009) on permanent
exhibition at Bishopbriggs Library (with a replica on exhibit
in Sydney, Australia, as discussed elsewhere in this volume by
Beverley Sherry), the equally superb painting by Ken Currie,
'The Trials of Thomas Muir' (2015; currently on display in
East Dunbartonshire) and the lovely embossed window (2015)
memorialising Muir at Cadder Kirk by Anita Pate, are all artefacts
attesting to the enduring heroic inspiration of our young lawyer.
In many ways these productions have been led by the remarkable

efforts of the Watson family (Alex and Jimmy Watson both
contribute to the present volume). Jimmy has also been largely
responsible, as Chair of the Friends of Thomas Muir, along with
Secretary, Don Martin, and other colleagues in the Society, for
establishing the successful 'Thomas Muir Heritage Trail' (even if
occasionally mistaken by some tourists with the legacy of John
Muir, the great environmentalist!). The Friends of Thomas Muir
are also now (in 2016) in their sixth year of the 'Thomas Muir
Festival' with the events of 'Thomas Muir 250' (2015) behind them
and so the commemoration of Muir is now stronger than ever
before. At the highest level of the Scottish political class (see Alex
Salmond's contribution to this volume), there are suggestions that
Muir might become much more of a national figure. It should also
be mentioned that the Watson family has delightful longstanding
form with Thomas: patriarch John Watson having established
his Huntershill Village business in 1995, across the road from the
remarkably extant Muir family home (an attractive eighteenth-
century mansion-house). The stone and brass memorial at
Huntershill Village, supported by efforts of local trade unions
(on occasion even personally polished by John) is quite simply a
beautiful tribute to Muir and his fellow martyrs. Much has been
done to remember Thomas Muir though much more might yet be
done.

Notes and References

1 See also, alongside the present essay, Pentland, 2016, pp.207-23.
2 McNaughtan, A, 1996. Last Stand at Mount Florida. Cockenzie, East Lothian: Greentrax Recordings.
3 Huch and Ziegler, 1985; and Chancellor, 1986.
4 Coleridge, 1971, p.17.
5 Coleridge, 1971, p.14.
6 Coleridge, 1971, p.16.
7 Coleridge, 1971, p.14.
8 Southey, R, 2009. *The Collected Letters of Robert Southey*, Part 1: 1791-97, ed L Pratt. In: *Romantic Circles*: https://www.rc.umd.edu/editions/southey_letters/Part_One/HTML/letterEEd.26.85.html
9 Epstein, 1994, p.193.
10 A forthcoming essay by Gerard Carruthers, Pauline Mackay and Ralph Mclean will discuss Cunningham and 'Scots Wha Hae' in more detail.
11 Burns, 1968, vol.2, p.770 (ll.39-42).
12 However, for a very different, indeed, hostile contemporary literary engagement with Muir see Leask, 2007, pp.48-69.
13 Galt, 2015, p.73.
14 See, for instance, another novel about Muir by Olly Wyatt, *The Democrat* (Azimuth, 2012).
15 Cockburn, 1856, p.99.
16 I am grateful to Dr Michael Shaw for pointing me towards this source. His own research here has been in the context of the Carnegie-funded project which will run from 2016 until 2018, 'The People's Voice: Poetry, Song and the Franchise in Scotland, 1832-1918' led by Catriona Macdonald, Kirstie Blair and myself.
17 Anon, 1842, pp.7-8.
18 Elliott, 1840, p.115.
19 Angus, 1993, pp.87-8.
20 Cockburn, 1856, pp.113-4.
21 The editors of the present volume are currently considering a project to collate the various versions of Muir's trial, in an attempt to compare and test their veracity.
22 Strain, 1908, pp.312-3.

In Search of Muir and Truth ... 250 years on

Jimmy Watson

While considering what I might contribute to this book I started to think about the sequence of events that brought me to this point. I certainly didn't set out to form a charity or to become the Chair of an organisation celebrating Thomas Muir; this all seems to have 'just happened'. I can remember knocking on doors and finding that there were other people who had a real interest in Thomas Muir. All of them said that Muir should be remembered and much better known. Contemplating their enthusiasm and sincerity I soon found myself faced with a decision on what to do. I was meeting some incredibly interesting people, who were all specialists in different areas of research. I also realised that their research seemed to overlap, but I became excited at the prospect of bringing them all together. And indeed this has become my role – one that I enjoy and have been privileged to be a part of. From starting out as an enthusiastic local resident dabbling in history who didn't see any harm in letting the truth get in the way of a good story, I've become someone who now doggedly attempts to seek out the truth ... wherever that may lead ... backed up by research and facts.

It began with the realisation that something needed to be done about the level of awareness in my own wee community of Bishopbriggs. This came about after hearing my father (John Watson) and Davie Waterston (alias 'the singing ex-polis') give their Thomas Muir of Huntershill presentation to a group of '1820 Society' members at the Thomas Muir Coffee Shop. My father had been championing the memory of Thomas Muir in our community for many years: he's proud of his Auchinairn upbringing. He left school at 15 to start his own business, which he established at the Huntershill Lodge House. This locality was his link to the 'world of Thomas Muir'. In the early nineties he purchased and converted an old derelict joiner's workshop opposite Huntershill House, which he named the 'Thomas Muir Coffee Shop'. It was also at this time that he read that a lump of stone had been purchased about 1838 to build a monument to Muir in the grounds of Huntershill. Charles Tennant of St Rollox, who appears to have been leading this project, died suddenly and along with him the opportunity to build the monument. To make up for this, my father, with some funding from Strathkelvin District Council, built the 'Thomas Muir Cairn' and mounted the 'Political Martyrs' Gate' on what was part of the grounds of Huntershill.

If I'm being honest, my belief for a long time was that if it had been left to my father and his friend Davie to keep this man's memory alive, he can't be that significant – so there it was, my own ignorance holding me back from listening, from learning. But something shifted in my head that afternoon in the Thomas Muir Coffee Shop with the enthused 1820 diehards ... for the first time I heard the essence of a young man fighting for a cause that he believed in. I started to read and find out more ... starting with books that my father had had on his book shelves ... Christina Bewley, Frank Clune, John Earnshaw, Michael Donnelly, Hector MacMillan ... amongst others.

Service of dedication at the unveiling of the Thomas Muir Cairn at Huntershill Village, Bishopbriggs on 24 August 1997; with the Reverend Dane Sherrard (Cadder Church), John Watson and assembled company.

I was surprised to discover very little reference to Muir on the East Dunbartonshire Council website. The website didn't even include the museum to Thomas Muir in Bishopbriggs Library or the specially commissioned bust of Muir by Alexander Stoddart exhibited there. I visited the Museum at the Library, which was looking a bit the worse for wear – a very small area, lights not working and in use for the storage of boxes of pamphlets. The centrepiece amongst the disarray of randomly stored brown cardboard boxes was Stoddart's magnificent bust of Muir ... quietly waiting to be remembered. When I met with Conservative Councillor Billy Hendry he promised that this would change and we set up the Thomas Muir Steering Group. I had met Don Martin with my father at a Doors Open Day event some years previously. My father explained that Don had arranged a Thomas Muir exhibition in earlier years and would wish to be involved. The Steering Group became the Friends of Thomas Muir, a registered charity. We drew up a list of aims and objectives, one of which was to raise the profile of Muir both locally and nationally. To achieve this, we realised that we needed historians and politicians at all levels discussing and debating Thomas Muir's contribution to democracy in a Scottish, UK and international context. In partnership with the University of Glasgow and East Dunbartonshire Council the Friends of Thomas Muir embarked on a Festival to begin the process. Included in the Festival was *Thomas Muir's Place in History,* a symposium at Tom Johnston House, Kirkintilloch, in 2011.

Group of contributors, along with East Dunbartonshire Councillors and others, at the first Friends of Thomas Muir Symposium, Tom Johnston House, Kirkintilloch, on 25 May 2011.

During this period Iain Arnott (former Mugdock Park Manager and Tourism Officer for EDC) encouraged the Friends of Thomas Muir to develop a walking trail within East Dunbartonshire. When we looked at options we realised that a number of our local communities had links to the Thomas Muir story; and so the Thomas Muir Heritage Trail was born. From our first red line drawn on an Ordnance Survey map, to a professionally designed map and accompanying booklet, we watched it develop. It is now firmly established, with signage, way markers and interpretation panels at key points along the route. It has featured in a number of publications, including BBC Scotland's website and *The Herald's* 'Scottish Walks' quarterly supplement.

First ceremonial walk along the new Thomas Muir Trail, Sunday 29 May 2011. Photographed at the John McFarlan memorial, Campsie Glen.

The present book is a wonderful opportunity to draw together the papers and research of recent years; also to draw a line under the work previously carried out and take it to a wider audience and hopefully inspire others to collaborate on the work of continuing and advancing research into Thomas Muir, his contemporaries and the rich period of political enlightenment of his day. We believe that there must be letters and papers in private collections waiting to be rediscovered. Perhaps what we find may not paint the ideal picture of Muir but this should not be seen as a disservice to his memory or as in any way undermining his achievements and the impact he had. We need to avoid linking Muir to personal political beliefs or ignoring his flaws. We need to put things into context. There was only one politics in Muir's time: you either had a vote or you didn't ... all other political ideas and assertions came secondary to this.

Having read, listened to and been part of many discussions involving Muir, it's my view that:

It is important to seek out the truth, in whatever form that it may take. To some Muir is a hero, to others he was foolish and reckless. Either way his story is significant and is rooted in an important period of Scottish, British and world history. Complicated and diverse – but what makes research into Thomas Muir so interesting and rewarding is that he was at logger heads with so many key people of the time. Thomas Muir becomes a means of navigation through a highly significant period in our history. His network and reach were truly far reaching and influential. The stance that Muir made at his trial enabled the concept of universal suffrage to be carried to a much wider audience; this is the essence of what the Friends of Thomas Muir remember and celebrate.

Over a few short years we established the Thomas Muir Festival as an annual event. It progressed from a local Bishopbriggs commemoration to an East Dunbartonshire-wide festival. Fundamentally, it was community-led and utilised existing community and business venues. In 2014 lamp post banners and venue banners went up across East Dunbartonshire. Every town and village had a contribution to make to it in one way or another. It was an unbelievable achievement in such a short space of time, especially as we were working to a very small budget and relying on goodwill and funding in-kind. Thomas Muir's place within East Dunbartonshire was firmly re-established.

Our next challenge was to take all this experience and goodwill to a national level. Realising that 2015 would be the 250th anniversary of Thomas Muir's birth we had an obvious focus, but we had to carefully consider ways of organising a local and national festival in tandem. We decided that for the anniversary year we would concentrate our energy and effort on a national celebration. We drew up a list of events and decided to advertise these widely throughout the year. We also decided that a national committee should be formed, which should reflect different aspects of Thomas Muir's character – these being faith, education, law and politics. Representatives were invited from the main political parties – Jo Swinson MP (Liberal Democrat), Fiona McLeod MSP (SNP), East Dunbartonshire Provost Una Walker (Labour) and Councillor Billy Hendry (Conservative). Other Committee members were Professor Gerard Carruthers (University of Glasgow), the advocate Brian Fitzpatrick, the Reverend Graham Finch (Cadder Parish Church), Don Martin (Secretary of the Friends of Thomas Muir) and myself as Chair of FOTM. In many ways this was a symbolic committee; we met only once, but we had the full support and assistance of all involved. More importantly, it established our academic and cross-party political endorsements.

Dennis Robertson, MSP for Aberdeenshire West, viewing the Thomas Muir Exhibition at the Scottish Parliament, Spring 2015.

During the earlier phases of the project, Fiona McLeod, the MSP for East Dunbartonshire, provided advice on ways that the Scottish Parliament could be involved and over a long period she provided valuable assistance with the celebrations. Through her guidance the Events Team at the Scottish Parliament suggested that mounting a Thomas Muir Exhibition at the Parliament would be an appropriate way of raising awareness of the 250th anniversary with MSPs. This was initially proposed for 2014, as advance promotion of Thomas Muir 250 events in 2015, but with the referendum dominating much of 2014 our slot was held over to the beginning of 2015 ... and so provided an extremely effective platform by means of which to launch 'Thomas Muir 250' year. This was soon followed by an exhibition of John Kay prints at the Thomas Muir Coffee shop in Bishopbriggs during East Dunbartonshire's Local History Week. Thirty original Kay prints were chosen to convey the Thomas Muir story in a way that had never been done before. They were professionally mounted with the assistance of an East Dunbartonshire Arts Council grant. At a related event the relevance of Kay prints to the Muir story and the way that the exhibition had been developed was explained by Don Martin and myself. The exhibition proved to be a great success and has become a permanent feature at the Coffee Shop. We were delighted when STV's Matty Sutton and BBC Scotland's Gillian Sharpe made contact to offer us welcome coverage on TV and radio. After a range of other events during the summer, including a 'Walk & Talk' at St Andrews House/Calton Hill, Edinburgh, on 12 June, organised by the Scottish Local History Forum, focus was placed on Thomas Muir's '250th Anniversary Month' in August.

On 22 August 2015 the Irish Heritage Foundation held an event at the Mitchell Library and invited John Watson, Davie Waterston and myself to talk about Thomas Muir and his link to the United Irishmen. In attendance was Vice Consul of Ireland to Scotland, Anne-Marie Flynn.

On 24 August (Thomas Muir's 'birthday'), East Dunbartonshire Leisure and Culture Trust unveiled a specially commissioned portrait of Muir by artist Ken Currie, titled 'The Trials of Thomas Muir', at the Lillie Art Gallery, Milngavie. This excellent work helps to make up for an undoubted shortage of Muir portraits. It's known that a portrait of Muir hung over the fireplace at

Huntershill at one time, but this has been lost. It is also speculated that the David Martin sketch of Muir that is held in the collection of the Scottish National Portrait Gallery is a preliminary sketch for an intended full size portrait, perhaps now held out of sight in a private collection somewhere. Does the owner know that it is a portrait of Thomas Muir? In the meantime we can anticipate that Ken Currie's new painting will in future play a full part in defining the Thomas Muir legacy.

Unveiling of Ken Currie's new portrait of Thomas Muir at the Lillie Art Gallery, Milngavie, on 24 August 2015; East Dunbartonshire Leisure & Culture Trust event. The artist is on the right, with Jimmy Watson on left.

Later the same day there was an inaugural Thomas Muir Lecture at St Mary's Cathedral, Edinburgh, organised by Word Power Books. Over 500 people attended to hear Alex Salmond present a range of imaginative suggestions as to how Thomas Muir might be commemorated, including: a call for a pardon for

Muir and his fellow political martyrs; renaming of the Scottish government residence at Bute House, Edinburgh, as 'Thomas Muir House'; inclusion of the story of Muir and his fellow Martyrs in the school curriculum; and for a high-profile film of the Life of Muir to be made. Also on 24 August, Murray Armstrong, author of the fictionalised story of Muir, *The Liberty Tree*, gave a lecture at Word Power Books' own premises in Edinburgh.

Donald Findlay QC starring as Lord Braxfield at the re-enactment of Muir's Trial, on 25 August 2015. Faculty of Advocates event at Parliament House, Edinburgh.
Courtesy of the Faculty of Advocates.

At Parliament House on 25 August the Faculty of Advocates restaged the Trial of Thomas Muir, in what turned out to be a truly unique experience. Advocate Ross Macfarlane's skilful editing and narration effectively restored the historic trial to life. The performance was preceded by an enlightening talk by Sir Tom Devine to set the scene of the trial in an appropriate historical context. The inspired casting included Donald Findlay QC as the infamous Lord Braxfield ('The Hingin Judge') and there were convincing performances by all those involved:

NARRATOR: Ross Macfarlane, Advocate
MUlR: Paul Brown, Advocate
DUNDAS: Iain McSporran, Solicitor Advocate
WEDDEL: Neil Murray QC
FREELAND: Frank Burr, Advocate
HENRY: Brian Crook, Advocate
McKlNLAY: David Nicolson, Advocate
WILLIAM MUIR: Gordon Jackson QC, Vice Dean of Faculty
FISHER: Anna Poole QC
JUROR: Alex Prentice QC, Principle Crown Counsel

The restaging of the trial gave valuable insight into the timing and delivery of speeches. In particular it was enlightening to see Muir's reaction when Annie Fisher was called as a witness, giving a completely different interpretation to the usual assumption that he was rude and arrogant about her station in life. In this version it was presented as an exchange between Braxfield and Muir over the sacrosanct nature of a person's home, seen by Muir as a basic civil liberty, with Braxfield and the Lord Advocate setting a dangerous precedent by undermining its privacy.

Professor Nigel Leask and Professor Gerard Carruthers leading the 'Thomas Muir in Literature' guided tour of the Scottish National Portrait Gallery, Edinburgh, on 26 August 2015.

On 26 August Professor Nigel Leask and Professor Gerard Carruthers delivered an imaginative tour entitled 'Thomas Muir in Literature' at the Scottish National Portrait Gallery in Edinburgh. Works were selected from the Portrait Gallery collection to illustrate the life and times of Thomas Muir of Huntershill and his circle. The tour leaders discussed Muir's relationship to Scottish culture in his own day and afterwards. It was a rare and insightful afternoon with impressive literary references.

During the autumn of 2015 East Dunbartonshire Leisure & Culture Trust mounted a commemorative '250th Anniversary Exhibition' at the William Patrick Library, Kirkintilloch, telling the story of Muir's life and times and featuring items from the Thomas Muir collection held by East Dunbartonshire Archives & Local Studies. In a similar way, Edinburgh Central Library agreed to host a Thomas Muir Exhibition at their Edinburgh and Scottish Collection. Provost Una Walker of East Dunbartonshire Council had previously arranged for a formal letter to be drafted and sent to Edinburgh City Council, suggesting that a motion be brought to the Council requesting support for Thomas Muir 250 celebrations. The City Council responded in a magnanimous way and the library exhibition was part of the outcome.

Young musicians at the Friends of Thomas Muir Scottish Parliament reception on 23 September 2015.

An event that took a great deal of planning over a full year from initial contact was the reception to commemorate the 250th Anniversary of Thomas Muir's birth. Fiona McLeod MSP very willingly agreed to act as sponsor and helped to steer this event through to its realisation. She enlisted the help of the Events Team at the Scottish Parliament on the basis that this would be one of the stand-out events of the year. Both the Friends of Thomas Muir and Fiona McLeod were keen to showcase East Dunbartonshire Schools at the reception, in recognition of the cooperation of local schools over the running of annual Thomas Muir symposia in East Dunbartonshire. Each year the symposium is hosted by a different secondary school, with pupils invited to perform music and deliver a short paper on a historical theme, to complement the contributions of academic and other speakers. The 250th Anniversary event was held at the Scottish Parliament on Wednesday 23 September 2015. Speakers included Professor Gerard Carruthers (University of Glasgow), Fiona McLeod (MSP), Rosie Duthie (a pupil from Douglas Academy, Milngavie) and myself. Music was performed by the very talented pupils of Douglas Academy and by professional musicians Stevie Lawrence and Fiona Cuthill. Bishopbriggs Academy pupils performed a short original play. Ryan Corbett, the remarkable young Douglas Academy accordionist, presented the Friends of Thomas Muir with a framed music score of his arrangement of the traditional music that Ryan and his fellow pupils had performed.

From the earliest stages of planning of the Thomas Muir 250 commemoration I had been keen on the idea of a procession through the streets of Edinburgh. I had read about the laying of the foundation stone at the Calton Burying Ground in 1844, with an associated walk through the streets of Edinburgh and this seemed well worth re-enactment, perhaps by re-treading the exact route through the streets, 'marching for democracy'. However, when Friends of Thomas Muir representatives met with Susan Lanham (Senior Events Officer, Edinburgh City Council) she was concerned that the original route posed a problem for modern Edinburgh and its traffic. She suggested that we look at alternatives. This at first caused us concern, as the whole idea was to march 'in the steps of our ancestors', but the idea of setting off from where our ancestors had stopped marching (*i.e.* the site of the Martyrs' Monument in the old Burying Ground) and walking from there to the Scottish Parliament, captured our imaginations. We could be seen as picking up the metaphoric baton from our ancestors, and taking it to its new spiritual home. Having navigated our way through several planning meetings, we had an eleventh-hour hiccup when I was summoned to an emergency licensing meeting to be told that a 'Scotland for Elephants' march and a National Front march were intended for the streets of Edinburgh on the same day. Fortunately, the priority of our plans was respected, but not before a front page headline 'Scottish Defence League thwarted by Elephants and Thomas Muir' appeared in the national press.

'Democracy 250 Walk' through the streets of Edinburgh to the Scottish Parliament, 3 October 2015.

The great event took place on Saturday 3 October. Following a short dedication service at the Martyrs' Monument, the 'Democracy 250 Walk' started out from where our ancestors left off, led by Milngavie Pipe Band and with an 8ft wide banner with the words 'Thomas Muir of Huntershill, Father of Scottish Democracy' emblazoned upon it, hoisted above our heads. So down we went, through the streets of Edinburgh via North Bridge, then onto the Royal Mile, along the Canongate and finally to the Scottish Parliament. Tourists and Edinburgh shoppers were enthused by the spectacle before their eyes. It was a truly memorable experience to walk across the North Bridge with the sounds of pipes resounding and echoing off the ancient buildings of Edinburgh. At the Parliament Fiona McLeod MSP was waiting to meet us and to welcome us on behalf of her Parliamentary colleagues. I said a few words as well, reiterating our motto for the day: 'Celebrating history, by making history'. We then made our way to the Edinburgh City Council offices, where the Lord Provost Donald Wilson of Edinburgh was waiting for us to very kindly host a civic reception. Four other Provosts of Scottish local authorities were also in attendance: Provost Una Walker of East Dunbartonshire, Provost Helen Moonie of South Ayrshire, Provost Mike Robins of Stirling and Provost Pat Reid of Falkirk.

Edinburgh City Council reception, with provosts of Scottish local authorities, 3 October 2015.

On Sunday 25 October, I gave a talk on 'Thomas Muir – a Contemporary of Burns' at the Robert Burns Birthplace Museum, Alloway. There is no historical evidence that Muir and Burns met in real life, but they certainly shared the same period of history and had many personal friends and acquaintances in common. A possible link that has interested many people is the letter Burns wrote with the first draft of 'Scots Wha Hae' to his then publisher George Thomson concerning the air then proposed for the song, namely 'Robert Bruce's March To Bannockburn', and especially a postscript stating that he had been inspired by Bruce's 'glorious struggle for Freedom, associated with the glowing ideas of some other struggles of the same nature, not quite so ancient'.

'Thomas Muir 250' Symposium at the University of Glasgow, 30 October 2015.

On Friday 30 October, a Thomas Muir Symposium, hosted by the University of Glasgow's Burns Centre, was held in The Humanities Lecture Theatre as another 'Thomas Muir 250' landmark event. A newspaper carried the heading, 'Thomas Muir comes in from the cold'. It was significant that after 200 years, Muir's place in history was being discussed and debated where as a young student he had voluntarily expelled himself. Speakers included Dr Rhona Brown, Dr Gordon Pentland, Professor Nigel Leask, Professor Gerard

Carruthers, David Brown, Satinder Kaur and myself. Satinder Kaur also prepared a most interesting exhibition of Thomas Muir documents from the University of Glasgow's archives for participants in the Symposium to inspect.

Unveiling of the Thomas Muir commemorative window at Cadder Church, 14 November 2015.

On the afternoon of Saturday 14 November 2015 a dedication service and unveiling of the Thomas Muir Memorial Window took place at Cadder Church, near Bishopbriggs. Thomas Muir had been an elder of the church and had successfully defended the congregation's right to choose their own minister. The Reverend Graham Finch, who was the minister of Cadder Church during the Thomas Muir 250 commemoration, was one of its most enthusiastic supporters. When he suggested that a new memorial window for Cadder Church might be unveiled during 250th Anniversary Year we were surprised and delighted. It was an ambitious proposal that would catch the imagination of all involved including the congregation and the wider community. Graham formed a memorial window committee to manage and steer the whole process through from the initial engagement of an artist, to congregational approval, to commissioning and the final installation. At the unveiling a few people were surprised that the window was of etched glass rather than stained glass. Graham had suggested Anita Pate as a specialist in engraving. She prepared an extremely attractive proposal that was soon adopted. The unveiling day was a wonderful celebration with representatives from a wide range of organisations. The unveiling was carried out by Sofia Gibson of the 92nd Girl's Brigade and Neil Young of the 212th Boys Brigade. In attendance was Provost Una Walker of East Dunbartonshire Council and there were tributes to Muir paid by Professor Gerard Carruthers (University of Glasgow), Iain McSporran (The Glasgow Bar Association), John Nicolson MP, John Watson and the Reverend Graham Finch.

Gabrielle Joy Henderson, with Scottish Parliament presiding officer Ken Macintosh, at the unveiling of Gabrielle's Muir portrait on 20 September 2016. Photograph by Andrew Cowan

The Friends of Thomas Muir organisation has made a conscious decision to reach out to the local community and engage with people of all ages. In this respect one of the main initiatives is the East Dunbartonshire Schools Art Competition. During 2015 the theme requested was for a 'Thomas Muir 250 Portrait' – the idea being that as one of Scotland most famous artists had been commissioned to paint a 'Portrait of Muir' for display in East

Dunbartonshire, this could be neatly complemented by East Dunbartonshire pupils competing to paint a portrait of Muir to hang at the Scottish Parliament. Artist Ken Currie accepted our invitation to join the judging panel along with Peter McCormack (East Dunbartonshire Leisure & Culture Trust) and Melanie Sims (East Dunbartonshire Arts Council). A portrait by an S6 pupil from St Ninian's High School, Kirkintilloch, Gabrielle Joy Henderson, was selected as the overall winner. Category winners were: John Watson, P1-P3, Meadowburn GU; Eilidh Dolan, P4-P7, Meadowburn; Rhea Williamson, S1-S2, Kirkintilloch High School; and Jeremy Phillips, S3-S4, St Ninian's High School. The following schools were represented in the final: Auchinairn Primary, Baldernock Primary, Bearsden Primary, Craigdhu Primary, Killermont Primary, Kirkintilloch High School, Lenzie Academy, Meadowburn, Meadowburn GU, St Machan's Primary and St Ninian's High School. The portraits were exhibited at the Thomas Muir Coffee Shop, Huntershill Village, Bishopbriggs, during the period 14-28 November 2015. Gabrielle's winning painting was unveiled at the Scottish Parliament on 20 September 2016 by Scottish Parliament Presiding Officer Ken Macintosh.

Other Thomas Muir events during November 2015 included a Thomas Muir 250 Memorial Concert at the University of Glasgow, where the performers included Dick Gaughan, Rallion, Kirkintilloch Male Voice Choir and John McLaughlin (20 November); and on 24 November there was a Schools Debating event 'Thomas Muir and his Legacy' at the National Galleries of Scotland Hawthornden Lecture Theatre on The Mound, Edinburgh. At this event, pupils from across Scotland come together for a debate in celebration of the 250th anniversary of the birth of Thomas Muir. It was organised in partnership with Mr Kenny Gray and Mr Stephen Sinclair (Douglas Academy, Milngavie), the National Portrait Gallery and the Friends of Thomas Muir. The audience watched the participants debating and discussing a range of issues relating to the development of democracy, significantly including the idea that 16 and 17 year-olds should have the right to vote. The QT panel included: Peter Arnott (Playwright), Janette Foggo (Actress), Michael Gray (Journalist), Satinder Kaur (University of Glasgow) and Jimmy Watson (Friends of Thomas Muir, Chair). School pupils asked the panel questions and offered their own views for discussion on democracy and current political events.

As the 'Thomas Muir 250' year came to a close we were all delighted that it had been so well attended and so well received. We believed we had achieved our aim of raising Muir's profile both locally and nationally. New archival sources had been identified and we had generated interest among a wider and growing audience.

Where is all this leading? I can't really say ... academics and future generations will perhaps have access to further sources of information and be able to discuss and debate the strengths and weaknesses of Muir's character much further.

> The records of this trial will pass down to posterity; and gentlemen, when our ashes shall be scattered by the winds of heavens, the impartial voice of future times will rejudge your verdict. *Thomas Muir. August 1793.*

Having read the original trial transcript, I had a very conscious feeling that the stance that Muir and his fellow political martyrs had taken needed to be revisited and reviewed. I would not be so presumptuous as to say that I could for one second truly know what Muir was thinking ... but what he said at his trial and the passion with which he lived his life are truly remarkable – I believe we should attempt to understand these things and to place them both in context; whatever Muir did before or after his trial pales into the background. For by defending himself in the way he did, by stepping into the public arena and pronouncing the idea of Universal Suffrage to a much wider audience, and in doing so using a loop-hole by means of which the court case could be transcribed and reported, he called the Dundas's bluff. The transcript of the trial sold out and then ran to a number of editions, by various publishers. We therefore have a valuable primary source to turn to. One that speaks for itself ... this is where I suggest that the truth of Muir's moment in history lies, the moment that changed the course of democracy in these islands.

'The Father of Scottish Democracy'
1765 - 1799

Events: August to December 2015

National Youth Debate

Exhibitions

Alex Salmond on Muir

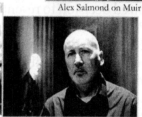

250 Concert
Dick Gaughan & Friends

Signings & Talks

Unveiling New Thomas Muir Portrait
by Ken Currie

'Democracy 250 Walk' from Calton Hill to Parliament with Milngavie Pipe Band

For full event details and to book tickets visit

www.thomasmuir.co.uk

'Thomas Muir 250' programme.

Muir's Trial: a Historical Context

TM Devine

This is an edited transcript of a short lecture given by Professor Emeritus Sir Tom Devine of the University of Edinburgh in Parliament Hall, Edinburgh on 25 August 2015, on the occasion of the reconstruction by the Faculty of Advocates of the trial for sedition in 1793 of the political reformer, Thomas Muir.

Many thanks, Mr Dean, for your generous introduction.

I would like to begin by congratulating the Faculty on its inspired decision to re-enact the historic trial of Thomas Muir here in Parliament Hall on the 250th anniversary of his birth. I note that some distinguished members of the Faculty will take leading roles in the proceedings. This tribute can therefore be regarded more than a piece of fascinating theatre. In March 1792 Muir was unanimously expelled from the Faculty of Advocates and his name struck from the register. In one way, this evening can therefore be seen as a form of rehabilitation for Muir delivered by current members of the Faculty to which he once belonged.

I have been asked to speak briefly on the context of Scotland in the early 1790s in order to provide some historical background to what follows. I will attempt to do this in two parts: first, the origins of Scottish political radicalism in the later eighteenth century; second, why radicalism failed and the old regime which it confronted managed to survive well into the nineteenth century.

Part One

To modern eyes it is scarcely credible that a movement in favour of reforming the political structure was only born in Scotland during the last two decades of the eighteenth century and not before. Even by the standards of that pre-democratic age, both Scottish local and national government were notoriously unrepresentative, corrupt and moribund. Across Britain, the governing assumption was that ownership of fixed property, preferably in land, should alone confer the right to vote. Only those with a firm stake in the land itself, so it was asserted, could be trusted to manage the affairs of the nation with prudence and responsibility. In securing their own property, as the thinking ran, they were also likely to act as the trustees of the country as a whole.

But in Scotland this time-honoured connection between property ownership and political representation was carried to bizarre extremes. Only 3,100 men or around 0.2 per cent of the Scottish population at the time had the right to vote for the 45 parliamentary seats in the counties and the 15 constituencies in the burghs. The electorate of the city of Dublin in Ireland at the time was almost the same size as the total number of voters in the whole of Scotland. Manipulation, brazen corruption and venality in burgh elections were rampant and ensured the perpetuation of self-perpetuating cliques and family oligarchies. The political process was therefore usually regarded with contemptuous indifference by many of those outside the charmed circle of power. In 1790, for instance, such was the lack of interest that only nine of Scotland's constituencies were actually contested in the elections of that year.

Perhaps opposition to such a regime was almost inevitable at some stage, especially in a country which prided itself on the recent flourishing of enlightened thinking and the old Calvinistic ethic of the equality of souls before God. But even modest criticisms only started to emerge in the 1780s with the demand that the franchise in towns be extended to more of the propertied middle classes. Scotland was experiencing by then the early phases of the industrial and urban revolution. At first glance, the political ancien regime with its foundations in ancient landed authority might no longer seem compatible with the changing economic and political structures of the country. The loss of the American colonies in 1783 also served to undermine confidence in government. The humiliation was widely regarded as a scandalous example of incompetence in power.

These, however, were yet but murmurings. It took explosive historic events beyond Scotland to trigger a movement for more radical political change. The outbreak of the French Revolution in 1789 had a catalytic effect not simply on Scotland but throughout

Europe. Crucially it demonstrated that despotic power could not only be challenged but successfully overcome by the collective action of the people. The pace of change across the Channel stimulated intense political debate and interest, not least because the British government continued to resist the modest demands for burghal reform in Scotland. Then in early 1791 the first part of Tom Paine's seminal text, *The Rights of Man*, was published. Unquestionably, it added fuel to the gathering fire. Written in clear and accessible prose, the book had a galvanic effect. It contained a coruscating denunciation of existing power structures, declared the unreformed state was totally incapable of reforming itself and offered a list of the kind of social benefits which could be enjoyed by the common man if universal suffrage came about. Paine showed that politics was not simply an elite game. On the contrary, it mattered a great deal because through reform of the franchise and the achievement of power for the people enormous material improvements in ordinary lives could be delivered. These ideas were revolutionary not reformist in intent. The government banned sales of Paine's writings in May, 1792. Predictably, demand for them became even greater as a result.

Out of this new ferment of political debate came the formation of reform societies across the country followed by the foundation of a national body, the Scottish Association of Friends of the People, in July 1792. The Association was not bent on revolution. Indeed, the objective was in part to steer popular unrest away from Paineite radicalism towards reformism and constitutionalism and so enable liberal-minded members of the propertied classes to support the movement.

However, before the inaugural meeting of the Friends of the People in December 1792 events in France took a dramatic turn. The bloodbath suffered by the French aristocracy and clergy in the 'September Massacres' was widely reported in the Scottish press and the newspapers did not spare readers any of the gory details of the grislier executions by guillotine. From this point on the Revolution, which had been warmly welcomed in Scotland, was increasingly portrayed as a political force which had gone wrong, careered out of control and slid to the depths of murderous anarchy. Plebeian disturbances along the Scottish east coast added to the alarm of the authorities. The French revolutionaries, after their victory over the Duke of Brunswick's great coalition army of European powers, then terrified the ruling classes across the continent by publicly offering military aid to all other peoples who wished liberation from oppression.

Part Two

The combination of the threat from France and fear of plebeian unrest rapidly caused a closing of the ranks of the propertied classes in Scotland. Even before its first meeting, the Friends of the People were already on the defensive. The government went on the attack by arresting Thomas Muir in January, 1793. His trial and the sentence of 14 years transportation to Botany Bay are the subject of the re-enactment which will follow this lecture. The authorities were now able to strike hard. A series of sedition trials were organised, the Act against Wrongous Imprisonment, the Scottish equivalent of Habeus Corpus, suspended and a general witch-hunt unleashed against any suspected radicals among the professional classes. The businesses of tradesmen thought to be sympathetic to radicalism also suffered from boycott and workers of the same ilk were often dismissed from their employment. Ministers of the Church of Scotland and other congregations railed against the Friends of the People from the pulpits and roundly condemned parliamentary reform as a mortal threat to the very existence of Christianity itself.

Not surprisingly the tiny Scottish electorate representing established power was well pleased. In the elections of 1796 the government won the largest number of seats ever recorded since 1707. Any opposition which survived now went underground. Radicalism did not disappear and indeed developed fresh sources of support among the industrial working classes after the Napoleonic Wars. Not until 1832, however, four decades after Muir's trial, was a successful attempt made to even partially reform the British constitution.

Clearly, the ancien regime of Scotland was much more resilient than its opponents had believed. The ruthless actions and revengeful reprisals enforced by government authorities in implicit alliance with a conservative judiciary is only part of the explanation for this. Events in France were also clearly decisive, showing as they did that constitutional reform could easily degenerate into social revolution which threatened the lives and property of the elites. When France declared war against Britain in February 1793 the days of public dissent were well and truly numbered. Those who had shown sympathy for the Revolution in France were now easily branded as the enemy within, not only disaffected from the state but potentially guilty of treason against the nation as well.

Moreover, unlike the nobility and petty landowners of France, the Scottish landed classes did not feel threatened by the new economic order which was beginning to emerge. Arguably, they were at the height of their powers, in possession of swelling rent rolls as urban markets expanded for the produce of their estates and new opportunities emerged for their male progeny in the territories of the British empire across the globe. The unreformed state may have been archaic in terms of political representation but it was more in tune with current economic developments. Its trade tariffs, naval power overseas and accommodating commercial law all gave direct or indirect support to the rapid advance of capitalism. The merchants and manufacturers of the towns may have resented landed power but were aware that its policies often coincided with their own economic interests. Thus was exclusion from political representation assuaged and compensated.

Indeed, landed authority was further consolidated as the wealthiest from the urban areas commonly bought into land as a public demonstration of their success in life. But this practice did not threaten bourgeois conquest of the landed interest's traditional preserves. Only the really affluent managed to secure broad acres of any extent and even their estates were relatively small in size compared to the vast properties of the ancient aristocracy and greater laird classes. As a result, for a time at least, their power remained undisturbed and potential urban opposition easily absorbed within the existing order. In that solid elite world of the eighteenth century the failure of Thomas Muir and the other radicals of the time was hardly surprising.

Reviving the Spirit of the Country: ideas for the commemoration of Thomas Muir

Alex Salmond

This essay is the edited text of the inaugural Thomas Muir Memorial Lecture delivered by the Right Honourable Alex Salmond MP PC on 24 August 2015 in St Mary's Cathedral, Edinburgh. It has been edited by Professor Michael Russell from a recording made at the event.

I was invited to give this inaugural Thomas Muir lecture at the Thomas Muir Memorial Exhibition held in the Scottish Parliament earlier this year.[1] The invitation came from Elaine Henry of Word Power Books. Whether as precaution or not, she did have a very large dog beside her when she asked me but that type of persuasion, or any type of persuasion, was unnecessary as I have long nurtured a passion for the memory and the influence of Thomas Muir. I want to see him commemorated in a number of different ways in Scotland and abroad and this inaugural lecture gives me the chance to outline some ideas about those commemorations. Word Power Books has been responsible for publishing many important contributions to Scottish thought and amongst those is Murray Armstrong's account of the life of Thomas Muir which of course is featured at the Edinburgh Book Festival this year. The detailed facts of Muir's life are still obscure but what we know, and what Murray has now presented us with, is an astonishing tale.

It is primarily a tale of the power of radical thought and that is a strong message for our times. But it is also a tale of how that radical thought developed in Scotland in the 1790s – and indeed elsewhere in Europe – thanks to the emergence of an educated and literate working class, able to be mobilised. That fact alone calls into question the charge of 'unconscious sedition' brought against Muir, for workers in Scotland and elsewhere were increasingly keen to be informed and motivated. They consciously, not unconsciously, sought change. It was the extraordinary Lord Braxfield,[2] the presiding judge at Muir's trial, who used that phrase of course and invented that legal concept in order to secure a conviction. Braxfield is the classic villain in this tale, the man who appears to want to be hated. Yet Braxfield is also the pithiest contributor to this story, and my favourite Braxfield remark is his repost to one of Muir's co-accused, Joseph Gerrald. When Gerrald pointed out to the court that Jesus Christ was a reformer, Braxfield growled in reply 'an muckle guid it did him, he was hangit'.

The Right Honourable Alex Salmond MP PC delivering the Thomas Muir Memorial Lecture in St Mary's Cathedral, Edinburgh, on 24 August 2015. Photograph by Lisa Ferguson, courtesy of The Scotsman.

It is not my intention here to tell the story of Muir's life either before or after the famous trial of 1793. Others are researching those facts with great skill and discovering more and more about the man himself, including his amazing ability to annoy and upset so much of any establishment with which he came into contact – church, university or the law. They are also discovering more about his amazing courage and daring. Muir was in Botany Bay for two and half years before he escaped but when he did get away he did it with style. He crossed the pacific to Vancouver Island, and then went on to California. California was under Mexico's control at the time so he travelled on from there and subsequently to Havana. From there he went to Spain and then to France – a complete circumnavigation of the globe – and it was in France that he spent the last year of his too short life. Those incidents alone make Muir's life a most extraordinary tale of courage and determination which is worthy of a telling. But of course we remember him for something even greater – his contribution to radical thought and democratic progress.

Because the tale of Thomas Muir has been so well told, by Murray Armstrong as well as by an increasing number of others including Professor Gerry Carruthers (who later this week will give a talk and guided tour at the National Portrait Gallery, focussing on Muir) I am not going to spend this lecture retelling it. What I want to do is to draw some lessons from the tale and make some proposals about how we can get the name of Thomas Muir, and others, as well as the story of this hugely important period of Scottish history better understood and better known.

Like many people, I first came across the name of Thomas Muir listening to the singer Dick Gaughan.[3] The last verse of a song, called *Thomas Muir of Huntershill* and written (words and music) by Adam McNaughtan[4] says this :

Gerrald, Palmer, Skirving, Thomas Muir and Margarot
These are names that every Scottish man and woman ought to know
When you're called for jury service, when your name is drawn by lot
When you vote in an election when you freely voice your thought
Don't take these things for granted, for dearly were they bought

I was ignorant of Muir at that time but of course his influence was great even whilst he was alive, though given the political persecution he suffered those who admired him had to be circumspect.

There is a tradition that Robert Burns finished *Scots Wha Hae* on the first day of Thomas Muir's trial in Edinburgh. What is more precisely true is that Burns wrote to George Thomson,[5] his publisher, about how he was inspired by the story of Wallace and then added a detail about how he was also inspired by the 'glowing ideas of some other struggles of the same nature not quite so ancient'.[6] That is a reference, in dangerous times, to the trial of Muir and it lies at one end of a tradition of song inspired by Muir and his ideas, at our end of which are Gaughan and McNaughtan. But that thought also leads to another which might make us pause for it is strange that whilst we know Burns' name, and Wallace's, many still do not know Muir's let alone those others who stood with him.

Muir addressed the bench at his trial, on the 30th of August 1793, with these words: 'Gentlemen from my infancy to this moment I have devoted myself to the cause of the people, it is a good cause, it shall ultimately prevail, it shall finally triumph'. That is a stirring statement and a reminder of the purpose of democratic politics – that purpose being to see that the cause of the people does ultimately prevail and finally triumph. But for Muir the statement was also a step on a journey for Muir did not start his life as a radical.

Muir started as a reformer but was radicalised by the experience of trying to bring forward reform in difficult times. Oppression made that reformer into a radical and then – in the state's terms – turned the radical into a revolutionary. That is a process not unknown in our own age. There was therefore a transition in what Muir was proposing and for which he was arguing though that transition was from and to things that could not in our age – and not without extreme prejudice in that age – be described as sedition, either conscious or unconscious. Certainly today we would regard them as basic democratic entitlements.

But within the journey, there is also a fixed point. What was consistent in Muir's argument was the context and that context was the necessity to restore Scotland's independence. In the preparation for the convention of the Friends of the People Muir was much influenced by, and became supportive of, the views of the United Irishmen. He introduced to Scotland the ideas of, and letters from, William Drennan[7] of Belfast and they made a direct appeal to Scottish notions of nationalism and independence. Those ideas caused some division within the Convention itself and that can be directly attributed to Muir's espousal of them.

I make the point because it has been argued in later years that Muir only developed into a supporter of Scottish independence as a result of his final experiences with the judicial system. In fact Muir was arguing the cause of independence from an early stage in his activities and further evidence of that comes from Lord Daer,[8] a liberal and progressive politician, but nonetheless a unionist, who in 1792, in correspondence with Charles Grey[9] of the London Friends of the People candidly admitted that 'Friends of Liberty in Scotland have been almost unanimously enemies of the union of England, such is the fact whether the reasons be good or bad'.[10] Muir is therefore not just an interesting figure for the ideas we associate with him but also because of the way those ideas developed from a firm base of nationalism. But Muir was even more than that. He was a believer in the laws of Scotland no matter how perverted their operation had become. So Muir returned to Scotland from the safe haven of France in early 1793 to face a judicial process which he supported though many others would have chosen not to do so.

Muir had faith, of course, in his own ability to disprove the unjust charges against him, a faith that is admirable though also a faith that was over confident given the forces ranged against him. It was a faith buttressed by the courage he undoubtedly possessed and which was to show again in his last year in France when, although facing certain death if he returned, he was still planning to attempt to come to Scotland and as a result was meeting delegates from the new organisations that had replaced the Friends so that he could discuss his role in the next phase of the campaign for democracy and independence. There is little precedent for that courageous determination. Many others – from James VII through to some other radicals of the late eighteenth century – decided that when the circumstances in Scotland were uncongenial, difficult and dangerous as a result of their belief they would ply their trade somewhere safer and more amenable.

Muir is therefore worthy of remembrance for all sorts of reasons – personal, political, progressive and historic. It thus seems pretty self-evident that we should do something about the fact that he has not been properly or adequately remembered or commemorated for two centuries or more.

What should be done?

Firstly we should and pay tribute to the work of those like the Friends of Thomas Muir who have campaigned so hard and vigorously to put this founding father of Scottish democratic reform back into a proper position of historical eminence. One of the arguments such campaigners have developed and promoted over the past few years has been the idea of a posthumous pardon for Muir, Palmer, Skirving, Margarot and Gerrald, his associates and fellow transportees. I think this is a cause very much worth supporting and I have experience of it in another matter. In my own recent book on the Referendum I record a moment, as First Minister, when I became active in considering a pardon in a case being brought by petition to the Scottish Parliament as I was hoping to be able to assist. This is from the relevant entry in *The Dream Shall Never Die* dated Monday 30th June:[11]

I've tracked down one of my old professors for help with some historical rough justice. I asked Bruce Lenman for a quick opinion on the Appin trial, there is a petition before the parliament from a Campbell no less, asking for a royal pardon for James Stuart. Devotees of Robert Louis Stevenson will recall that Alan Breck Stuart (who bore the king's name) may or may not have shot the Red Fox at Appin. What did happen for certain in historical terms is his stepfather James Stuart was strung up by a Campbell Jury with a chief of the Clan Campbell in the bench just to make sure there was no mistake.

Cases such as this are usually turned down for fear of opening a can of worms and setting a difficult precedent. However I decided to make a check or two with Frank Mulholland, the current Lord Advocate before we decide on this one.

It is not often in life that you get the chance to right what seems a clear historical wrong. Hence I've asked my old history prof for an informed opinion.

As a boy I use to love the lectures of Dr Ian Grimble.[12] Looking at this audience tonight there are some who will remember those broadcasts. They will recall that Grimble usually came to the podium with no notes, seeming to tell the stories of great figures in Scottish history from his memory. I still remember his account of Thomas Cochrane[13] the 10th Earl of Dundonald. Cochrane was the radical naval admiral who, when he was a member of Parliament was impeached, tried, found guilty of stock market fraud and utterly disgraced but he then went on to liberate Peru, Brazil, and Chile and had a go at liberating Greece. He was an extraordinarily able naval commander but a very poor politician as he kept falling out with everybody and anybody. That is not something I would recommend in politics. Cochrane was eventually restored to public favour and recalling that I looked again at his trial. There was, without a doubt, much more evidence against Cochrane compared to the evidence that convicted Muir yet Cochrane was pardoned in 1832. And to take an even more pertinent case, the 1820 Martyrs[14] were – no matter what you think of their cause – guilty of an actual act of rebellion against the Crown. They were pardoned in 1835 when the political pendulum swung, but there was no pardon at that time for Muir or any of his associates whose convictions took place more than a quarter of a century earlier.

I think there should be such a pardon. I know that there remain arguments against such actions, one being that it sets dangerous precedents. Lord Advocates and Solicitors General worry that if you start pardoning figures from history then you are taking the context of judgements away from their time and moving it to the present day which could be dangerous in the future. Yet even at the time Braxfield's conduct of the case and the sentences handed down were seen as unacceptable to most and unduly harsh and extreme to many. The second reason for opposing pardons is more technical. We now have in existence something called The Scottish Criminal Case Review Commission which is charged with looking at all potential current and recent miscarriages of justice. This allows a view to be taken without expressing bias about previous judgements or actions. This is a good way to proceed and it is a good institution. It might therefore be an important next step to involve that body in considering a posthumous pardon not least because it would right a wrong and draw attention to the unjust treatment of those who took forward our basic freedoms. A pardon would be one tangible way of recognising and publicising the contribution of Muir and his colleagues.

Another would be to respond positively to the call from the Friends of Thomas Muir for a new statue of Muir to be erected in Edinburgh. That is a good and worthy idea but Edinburgh is not a city which is short of statues and particularly not short of statues to white men from history. There could be a place for such a statue inside or even outside the Scottish Parliament but we should not forget that Muir already has a memorial in the city of a distinctive and indeed unique kind. The 'Martyrs Memorial' in Calton Cemetery is a very striking granite obelisk the idea of which was successfully promoted by the radical liberal MP Joseph Hume in 1844. It dominates the cemetery and the skyline and commemorates exactly who we are talking about this evening – Muir, Palmer, Skirving, Margarot, and Gerrald. It would be hard to better it but it is not nearly as well known as it should be. Perhaps that is the real task – to make it better known and I did have an idea about that some time ago.

A few years back in what I have to confess was one of my less glorious moments I decided not to do something which in my opinion was undoubtedly the right thing to do because I thought my critics in the Scottish press corps would have a field day with it and as a result distract attention from the greater business in hand which was the referendum campaign. That thing I didn't do was to agree to the proposal, which arrived on my desk one day from the civil service, to move the residence of the First Minister from Bute House to the Governor's House beside St Andrew's House on Calton Hill and right beside Old Calton Cemetery with the Martyrs Memorial in sight.

There were a number of advantages in this proposal including the fact that the house is already owned by the Scottish government, it is within the St Andrew's House complex and therefore has secure access and decent parking and it is, not least, a very important and very unusual historic building which was indeed the House for the Governor when the site of St Andrew's House was the Calton Prison. However whilst there was a great deal of sense in making the move there were some drawbacks, chief amongst which would have been the inevitable over the top and negative presentation of it by large sections of the Scottish press corps, rather than a positive take on what would have been a sensible, modern and cost effective use of one of the Scottish Government's own historic buildings, which would have saved renting one from the National Trust.

Now however there might be a way to square that circle. My successor, who is a much braver politician than I, could not only move closer to the shop, so to speak, but she could also build a new public reception area (which was to be part of the plan in any case) which would allow people to see right into the seat of Government in this great capital city. Then she could crown the whole achievement by renaming the house after Thomas Muir. Moreover if Historic Environment Scotland were to take over the Old Calton Cemetery and restore it to the condition it deserves but alas doesn't presently meet, the house could become part of a landscape which was redolent of, and a testament to, the achievements of the democratic reformers.

It is high time that the Old Calton Cemetery was restored in any case. Apart from the Martyrs Memorial it contains many important things which need to be part of the experience of visiting the capital of Scotland. The tomb of David Hume is there, for instance, engraved with just one word – Hume – as nothing more needed to be said. It also has a memorial to Abraham Lincoln and the dead of the American Civil War, the first raised outside the USA and containing the only statue of an American President to be found in Scotland. This story of that statue and memorial also speaks of Scotland's passion for justice because it commemorates six Scots who fought in the Union Army because they opposed slavery. The monument has on it the representation of a slave being freed from his shackles. I used to sometime watch buses and individual tourists arriving at the cemetery as I went to and from St Andrew's House and I was sorry that it was not better presented so that all the markers and monuments could properly speak of our history and the great figures that lie there. That needs to change.

But let me go back for a moment to the Martyrs Memorial itself. Joseph Hume, whose efforts led to its erection, was the Radical MP for Montrose Burgh, the same constituency which was represented a century later by John Scott Maclay who was the National Liberal Secretary of State for Scotland. He was of course a Liberal in a Tory Government (we know how that always ends up) and in his case he is largely forgotten even by those who should know better in the Liberal Democrats who claimed that Jim Wallace was the first Liberal Minster in Scotland since the Second World War – but he wasn't. Maclay finished his elected political career as the MP for West Renfrewshire (before becoming Viscount Muirshiel) and his successor was Norman Buchan,[15] who was still in Parliament when I was elected as member for Banff and Buchan back in 1987.

I make those points to stress the issue of continuity because when we talk about Scottish politics we need to talk about that line of continuity. It is that line of continuity of thought and intention that links us to the events of two centuries ago and it is that line of continuity that has been enriched by the influence of Thomas Muir. So 'Thomas Muir House' overlooking the Martyrs Memorial in a restored Calton Cemetery could provide a physical manifestation of that influence and continuity in the heart of our capital. Yet continuity is not a straight line – times change, often rapidly. Muir was deported to almost certain death in 1793 but by 1844 the town council of Edinburgh had agreed to have a monument erected to him and his fellow deportees. As I have said the martyrs of 1820 were pardoned within fifteen years. Resolute action and positive thought – leadership against the odds – can move mountains and remove the most serious and seemingly entrenched political and social blockages.

One of the things I am most pleased about doing during my time as First Minister was ensuring that the contribution of the late Jimmy Reid,[16] to Scottish political thought in the late twentieth century was made available to schools throughout the country. He stood up to be counted when that was essential for the future of his industry, his comrades and his country. He moved mountains and he remained positive and determined to the end of his days. What he can teach needs to be taught. We must do the same for Thomas Muir. Education Scotland, the national body that supports teaching in Scotland, should be approached to allow that to happen and to help prepare the materials so that the story of Muir – a great story as I said at the beginning of this lecture – is understood by all our children. They should be inspired by it and they would also be – a great advantage – entertained and thrilled by it.

That task of inspiring by entertainment could also be achieved by ensuring that the story of Muir is presented to the widest possible audience by television or film and I am happy to offer Murray Armstrong whatever help I can give in that regard. There is a lesson to be taken from another Scottish epic story that made it to the big screen. 'Braveheart'[17] often gets criticised as being dreadful history but it has made William Wallace and the cause of Scottish independence known through the world. That is what it was meant to do. I remember talking to Randall Wallace,[18] the writer of the original screenplay. He told me that he first got interested in William Wallace when he saw his statue in Edinburgh Castle. Having the same name but knowing virtually nothing about Wallace he started to read about him, became inspired by the story and eventually went to the Wallace Monument. It is not the easiest place to find and he got lost so he stopped and asked three young lads on a street corner in Bridge of Allan how to get there. They gave him directions and then he asked them who William Wallace was. He was stunned when none of them could answer and he resolved there and then that he would ensure that, if nothing else, his screenplay would make sure that no young person in Scotland or around the world was ignorant of such a great hero. If that can be done with the epic tale of William Wallace, then I think it can be done with the epic tale of Thomas Muir.

The last thing I want to say is this: Muir developed his political views by thinking on, and learning from, the experience that he had. I don't think he ever lost his faith in the judicial process, harshly though it had treated him, but he certainly lost his faith in those who administered the political process in his time. What encouraged him, however, was the attitude of the people themselves and by their slow but steady radicalisation. The last recorded quote of Muir before his death in January 1799, is this:

We have achieved a great duty in these critical times, after the destruction of so many years, we have been the first to revive the spirit of our country and give it a national existence.

I am sure that you will not be surprised if I, in closing, suggest that there is an analogy with recent experience in our country for I am strongly of the belief that the referendum last year galvanised and mobilised the nation – it 'revived the spirit of our country' in Muir's terms.

That is clear from the figures alone. 98% of those eligible registered to vote. 85% of those registered actually voted. These are remarkable figures in any modern democracy and as a close to a full turnout as it is probably possible to get given illness, absence and death all of which affect the register and the final figures in any poll. Hundreds of thousands of our fellow citizens were, for the first time in their lives, activated and mobilised and were willing to articulate and build on political ideas and experience – in both camps it should be said. I think that was and is a marvellous thing.

Muir believed that history would vindicate his position. Despite parliamentary failure he was encouraged by the flow of what was happening. He was certain that a mobilisation of the people would bring about the democratic reforms he sought. Now not all those democratic reforms have as yet been achieved. Certainly 98% of people can now register to vote in a referendum but it is telling that many of them weren't on the electoral register for a normal election. Disenfranchisement is still rife, even if it is now usually – though not always – driven by disaffection from the political process rather than by legal or administrative exclusion. Moreover we still have the House of Lords, the most extraordinary relic of the undemocratic past, which is – astonishingly – defended on a regular basis by otherwise perceptive people some of whom even agree to join it 'just for a ribbon to wear in their coat'[19] to quote Browning on Wordsworth.

Nor have we yet established Scotland as the bastion of liberty and human rights that Muir would have expected and many of us still want to see. We can, I think safely say that in Scotland no First Minister would appoint a Lord Braxfield as Lord Justice Clerk. Indeed our system of choosing the justiciary and holding them accountable – not to politicians but to society – has improved out of all recognition. But we still have people – intelligent people – who argue that the lesson we should take from the history of Thomas Muir and his confederates is that of the supposed liberalising effect of the southern part of these islands which has mollified the harsh treatment of radicalism in Scotland. In other words that we need the Union to ensure we do not revert to a brutal backwater.

In reality I believe that the story of Thomas Muir teaches us something entirely different: that the development of the democratic scrutiny of the institutions of Scotland is not only good and has good historic roots but that it will only improve the more we take full responsibility for those institutions. It is, I think, self evident that those over which we presently have democratic control have improved greatly in recent years but those which are still controlled by Westminster are amongst the most pernicious in the land. So we should complete the job that Muir started. We need what Muir wanted – an independent, democratic country. We need to go on building the institutions which will allow – which indeed are designed to ensure – positive human expression of thought, positive human application of ability, and positive human development of creativity so that all those attributes can be used to build and benefit the Scottish body politic.

Much of the institutional thinking of our country is still rooted in the idea of a passive population who vote occasionally and then allow the politicians to get on with the real business of running the show. In the age of the internet we can do better than that. Social media electrifies the political debate (sometimes to the extent of almost frying it, it must be admitted) but it does so because, as Muir understood clearly, ideas can only take root, grow and bear fruit when there is an educated, participative, involved and committed population. The prospect of that excited him. That prospect gave him belief in a distinctive Scottish radicalism in which he invested not just so much hope but also his very life. We can find the means to take that belief and use it to light a torch of creativity that transforms our democracy and our nation. In fact we have already started on that process as the Referendum last year showed for we now have that educated, participative, involved and committed population which is the medium in which democracy and democratic institutions flourish.

Even without the persuasion of the large dog I would have been delighted to deliver this lecture tonight or at any time. Thank you once again for asking me. We must now take practical steps to support and obtain a pardon for Muir and his associates. We should celebrate in a tangible way Muir's legitimate claim to be the father of modern Scottish democracy, perhaps by recognising it in bricks and mortar, whilst maximising the impact of the monument we already have. And we must ensure that our young people have the opportunity, which I did not have until I heard Dick Gaughan sing of *Thomas Muir of Huntershill*, to learn this amazing story and be inspired by it. There is nothing more powerful than the democratic intellect of a country, applied to ensuring democratic choice about its future. That was the view of Thomas Muir and it is mine too.

Notes and References

1 As part of the 250th anniversary celebrations there was an exhibition at the Scottish Parliament from 31 March to 2 April 2015, organised by a National Committee formed by the Friends of Thomas Muir to co-ordinate the many events planned for the year.

2 Robert MacQueen, Lord Braxfield (1722-1799). Appointed Lord Justice Clerk in 1788.

3 Richard Peter Gaughan. Folk singer born 1948.

4 Adam McNaughtan. Scottish folk singer and song-writer, mostly celebrated for his songs about working class Glasgow.

5 George Thomson, 1757-1851. Musician, collector of Scottish music and music publisher.

6 Robert Burns: Letters 2,235.

7 Dr William Drennan, 1754-1820. Physician, poet and political radical; one of the founders of the Society of United Irishmen.

8 Basil William Douglas-Hamilton, Lord Daer, 1764-94, second son of the Earl of Selkirk . Burns wrote of him:
Nae honest, worthy man need care
To meet with noble, youthful Daer,
For he but meets a brother.

9 Charles Grey, 1764-1845, later Earl Grey, Politician and Reformer. Prime Minister, 1830-4.

10 Lord Daer, letter to Charles Grey, 17 January 1793.

11 Alex Salmond, *The Dream Shall Never Die*. HarperCollins, 2015.

12 Iain Naughton Grimble, Historian & Broadcaster, 1921-95. Herald obituary at http://www.heraldscotland.com/news/12671849.Dr_Ian_Grimble/

13 Admiral Thomas Cochrane, 10th Earl of Dundonald, Marquess of Maranhão, 1775-1860. Naval Officer and radical politician.

14 After an insurrection of 1-8 April 1820 in west central Scotland a number of people were charged with treason. After trial Wilson, Baird and Hardie were hanged and twenty others sentenced to transportation.

15 Norman Findlay Buchan, 1922-1990. Left-wing Labour politician, MP for Renfrewshire West and then Paisley South.

16 James 'Jimmy' Reid, trade unionist, writer, activist, 1932-2010, who led the work-in at Upper Clyde Shipbuilders during 1971-2. Elected Rector of Glasgow University in 1971, he delivered a Rectorial address described by the *New York Times* as the 'greatest speech since the Gettysburg Address'. It contains this famous passage: 'A rat race is for rats. We're not rats. We're human beings. Reject the insidious pressures in society that would blunt your critical faculties to all that is happening around you, that would caution silence in the face

of injustice lest you jeopardise your chances of promotion and self-advancement. This is how it starts and before you know where you are, you're a fully paid-up member of the rat-pack. The price is too high. It entails the loss of your dignity and human spirit. Or as Christ put it, "What doth it profit a man if he gain the whole world and suffer the loss of his soul?" '

17 1995 Feature film: a historical drama based on the life of William Wallace, directed by Mel Gibson and the winner of five Academy Awards at the 68th Academy Awards Ceremony, including those for best picture and best director.

18 Randall Wallace, born 28 July 1949 in Jackson, Tennessee. Screenwriter, director, producer and songwriter whose script for 'Braveheart' was nominated for best Original Screenplay at the 68th Academy Awards.

19 Robert Browning, 'The Lost Leader', 1845.

The Essential Thomas Muir: the roots of his inspiration

Don Martin

The purpose of this essay is to examine the factors and circumstances that caused Thomas Muir to act in the way that he did, especially during the years 1790-93. As it is clearly impossible to recover Muir's thought processes none of the suggestions made here can be proved with certainty, but some probabilities are identified. Future research might strengthen the likelihood of individual suggestions but equally this likelihood might be diminished or in some cases removed altogether.

In her 1981 biography of Thomas Muir, which arguably remains the most useful work on her subject, Christina Bewley casts doubts on the value of Peter Mackenzie's *Life of Thomas Muir*, published in 1831. She makes frequent reference to Mackenzie's work, but often with the qualification that we must take what he says with a pinch of salt. For example, she invites us to consider the probability of Mackenzie's suggestion that Muir caught yellow fever at Vera Cruz in Mexico but cautions us to remember that Mackenzie is 'never a very reliable source'.[1] Most of the inaccuracies she mentions come from the part of Mackenzie's narrative that relate to Muir's adventures around the world, but this has not prevented subsequent writers from following Bewley's lead in labelling Mackenzie's writing with a tag of general inaccuracy. In truth it seems fair to state that his Scottish-based information reflects a view of Muir that was held by many people in the Glasgow area in the early 1830s. Mackenzie tapped into a vibrant oral tradition, often drawing on the memories of people still alive who had lived through the upheavals of the 1790s.

Muir the Committed Churchman

Much of the long-accepted wisdom about Muir can be traced back to Mackenzie's writings. He suggests that Professor John

Millar 'was probably one of the best Jurists that this country ever produced' and that 'Mr. Muir was particularly attached to this good and eminent man'.[2] He tells us that Muir was a 'popular member' of reform societies in Glasgow, Kirkintilloch and other places in Scotland and that when he addressed them 'with energy, propriety and effect' he urged them 'to adhere to the great principles of the Constitution', putting them on their guard 'against the villanous [sic] seduction of hired spies who then unhappily had begun to brood in the land'. Above all, Muir had pointed out to them 'the dangerous consequences of the least tumult or insurrection [...] which would be fatal to the object of their Association, and highly criminal'.[3]

Mackenzie quotes *verbatim* from letters written by Muir and others received by him. Those carry an apparent badge of authenticity and there seems no reason to doubt their accuracy. Correspondence between Muir and the Reverend William Dun, Parish Minister of Kirkintilloch[4] is particularly illuminating because it appears to confirm Muir's essential integrity and character. On 8 June 1792 Dun wrote to Muir in Edinburgh in the following terms:

MY DEAR SIR, – The unanimous wish of the Session of Cadder, and I am desired to say, the prevailing wish of the people of Cadder, is, to have the Sacrament of the Lord's Supper dispensed among them this season; – of this they have desired to inform you, hoping it will meet with your approbation. The Presbytery of Glasgow is to be advised of it on Wednesday first, and requested to appoint a day for the purpose, and the fourth Sabbath of July has been thought of by some. As an ordinance of holy religion, it is surely proper – in other respects it may do good, and can do no harm.

To have your approbation of this design before the meeting of the Presbytery, would be agreeable to the Elders, and also to him who has the pleasure to be,
DEAR SIR,
With respect,
Your most humble Servant,
WM. DUN

Muir replied from Edinburgh three days later, as follows:

DEAR SIR, – The proposed celebration of the Sacrament
of the Lord's supper in the parish of Cadder, is a measure
to which I cordially give my highest approbation. Whatever
political opinion may be entertained by different parties, in
this instance, I should consider their interference as a crime
of the deepest guilt. I therefore hope that on all sides there
will be universal unanimity. No exertion on my part shall be
wanting to render everything convenient for the Ministers
who may attend.
You are, however, sensible that from the various
altercations which have lately occurred, much of the utility
of the measure will depend upon a prudent choice of these
Ministers. I could wish that gentlemen, obnoxious to no
party, should be invited, whose ministrations will not be
associated in the minds of the people with prior political
conduct – whom they will regard solely as Ministers of
religion, and not as the partisans of any particular party.
Upon this subject I beg your advice. I value the interest of
religion, and I consider this to be to them of the highest
moment.
Returning you my sincere thanks for your attention to the
parish in a matter of such superior importance,
I remain,
DEAR SIR,
Yours most respectfully,
THOMAS MUIR

The appeal for political neutrality in church might seem
surprising from the pen of a recognised political campaigner, but
in the opinion of the present writer it should be accepted at face
value. Muir enjoyed the trust of many of the Cadder congregation
and there were people in neighbouring parishes who would have
wished to interfere in the proposed Sacrament at Cadder. Peter
Mackenzie makes the following observation in a footnote:

To the scandal of the Church of Scotland, political
animosity, at this time, frequently displayed itself from the
pulpit.[5]

Thomas Muir was a devout Presbyterian and apart from his deep sense of political injustice this was perhaps the most significant factor in his outlook. There seems no reason to doubt that the integrity of his religious principles was every bit as strong as his political conviction. As a ruling elder he had entertained clergy and elders at Huntershill during periods of communion at Cadder Church.[6] As noted by Bewley, his faith was of a specific kind:

Muir followed his parents in supporting the Popular Party.[7]

This bland statement is one of the most significant in Bewley's book. Unfortunately she does not elaborate on it or provide a source for the information, but Muir's support of the Calvinist Popular Party fits well with everything else we know about him and there seems to be little doubt about the truth of Bewley's statement. Muir's adherence to this extremist wing of the Church of Scotland has puzzled some modern writers and it has been suggested that when Muir acted as Counsel for Popular Party interests in church courts he could simply have been fulfilling the brief 'in the time-honoured manner of his profession [...] with a view to his own professional advancement'.[8] However, Muir's principles were such that he would surely have been unhappy to act in this way over religious matters and it seems much more likely that he was supporting arguments that fitted well with his own personal beliefs.

In his June 1792 letter to the Reverend William Dun, mentioned above, Muir referred to 'various altercations which have lately occurred' and to his wish that 'gentlemen, obnoxious to no party should be invited, whose public ministrations will not be associated in the minds of the people with prior political conduct'.[9] Without doubt his concern was directed at one particular individual, the Reverend James Lapslie, Parish Minister of Campsie, who had clashed with Muir at a meeting of the Synod of Glasgow and Ayr, in April 1791, over the 'McGill Affair'[10] which was basically a dispute between the Popular Party and the Moderate Party, the latter regarded as the ruling elite of the Church of Scotland at the time.[11] As such the dispute was largely theological in nature, but Muir also related it to the Popular Party struggle against the Moderates over patronage in the appointment of ministers.[12] After the Popular Party case was rejected by the General Assembly, comments in a pamphlet (probably authored by Muir) blamed the Kirk's theological stance over the McGill affair on its culture of patronage, which they suggested might still be broken, so enabling reunification of the national church:

> [...] there is still an expedient left us, and *but one*, by which
> we may, through the divine blessing, repair the breaches,
> and raise up the broken down walls of our Zion, namely, an
> application from the people of Scotland in general, to the
> legislature, to repeal the patronage laws![13]

There followed several pages of bitter invective against ecclesiastical patronage, justified by the following comment:

> We have insisted at some length on this subject, because
> patronage is at the foundation of all the evils which our
> church labours under.[14]

The families of both Lapslie and Muir had formerly been resident in Campsie parish for a long period of time, so the two men knew each other well and Lapslie had socialised with the Muirs at Huntershill House.[15] However, as a recipient of Crown patronage he was a supporter of the Moderate Party[16] and in line with this enjoyed close links to the political establishment of the day. As a young man he had been employed as a tutor and companion to Sir James Suttie (later of Prestongrange) on a 'grand tour' of Europe.[17] Suttie was closely related to the Dundas family, the most powerful political family in Scotland at that period; indeed it seems that Lord Advocate Robert Dundas was his first cousin.[18]

Not much more than a year after the correspondence between William Dun and Thomas Muir on the proposed Sacrament at Cadder, Muir was on trial at the High Court of Edinburgh on a charge of sedition. In between times much had happened, but the interfering presence of the Reverend James Lapslie had remained as a constant. The indignant tone of Peter Mackenzie's description of Lapslie's behaviour at the time of the trial is worth recalling, because it confirms that nearly forty years after the trial Lapslie's enthusiastic desire to contribute to Muir's downfall was still remembered:

Thomas Muir's arch-enemy, the Reverend James Lapslie of Campsie Parish. John Kay Etching (Jimmy Watson Collection).

129

Robert Dundas, Lord Advocate at Thomas Muir's Trial. Dundas's Cousin, Sir James Suttie of Prestongrange, was accompanied on a tour of Europe by the Reverend James Lapslie. John Kay Etching (Jimmy Watson Collection).

[...] the moment the ministers of the Crown denounced Mr. Muir, that moment this minister of religion turned upon him like a serpent. His own sting would have been powerless, because, for aught that appeared, Mr. Muir had

never uttered one syllable in his presence of a criminal or
seditious nature: – but, in order to supply that deficiency,
he did not scruple to fish for evidence against him in
every quarter where he thought he would be successful.
He attended the initiatory examination of some of the
witnesses for the Crown before the Sherriff, and "coaxed
them to speak out." And so great was his zeal for the
prosecution, that when the Trial itself drew nigh, he left his
parish and voluntarily journeyed to Edinburgh, a distance
of forty miles and, *without being subpoened* he actually
attempted to plant himself in the witness box [...][19]

Mackenzie is inaccurate in one respect. He suggests that the
friendship between the Muir and Lapslie families had been
maintained right up to the time of the trial and in his view this
made Lapslie's action especially distasteful, but he seems to have
been unaware of the long-standing dispute between Muir and
Lapslie over the McGill affair. Without doubt the latter would have
generated bad blood between the two and would certainly have
provided an element of motivation for Lapslie's conduct relating
to the trial.

Muir objected to Lapslie as a witness at his Trial on the basis
that he had coached and prejudiced other Crown witnesses:

[...] I offer to prove, that he has assisted the Messengers
of the Law, in exploring and citing witnesses against me;
that he attended the sheriffs in their different visits to the
parishes of Campsie and Kirkintiloch, that previously to the
precognition, he conversed with the witnesses of the Crown,
that he attended their precognition, put questions to them
and took down notes [...][20]

Muir then proceeded to call witnesses in proof of these allegations:
Henry Freeland, a Kirkintilloch weaver, Robert Henry, a printer
at Kincaid Printfield, and Robert McKinlay, a Paisley print-cutter.
He was about to call James McGibbon, another Kincaid printer,
when Lord Advocate Robert Dundas intervened, saying that there
was no need for further witnesses as to Lapslie's conduct, as he
was willing to forego the latter's evidence:

[...] not on the ground of his being present at the precognitions, but because he appeared, if not an agent, at least to have taken an active part in the business.[21]

Muir had earlier stated that his objection to Lapslie was so strong that if allowed the opportunity in future he would proceed with a criminal prosecution against him 'when he and I shall exchange places at this bar'.[22]

Chryston Chapel of Ease. The Reverend Archibald Provan, whose claim to be Minister of Cadder was promoted by Thomas Muir, was minister here from the Chapel's opening in 1780, until he eventually became Minister of Cadder in 1793. Photograph courtesy East Dunbartonshire Archives & Local Studies.

As noted above Thomas Muir seems to have enjoyed the trust of a majority of the Cadder parishioners. It is unclear how many of them shared his support for the Kirk's Popular Party, but it is likely that many of them did so, because when trying to ensure that the minister they wanted for their church was appointed they found themselves in clear opposition to the Moderate-driven imposition of patronage. This came about in June 1790 when the minister of Cadder, Alexander Dun, passed away and a successor was needed. As it happened, the members of the congregation were happily confident about the man they wanted to take over. The Reverend Archibald Provan had been the minister of Cadder's own Chapel of Ease in the village of Chryston from its opening in 1780 and was highly regarded. He seemed the obvious choice, but James Dunlop, the local laird of Garnkirk, disagreed. New ministers of Cadder Church were chosen by the heritors and Dunlop had his own favoured nominees for this responsibility, including, it has been claimed, 'parchment barons' installed as feudal superiors of small tracts of land for the purpose.[23] Using his skill as an advocate Thomas Muir opposed Dunlop's definition of 'heritor' and the dispute dragged on for three years, via the Presbytery of Glasgow, the Synod of Glasgow and Ayr, the General Assembly and the Court of Session. Eventually the will of the congregation prevailed and to their satisfaction Archibald Provan was appointed. Ironically this success was confirmed in April 1793, just a few months before Muir was found guilty of sedition and banished as a convict to Australia, but the appointment of Provan as Minister of Cadder must have given him comfort and satisfaction in his time of trouble.[24] The following note about the Reverend Archibald Provan appears in a church history of Cadder published in 1908:

1793. Archibald Provan. Minister of Chryston Chapel-of-Ease, and elected to Parish by Heritors and Elders, in whom the right of election was now vested, on 24th December 1790, but owing to dispute as to validity of election was not inducted till 25th April, 1793. Died at Hutchesontown, 21st April, 1814.[25]

Without doubt Muir would have been something of a hero with many of the people of Cadder and this perhaps explains the warmth of his correspondence with William Dun. There is an interesting entry in the Cadder Kirk Session minutes of 27 March 1791:

Mr Thomas Muir made a motion to appoint a meeting of Session in Monday se'enight to chuse a ruling Elder as he said he was then to resign. To which the Moderator [James Furlong] would not agree as being competent.[26]

Cadder Church. The present church dates from the 1820s, but is built on the site of the church that existed in Thomas Muir's time.

When considering the dynamic of Muir's life and varied activities during the early 1790s his reasons for resigning are of the greatest interest. Did he feel that his role as a professional advocate promoting the case for the appointment of Archibald Provan as minister was inconsistent with his duties as elder? Indeed, what was his foremost concern in this issue? Did he see his involvement primarily in terms of an advocate concerned with the mechanisms of law? Or was the opposition to patronage at his local church of more fundamental importance to him, and therefore an issue of passion? With extra responsibilities did he feel the pressure of frequent stagecoach journeys between Glasgow and Edinburgh difficult to cope with?[27] Or did James Furlong's intervention prove crucial and was Muir's resignation therefore rejected outright?

Opposition to Patronage, in Every Walk of Life

The answers to some of the questions posed in the last paragraph might well lie with Professor John Millar, Thomas Muir's mentor when at the University of Glasgow, and especially his views on patronage. American students of the Scottish Enlightenment have noted that most of its main figures were beneficiaries of patronage, in one way or another, but have been perplexed by Millar's ingratitude, noting that 'Millar was alone among the enlighteners in putting forth an all-out indictment of the behemoth that patronage had become in British political life'.[28] For indeed Millar was the arch-opponent of patronage. His views are clearly set out in volume 4 of his *Historical View of the English Government from the Settlement of the Saxons in Britain to the Revolution of 1688*, published in 1803:

> From the time of the revolution [...] we may trace, in
> some measure, a new order of things; a new principle of
> authority, which is worth the attention of all who speculate
> upon political subjects. Before that period, the friends
> of liberty dreaded only the direct encroachments of the
> prerogative; they have since learnt to entertain stronger
> apprehensions of the secret motives of interest which the
> crown may hold up to individuals, and by which it may
> seduce them from the duty they owe to the public. To what
> height in fact, has this influence been raised in all the
> departments of government, and how extensively has it
> pervaded all ranks and descriptions of the inhabitants: in
> the army, in the church, at the bar, in the republic of letters,
> in finance, in mercantile and manufacturing corporations.
> Not to mention pensioners and placemen; together with the
> various officers connected with the distribution of justice,
> and the execution of the laws, the corps diplomatique, and
> the members of the king's confidential council. With what
> a powerful charm does it operate in regulating opinions,
> in healing grievances, in stifling clamours, in quieting the
> noisy patriot, in extinguishing the most furious opposition!
> It is the great opiate which inspires political courage, and
> lulls reflection; which animates the statesman to despise
> the resentment of the people; which drowns the memory of

his former possessions, and deadens, perhaps, the shame and remorse if pulling down the edifice which he had formerly reared.[29]

Effigy of John Millar in Nelson Mandela Place Glasgow.

If we accept the tradition that Muir was deeply influenced by Millar's teaching, then it is reasonable to assume that he was impressed by Millar's views on patronage. Millar opposed patronage in all walks of life but in the first instance Muir would have been most interested in Millar's views on patronage in the church. This seems to provide a possible third strand of motivation for Muir's involvement in the Cadder Church minister issue of 1790-3. As well as providing an opportunity to practice his skills as a young advocate and a context in which to express principles derived from his upbringing in a Popular Party family traditionally opposed to patronage in the Kirk, there seems also to have been a legacy from his time at Glasgow University, inspired by the teaching of John Millar. But to what degree did Muir's opposition to Kirk patronage lead him to oppose patronage in other walks of life? To what extent did it increase his awareness of its workings 'in all the departments of government' and indeed in 'the army [...] at the bar, in the republic of letters, in finance, in mercantile and manufacturing corporations'? This is perhaps a key question of relevance to an understanding of Muir's thought processes. It might well lead to the conclusion that Muir's Popular Party background was fundamental to his radical stance on matters of electoral and parliamentary reform. John Millar's teaching could well have dovetailed with a conviction already held. Although adopting a severely dependent form of faith, Calvinist groups like the Popular Party of the Church of Scotland inclined towards a levelling of barriers in society, in line with their opposition to the hierarchical arrangements of the medieval church, and this could sometimes lead to a bravely *independent* view of radicalism in politics.[30] To people like Thomas Muir this would have seemed consistent with the ongoing dynamic of the Reformation but they were all too aware of the factions in the Church which failed to see its logic.

During the latter part of the eighteenth century patronage was a high-profile subject, very much to the forefront of people's minds. In fact, it has been noted that it was 'far and away the biggest item of business for Scottish government'. The most prominent Scottish politician of the period, Henry Dundas, was then as now regarded as its arch proponent. The types of patronage bestowed by Dundas synchronize well with those noted above as condemned by John Millar. In approximate order of frequency they included:

commissions in the armed forces, posts in civil administration, pensions, church patronage, university appointments, patronage of literary works, legal posts, jobs in the colonies and applications for peerages.[31] Dundas's involvement in church patronage was undertaken in conjunction with his nephew Robert Dundas and with the Moderate Party. The appointment of Church of Scotland ministers under the patronage system was especially controversial during the early 1780s when a plethora of pamphlets and other publications on the subject appeared.[32]

Rooted in the Enlightenment

Without doubt John Millar's influence on Thomas Muir is a pertinent link between Muir and the Enlightenment, for Millar is widely recognised as one of the key figures of the latter in Scotland.[33] Indeed, many other such links can be discovered by careful investigation. But in the vast literature relating to the Scottish Enlightenment Muir is nowhere to be seen, while none of the existing books about Muir make much mention of the Enlightenment as such. With a view to highlighting this anomaly the present writer published a short article on 'Thomas Muir and the Scottish Enlightenment' in 2011.[34]

Muir transferred his legal studies from the University of Glasgow to the University of Edinburgh in 1785, just at the time when Dugald Stewart was succeeding Adam Ferguson in the chair of Moral Philosophy there. Although difficult to find evidence it seems very likely that the opinions of both men would have had a profound effect on the young Muir. He would have taken an interest in some of Ferguson's ideas, especially, perhaps, because of the didactic way in which they were presented:

> Liberty is a right which every individual must be ready to vindicate for himself; and which he who pretends to bestow as a favour, has by that act in reality denied. Even political establishments, though they appear to be independent of the will and arbitration of men, cannot be relied upon for the preservation of freedom; they may nourish, but should not supersede that firm and resolute spirit, with which the liberal mind is always prepared to resist indignities, and to refer its safety to itself.[35]

During his earliest philosophy lectures at the University of Edinburgh Dugald Stewart taught that sovereigns have no right of obedience on the part of their subjects except in the context of power vested in them by society 'for preserving regularity and order in the state'; also that when people perceive that government is inconsistent with the natural liberty of men 'it is not only lawful but it is incumbent on us to resist the reigning power'.[36] Interestingly, Dugald Stewart and Thomas Muir shared a personal friend in William Drennan of the United Irishmen. The precise relevance of this connection will require further research, but it nevertheless strengthens the conviction that Muir was close to Stewart not just in space and time but perhaps in political ideology as well.[37] It seems possible that Muir's enthusiasm for the Constitution at the time of his trial owed something to the teaching of Dugald Stewart who during the late 1780s had been taking an interest in its virtues.[38]

It is worth noting that links between Muir and some of the Enlightenment literati can also help to provide a radical context for the Scottish Enlightenment itself. Any perceived connections between radicalism and the Enlightenment have tended to be brushed aside as irrelevant. As Professor Smout has pointed out:

There was [...] in Scotland no equivalent to the French revolutionary philosophers like Voltaire and Rousseau, to England's Tom Paine, or even to John Wilkes, John Cartwright, Thomas Spence and William Cobbett.[39]

More controversially, and citing no fewer than twenty-one modern authorities in support of his contention, Charles Camic has pronounced:

Neither popular democracy, a fundamental redistribution of economic resources, nor the eradication of social classes formed any part of the program of the Scottish Enlightenment.[40]

However, if it can be shown that Thomas Muir and perhaps other Scottish radicals of the late eighteenth century derived inspiration from the writings of the Scottish literati then perhaps a modification of Camic's sweeping statement will be achieved.

Muir also admired the Enlightenment ideal of a 'Republic of Letters'. The literati of the Scottish Enlightenment saw themselves as part of an international community of citizens of the Republic of Letters whose aim was to place intellectual property in the public domain.[41] Thomas Muir heartily concurred with this sentiment, but believed that it was vital for the spread of information to extend to all levels of society. Right at the start of his trial in August 1793 he presented the following manifesto, in the context of his proposal for equal representation of the people in the House of Commons:

> I grant that I advised the people, to read different
> publications upon both sides, which this great national
> question has excited, and I am not ashamed to assign my
> motives. I consider the ignorance of the people, on the
> one hand, to be the source from which despotism flows.
> I consider, upon the other hand, an ignorant people
> impressed with a sense of grievances, and wishing to have
> their grievances redressed, to be exposed to certain misery
> and to complete ruin. KNOWLEDGE must always precede
> REFORMATION, and who shall dare to say that the
> PEOPLE should be debarred from INFORMATION, where
> it concerns them so materially.[42]

To support the dissemination of information Muir maintained an extensive library at Huntershill[43] and made the contents freely available to interested people. However, as the drama of his trial unfolded it became clear that the prosecution was developing its case in the context of a need to suppress information that had hitherto been published and therefore freely available. It was obvious that libraries like the one at Huntershill were being attacked and their future threatened. So it was apparent that the Republic of Letters was in great danger. It has been suggested, in fact, that one of the unintentional consequences of the crisis of the 1790s was the end of the Scottish Enlightenment.[44] If this is indeed the case then the Trial of Thomas Muir was a key event. Lord Cockburn later concluded that: 'The intentions of these reformers may have been good, but in effect they were the enemies of liberty'.[45] There was some truth in this, but the damage was not permanent; although even in Cockburn's day the stance taken by

Muir and his fellow radicals, in the name of democracy, was still to be fully appreciated.

Defining Democracy

Many extracts from Muir's oration at his Trial have been widely quoted but for the present writer one stands out as head and shoulders above the rest:

> What then has been my crime? Not the lending to a
> relation a copy of Mr Paine's Works; not the giving away to
> another of a few numbers of an innocent and constitutional
> publication; but, for having dared to be, according to the
> measure of my feeble abilities, a strenuous and active
> advocate for an equal representation of the People – in the
> House of the People.

The significance of this statement is in the clear way that it reveals Muir's grasp of the political nature of his trial and also his determination to deal with his enemies on their own terms, meeting politics with politics, rather than attempting a conventional legal defence. The circumstances that determined this essential nature of the trial are therefore worth examining. Their origins can be traced back to May 1792 when the British Government issued a proclamation against seditious meetings and publications. This was met with defiance in Scotland and failed to inhibit the establishment of a Friends of the People Society in Edinburgh, on 26 July, and other such societies across Scotland soon afterwards.[46] Government spies were present at these meetings and duly reported on the proceedings in each case and also on the plan to hold a Convention of the different Scottish societies in December. Doubtless motivated by the spies' reports, as well as the increasing likelihood of war with Revolutionary France, a second proclamation against sedition was issued on 1 December.[47] Thereafter, as an example to others, Henry Dundas and his government acolytes decided to identify some clear instances where acts of sedition might be prosecuted. They soon earmarked Thomas Muir's determination to read an allegedly treasonable address from the United Irishmen at the December Convention as a circumstance that placed him in the firing line.

Among others attracting attention was the polymath James Tytler, pioneer hot-air balloonist and editor of *Encyclopaedia Britannica*, who in early December published a pamphlet advocating the use of passive resistance as a means of promoting reform. Moves to quash the activities of these two men became linked together in an event of 2 January 1793 when Muir was arrested at the Holytown stop while on his way by stagecoach from Glasgow to Edinburgh to defend Tytler at the High Court.[48]

Muir remained fairly relaxed about the situation. After being freed on bail he spent a short spell among radical friends in London before travelling to France on 15 January, apparently with a vague notion of adding his voice to the clamour to save Louis XVI from execution. At this stage he felt confident about being able to return to Scotland as soon as the date of his trial on a charge of sedition was set.[49] However, with the French king's execution on 21 January and the outbreak of war between France and Britain on 1 February, travel between the two countries became very difficult. Muir's trial was fixed for 11 February (later postponed to 25 February), but it soon became obvious that he could not manage back in time and would therefore be classed as a fugitive from justice.[50] Muir now had a moral dilemma. Should he persevere in his attempt to return for trial or should he simply lie low in France for a period? To his fellow radical William Skirving he had earlier expressed the intention of defending himself at his trial, so this had been his preference, perhaps even from the moment he was arrested.[51]

Peter Mackenzie later published a letter from Thomas Muir 'to the Friends of the People in Scotland', dated 13 February 1793. It included the following words:

> I will return to Scotland without delay. To shrink from dangers would be unbecoming my own character, and your confidence. I dare challenge the most minute investigation of my public and private conduct ...[52]

Hector MacMillan has suggested 'that there is reason to believe he [Muir] had now decided to return and use Edinburgh's High Court as a political platform', especially as Thomas Paine had suffered criticism in Paris for not returning to defend his *Rights of Man* personally instead of leaving it in the hands of Thomas Erskine, brother of Edinburgh's Henry Erskine.[53]

The suggestion that Muir fully intended to return to Edinburgh in due course crops up regularly,[54] so MacMillan's assessment seems reasonable. Muir appears to have considered crossing to America and indeed he sailed from Le Havre in mid-July on the American-bound ship *Hope*, but left it again at Belfast and after a few days in Ireland was back in Scotland. At Muir's Trial in August the Lord Advocate made much of the secret nature of Muir's return to Scotland:

> He informed nobody of his coming home. How wonderful
> that no letter was driven by the winds or impelled by the
> waves, to give notice of what he says was his earnest wish.
> The reverse in fact appears to have been the case [...][55]

Muir was incensed at the Lord Advocate's suggestion that his return to Scotland had been of a clandestine nature. He was dismayed that although cited to appear for the prosecution James Carmichael, the customs officer who had recognised Muir when he landed at Portpatrick, and William Ross, the magistrate before whom he appeared at Stranraer, had not been called. He claimed that:

> I would have adduced them as witnesses to prove that so
> far from concealing myself I announced myself publicly,
> and without disguise; so far from attempting evasion, my
> only anxiety was to put myself in the hands of the Law; and
> under the protection of its magistrates.[56]

For Muir this was an extremely important point. He had returned to Scotland for the specific purpose of defending himself at his trial as he realised he would there have a very public platform to explain the principles in which he believed. And for this reason he had no intention of allowing anyone else to handle his defence and so deny him the unique opportunity that was available to him.

Some of Muir's friends had sounded out Henry Erskine, the Edinburgh Whig advocate, about the possibility of him defending Muir at his trial and to this he had agreed, subject to the proviso that he would have complete charge of the defence. When Muir refused the offer, Erskine confirmed his awareness of Muir's true purpose by prophesying that Muir would convict himself with his intended harangues, because these would establish his guilty intent;[57] but Muir was a knowledgeable and competent advocate and would have been as aware as Erskine of the risk he was taking. It was one that he was determined to shoulder.

Some historians seem to have missed this point. There are histories of Scotland that afford little space to Muir, but nevertheless succeed in mentioning his perceived incompetence in handling his own defence. In this way they invite readers to conclude that the alleged folly at his trial is a fundamental aspect of the Muir story:

> He opted to fight his own defence, but showed little grasp of forensic skills in doing so.[58]
> Muir handled his case atrociously, failing to challenge the relevancy of the indictment at the proper stage.[59]
> Muir's conduct of his own defence was neither calm nor competent [...][60]

For Muir his personal defence was of minor consideration. His purpose was to draw attention to the logic of the case for 'an equal representation of the People in the House of the People'.

He was not the first person to support this case, but he was arguably the most forthright and the most effective. His trial received widespread attention in the press of the day and the published reports were widely circulated. His stance was a major news story. It also passed into oral tradition across Scotland and remained part of the word-of-mouth version of Scottish/local history (then still supported and enjoyed by many people) for some considerable time.

Christina Bewley has suggested that 'Any claim Muir may have to a small niche in European history [...] rests largely on the enormous amount of campaigning and administrative work he carried out which resulted in the successful three-day meeting in December 1792 of the Scottish Convention'.[61] The Convention was certainly of significance, but we should recognise that the stance taken by Muir at his trial was of even greater moment; and perhaps Muir deserves more than 'a small niche' in democratic history. The epithet 'Father of Scottish Democracy' sometimes applied to Muir is difficult to justify, because democracy is a multi-faceted concept and political democracy just one part of it; but nevertheless his trial was surely a significant event in the history of democracy. His bravery there was *not forgotten* and knowledge of it spread far and wide, remaining vibrant in oral tradition for a very long time afterwards. Muir played a notable part in helping people to understand the significance of democratic principles, and to define what was meant by them.

Tolerating Alien Cultures

As a Calvinist Presbyterian and a supporter of the Church of Scotland's Popular Party, Thomas Muir might have been expected to dislike and distrust the adherents of other faiths, especially Roman Catholics. Traditionally the Scottish Calvinists roundly embraced 'particularism' (exclusive validity) relating to their faith and would extend no compromise to others.[62] Even respected members of the group did not hide such prejudice. Professor John Anderson compared 'the Papists to a Rattle-Snake, harmless when kept under proper restraints: but dangerous like it, when at full liberty; and ready to diffuse a baleful poison around'.[63] Quite possibly Muir displayed aggressive partiality of this kind in private. However, there is no evidence that he would have denied political democracy to Catholics or to people of any other faith. By universal [male] suffrage he meant just that. His promotion of an address from the United Irishmen at the Scottish Convention of December 1792 was in full knowledge that 'united' meant inclusion of Catholics and this inclusiveness did not inhibit him from joining that organisation the following month.[64] When he was in Mexico in 1796 he reported to the Viceroy of New Spain that 'Three Millions of Catholics [in Ireland] were denied the rights of our common nature, were excluded from all the priveledges [sic] of the social state, their properties exposed to sanctioned robberies & their persons to insult & persecution'. He added that with Presbyterians 'who were equally oppressed' they had formed a union. He then confirmed that it was against this background he had transmitted the address of the United Irishmen to the Edinburgh Convention of radical societies in December 1792.[65] In the twenty-first century it is difficult for us to appreciate how awkward it must have been in 1792 for a Popular Party Presbyterian to stand up for the rights of Catholics in this way, but it was indeed a quantum leap and speaks volumes for Muir's determination.

Remembering Thomas Muir

If there is any validity at all in the attributes suggested in this essay then Muir deserves to be remembered, certainly by the people of Scotland and the other countries where he was known. There is ample evidence to confirm that the memory of Thomas Muir and his radical activities lived on in the hearts and minds of the Scottish people long after his death. During commemoration of the passing of the second reading of the Reform Bill in March 1831 an illuminated transparency of Muir was displayed in Glasgow.[66] After the passing of the Reform Act there was a 'Reform Jubilee' in Edinburgh on 10 August 1832 when a vast crowd assembled on Bruntsfield Links, displaying numerous banners, including one presented by a group of chair and cabinet makers in memory of Thomas Muir and others who suffered in the cause of reform.[67] Lord Cockburn was extremely interested to see it:

Lord Cockburn. The Whig judge had strong views on Thomas Muir and his fellow radicals.

There was one most just black placard, which recalled as great a contrast as the same people could exhibit in the same age. *It was dedicated to the memory of Muir, Gerald and Palmer!* [Cockburn's italics] I knew that the atrocity of their punishment was deeply remembered among a higher class, and I was delighted to see it understood and proclaimed on the street.[68]

The difference was that the members of the 'lower class' were remembering the deeds of Muir and the others rather than the severity of their punishment. Cockburn's view was that the actions of the reformers had been extremely rash but that the trials of 1793-4 deserved to be remembered on account of the crass incompetence of the judges involved, and especially the draconian sentences imposed:

The truth is that if they [the radicals] had only been properly tried, and properly punished, the idea of raising a monument to their memory would never have occurred.[69]

Indeed, he was extremely critical of those responsible for the erection of a monument to Muir and the others in Edinburgh's Calton Burying Ground during the 1840s:

[...] no public monument is due to these men. Private friendship may mourn over Muir, Palmer, and Gerrald, and may erect some memorial of their virtues and sufferings; but on public grounds, they have no claim to any pillar.[70]

He also felt that the design of the monument was 'abominable'. However, his view on this later mellowed. In May 1846 he noted that '... the monument is now actually finished, and I don't think it looks ill at all', but his final comment remained true to his earlier opinion:

How the judges' names are omitted I cannot understand. For it is, in truth, *their* monument.[71]

Extract from a letter from Joseph Hume MP to Peter Mackenzie, promoting the idea of a memorial to Muir and his fellow radicals in Edinburgh.
Courtesy East Dunbartonshire Archives & Local Studies (Peter Mackenzie Papers).

Cockburn's surprise to see the banner displayed by cabinet makers during the 1832 Reform Act commemoration reveals how out of touch he was with the common people. Without doubt the banner reflected grass-roots views that were widespread in 1832.

Clearly an appreciation of the significance of Muir, and perhaps his associates as well, lived on in oral tradition throughout the nineteenth century. The Campsie historian, John Cameron, recorded a vibrant tradition that was still alive at the end of the nineteenth century, in a parish where the deeds of Muir's arch-enemy, the Reverend James Lapslie, were also remembered.[72] The historian of neighbouring Kilsyth, the Reverend Robert Anderson, provided information in support of this.[73] Perhaps of even greater interest was a paragraph headed 'A Link with the Past Severed' in the *Kirkintilloch Herald* of 6 January 1892 which explained in some detail why the death of Mrs Janet Martin of the Forth & Clyde Canal village of Tintock had severed a local link with Thomas Muir's trial. Her father, William Muir, had been one of the witnesses[74] and she had preserved the memory of significant events of his day. The local *Herald* reported that her stories and anecdotes connected with Kirkintilloch and its people of bygone years were much appreciated by all who had the good fortune to hear them.[75] The death of Janet Martin therefore serves as a reminder of the clear significance of oral tradition, right down to the end of the nineteenth century and beyond. This important source of information is now much less in evidence than in former years, but perhaps social media and other on-line facilities will have a part to play in sustaining the popular history of future years. Maybe in due course Thomas Muir will find his level there.

Notes and References

1 Bewley, 1981, p.156.
2 Mackenzie, 1831, pp.1-2.
3 Mackenzie, 1831, p.6.
4 Following the death of his namesake Alexander Dun, Parish Minister of Cadder, in 1790, William Dun frequently acted as moderator at Cadder Kirk Session meetings (volume of photocopied Cadder Session minutes 1723-98 in the William Patrick Library, Kirkintilloch LC 285.233).
5 Mackenzie, 1831, pp.112-3.
6 Mackenzie, 1831, p.113; Bewley, 1981, p.11.
7 Bewley, 1981, p.11.
8 MacMillan, 2005, p.18.
9 Mackenzie, 1831, p.113.
10 The author is grateful to David Roberts for this information. Details of the spat between Lapslie and Muir at the April 1791 Synod are provided in Robertson, 1792, pp.30-5, but without referring to either by name. However, Lapslie is identified in this context in Anon, 1792a, p.117 (footnote). See also Cowley, 2015, pp.53-5. Cowley confirms that Thomas Muir represented the Popular Party in church courts during the McGill affair.
11 For a general explanation of the McGill dispute see Drummond and Bulloch, 1973, pp.105-7.
12 Cowley, 2015, p.55. See also Anon, 1792a, pp.131-150.
13 Anon, 1792a, p.157.
14 Anon, 1792a, p.160.
15 Bewley, 1981, p.10.
16 Because of his establishment connections it is clearly correct to describe Lapslie as a Moderate, but in some respects, especially those relating his preaching style, he behaved more like an evangelistic member of the Popular Party. According to Cameron, 1892, p.18: 'He had a strongly emotional nature, on which he placed no restraint; a certain fervid eloquence, which was accompanied by an extraordinary amount of physical exertion'.
17 Kay, 1877, vol.2, p.112.
18 Sir James Suttie's mother Agnes (Nanny) Grant was a sister of Jane (Jean) Grant, mother of Robert Dundas, the Lord Advocate who was involved in the trial of Thomas Muir – therefore Sir James Suttie and Robert Dundas were first cousins. See ScotlandsPeople 713/00 0030 0273 Marriage of Sir George Suttie and Nanny Grant, 7 June 1757; 685/01 480 0300 Marriage of Robert Dundas and Jean Grant, 29 August 1756. The certificates confirm that Nanny and Jean Grant were both daughters of William Grant, Lord Prestongrange.

19 Mackenzie, 1831, pp.14-15.

20 Robertson, 1793, p.38-9.

21 Robertson, 1793, p.40.

22 Robertson, 1793, p.38.

23 This is the traditional view of the affair, but is perhaps too simplistic. See Gerard Carruthers' essay on 'Thomas Muir and Kirk Politics' elsewhere in this volume.

24 Bewley, 1981, p.11; Kidd, 1996a, p.8.

25 Watt, 1908, p.14.

26 Photocopy of Cadder Parish Session Minute of 27 March 1791 in the William Patrick Library, Kirkintilloch LC 285.233.

27 As Bewley notes (1981, p.9), the stagecoach journey between Edinburgh and Glasgow at this time took fifteen hours.

28 Camic, 1983, pp.220-3.

29 Millar, 1803, pp.95-6.

30 Camic, 1983, p.24.

31 Fry, 2004, pp.132-7.

32 Meikle, 1912, p.36.

33 Millar is one of five men identified by the American sociologist Charles Camic as the genuine 'intellectuals' of the Scottish Enlightenment, the others being Adam Ferguson, David Hume, William Robertson and Adam Smith (Camic, 1983, pp.48-51). Camic was concerned only with the philosophical/sociological side of the Scottish Enlightenment; in particular he did not consider the scientific side as having the same validity.

34 Martin, 2011, pp.14-7.

35 Ferguson, 1773, Part VI, Section V 'Of Corruption as it tends to Political Slavery', p.444.

36 Brown, 2007, pp.102-3.

37 Brown, 2007, p.1.

38 Brown, 2007, p.104

39 Smout, 1972, p.475.

40 Camic, 1983, p.82 and footnote.

41 Broadie, 2007, p.14.

42 Robertson, 1793, p.29. The capitalisation of certain words is the publisher's. James Robertson was well known as a sympathiser of Muir's views.

43 Robertson, 1793, p.51 and p.109.

44 Brown, 2007, p.126.

45 Cockburn, 1888, pp.249-50.

46 Bewley, 1981, p.26, p.30 and p.32.

47 Bewley, 1981, p.40.

48 Tytler's trial had been scheduled for 7 January 1793. According

to Lord Cockburn 'The accused did not appear and was outlawed, without anything being said either by the prosecution or by the court [...]' (Cockburn, 1888, Vol.1, p.95). Tytler seems to have fled to Ireland at the time (Bewley, 1981, p.52).

49 Bewley, 1981, pp.52-6.
50 Bewley, 1981, pp.59-60.
51 Bewley, 1981, p.53.
52 Mackenzie, 1831, p.16.
53 MacMillan, 2005, p.45.
54 According to Bewley, Muir had written from London to William Skirving in January 1793 to say that his stay in Paris would be short as he intended to plead his own cause in person (Bewley, 1981, p.53). See also Meikle, 1912, p.130 footnote.
55 Robertson, 1793, p.72.
56 Robertson, 1793, pp.77-8.
57 Ferguson, 1968, p.256.
58 Devine, 2006, p.207.
59 Ferguson, 1968, p.256.
60 Allan, 2002, pp.31-2.
61 Bewley, 1981, p.48.
62 Camic, pp.22-3.
63 Devine, 2006, p.80.
64 Muir's membership certificate of the United Irishmen, dated 11 January 1793, is held in the National Records of Scotland, Reference JC26/1793/1/5/25.
65 MacMillan, 2005, pp.182-3.
66 Meikle, 1912, p.236, Footnote 2, quoting from the *Scotsman* of 30 March 1831.
67 Meikle, 1912, p.236, quoting from the *Scotsman* of 11 August 1832.
68 Cockburn, 1874, Vol.1, p.34.
69 Cockburn, 1888, Vol.2, Appendix, p.250.
70 Cockburn, 1888, Vol.2, Appendix, p.249.
71 Cockburn, 1888, Vol.2, Appendix, p.252.
72 Cameron 1892, pp.10-13 and p.69.
73 Anderson, 1901, pp.44-5.
74 William Muir was the witness who interestingly refused to swear an oath on the Bible because it was against his religious principles, described as those of 'The Mountain'. For this he was threatened with permanent imprisonment until the Kirkintilloch parish minister, the Reverend William Dun, persuaded him to relent (Robertson, 1793, pp.42-4, pp.51-2 and pp.54-5).
75 *Kirkintilloch Herald*, 6 January 1892.

Thomas Muir and Staff and Student Politics at the University of Glasgow

Gerard Carruthers and Satinder Kaur

As well as in the later spheres of kirk and reformist politics, Thomas Muir was also embroiled in intense litigation relating to student and staff politics at the University of Glasgow. Like the ecclesiastical politics in which Muir was to become active, too little close attention is given to his university politics by those who attempt to summarise his life, and the documentary sources that we might utilise to account for his student activity have been surprisingly underplayed. This essay seeks to begin correcting this deficit, but other contemporary sources remain that are likely to shed further light on Muir's Glasgow days and which await examination in the future. Indeed, it should also be noted that the sources used in this essay need returning to for fuller examination than can be accomplished in the short space here.

We might begin with some earlier eighteenth-century University of Glasgow history, where we find that in the 1710s and 1720s, as later in Muir's time in the 1780s, there was controversy over university 'management'. *A Short Account of the Late Treatment of the Students at the University of G-----w*, a pamphlet published in Dublin in 1722 and usually attributed as the work of James Arbuckle (b.1700) begins:

> The right management of the universities is a
> matter of such importance to the whole nation, that
> it is apprehended, no one will think the following
> representation of the corruptions and disorders in the
> University of G-----w a work either unreasonable or
> useless.[1]

The *Short Account* makes much of the collocation of 'liberty and learning' and celebrates the historic right of students to choose

Glasgow University's Rector.[2] This right, Arbuckle tells us, was re-affirmed by the Treaty of Union in 1707, as a tradition that had lasted largely intact from 1492 until the seventeenth century, with brief periods of interference from a pair of tyrants, Oliver Cromwell and King James II. However, as Arbuckle sadly reports, 'soon after the late, happy Revolution' of 1688 this and other university rights were appropriated by a general meeting once a year whose committee (under the direction of the Principal) decided upon the appointment of the Rector and communicated the decision to the students.[3] The result was that from 1691 until 1718 Glasgow University had its longest serving rector, Sir John Maxwell, who to the chagrin of Arbuckle and like-minded men was far too secure in the position. Arbuckle complains against such clear signs of the breaching of the 'generous old Gothick rule of governing all by all', gothic here simply referencing the fact that the Goths were among the first of the Europeans, reputedly, to form a strong and effective tribal identity.[4] Arbuckle contends that following 1688, as a result of patronage by small groups and certain individual families, there had been too many ignorant Scottish clergymen employed at Glasgow rather than real scholars of talent. He cites one disastrous example of this, where the Principal employed a Professor of Oriental Languages who had to be sent to the University of Leyden to be taught Hebrew. In 1716, in response to student agitation for a rectorial election, the Chancellor of the University (the Duke of Montrose) was inveigled by the Principal into bringing a Commission of Royal Visitation, with the result that the Rector was for some years thereafter chosen by the Masters (most of whom were obedient to the Principal). Shortly afterwards, James Arbuckle, the student who had been so vocal about student rectorial voting rights, was denied not entry to classes but instead a ticket for communion at university worship, and in this way had a shadow cast over his faith and morality. So at this period the Presbyterian character of the University of Glasgow was part of the crucial territory of academic disputes, just as it was later in the eighteenth century.

Arbuckle's pamphlet, written after he had left Glasgow is an attempt to highlight what he takes to be the unfair patronage of his alma mater and the bullying against himself and other Glasgow students. He had continued his campaign against the university authorities after the events of *A Short Account*, by participating in a performance at Glasgow Grammar School in December 1720 of Nicholas Rowe's *Tamerlane*, a drama of 1701 that celebrated the coming to the throne of William III in 1689. The Glasgow performance included a prologue and epilogue that accused Principal John Stirling of squandering the benefits of the Glorious Revolution at Glasgow. In his contributions to *Tamerlane*, Arbuckle calls the university authorities a 'tyrannizing faction' to be compared to those masters of dark intrigue, the Jacobites. The period of Principal Stirling's custodianship of the university was, indeed, particularly factious with staff infighting and rowdy behaviour among the students. Having been Minister at Inchinnan and Greenock before becoming Glasgow's Principal, Stirling was appointed due to his closeness to the Rector, Sir John Maxwell. Stirling's predecessor during the period 1690-1700 was William Dunlop, another Presbyterian minister and an undistinguished scholar, appointed due to influential family connections. His supposed lack of wisdom was also to be seen in his investing of university money in the Darien Scheme, something which became one of many grumbles about finances at Glasgow that rumbled on through the eighteenth century. For Arbuckle, the Glorious Revolution of the Whigs was supposed to have done away with the obscurantist (Stuart) use of power, and of nepotism (at least outside the Monarchy) but what he saw instead was a rather narrow, albeit 'Moderate', Protestant culture of patronage in Glasgow University gathering power to itself. Arbuckle, on the other hand, a good Presbyterian himself, wanted a meritocracy with unfettered 'liberty & learning', an openness that came to some extent from the historic democratic kirk politics that were opposed to the ecclesiastical patronage (and patronage also in the public sphere including the universities), a particularly hot issue from 1711-12 with the Church Patronage Act (Scotland) and the restoration of the minister-appointing rights of nobles and patrons that the Glorious Revolution was supposed to have ended, or at least this was how Whigs of Arbuckle's stamp interpreted the disposition of 1688-89.

Arbuckle went on to become a periodical journalist editing the *Dublin Journal* where he adopted the pen-name of 'Hibernicus'. In this magazine he published the work of Francis Hutcheson, an

Ulsterman who became Professor of Moral Philosophy at Glasgow in 1729, and who instantly raised the standard of scholarship, not only by being a very clear writer and communicator but by being the first Professor in a Scottish university to lecture in English rather than in Latin. Hutcheson himself was very much seen as a 'new light' or Moderate, in keeping with the university authorities to whom Arbuckle was opposed in his student days. However, in his liberal theology, and in the fact that as a considerable minor poet he was very much non-puritanical in his aesthetic outlook (like Hutcheson who was one of the pioneers of theories of beauty in art), Arbuckle was a progressive figure in the emerging Scottish enlightenment. Hard-line Calvinist he was not. Hutcheson, for all his acceptability to the powers-that-be considered by Arbuckle as so corrupt, was also a pioneer at Glasgow of constitutional and personal rights, and the teacher of John Millar (Professor of Law with a similar interest in constitutional and personal rights). Millar taught and influenced Thomas Muir in the matter of rights (as we see in some detail elsewhere in this volume, in the essay by Ronnie Young). Millar, champion of democracy in the 1790s and opponent of slavery, was possibly the greatest 'political' influence on Muir, more so, for instance, than Thomas Paine the thinker with whom the young lawyer was most associated by the prosecution at his trial in 1793.

The foregoing sketch of Arbuckle's critique of the University of Glasgow has been intended to bring into view the long-rooted disputes about governance and patronage at the institution that Muir would enter. It also begins to show something of the complex entanglement in this history of figures of the Scottish Enlightenment, and indeed the nuanced spectrum of Presbyterian intellectualism in Glasgow and Scotland, that ran throughout the century. And it is provided also because, as we shall see below, the early eighteenth-century tenure of Principal Stirling rears its head again in the later contretemps at Glasgow involving Professor John Anderson, to whom Thomas Muir is seemingly an assiduous ally.

Thomas Muir (1765-99) was the son of James Muir and Margaret Smith. He was raised as an orthodox Presbyterian, entering Glasgow University with the likely destiny of church ministry.[5] His education began at the age of five through a private tutor, William Barclay, and he was admitted at the age of ten to the 'gowned classes' of the University.[6] After five sessions of study, he matriculated at the university in 1777 to study Divinity, one of several Master of Arts courses that the University offered. In 1782 he graduated as a Master of Arts at the age of seventeen, and fell under the influence of the teachings of John Millar, Professor of Civil Law, so that he abandoned his studies of Divinity in favour of Law.[7] In the session 1783-4, Muir became a student of Millar's classes on Law and Government, and also more involved in student life by joining clubs and societies that debated the important topics of the time, such as the Union of Scotland and England, and parliamentary reform. However, in May 1784, a dispute occurred between Professor John Anderson (1726-96) and other members of the Faculty, including Principal Leechman. Anderson had entered complaints regarding the misappropriation of college funds into the minute of a Faculty meeting, and the subsequent removal of these complaints from the minute caused him to make frequent comment on corruption at the University.[8] These remarks cost Anderson his privileges of the Senate membership, which in turn led him to petition the Chancellor (and Secretary of State), Henry Dundas, to procure a Royal Commission of Enquiry into the University's affairs. However, this was refused and upon returning from the summer vacation of 1784, Anderson announced his intention of submitting similar petitions to the Secretary of State in London, intentions which were never realised.[9] Following his suspension from the Senate, Anderson remained at the University of Glasgow, but became 'an embittered and somewhat isolated figure in the college'.[10] He took revenge on his Glasgow colleagues by drawing up a will in 1795 to use his estate to found a new university in the city following his death. Upon his death in 1796, the Andersonian College was swiftly established, with courses being offered from November of that year.[11] Anderson's vocal outrage against the University of Glasgow earned him widespread public popularity as well as influential allies in public life who later helped establish the new institution. The support for Anderson had previously peaked on 24 February 1785 when the Glasgow Trades, by a large majority, voted in support of Anderson's cause.[12] This had angered the elderly Principal Leechman to the extent that he made an impassioned appeal to the Trades, which led to the vote being reversed. The students who had been active on Anderson's behalf responded to this very public extension of the dispute by publishing a pamphlet entitled 'A Statement of Fact', which unceremoniously rounded upon Leechman and the Faculty for disregarding Anderson's complaints. The Faculty, probably with justification, saw this publication as guided by Anderson and as an act of gross insubordination. Upon Anderson's departure on a trip to London, there was retaliation. Disciplinary proceedings

John Anderson's support for students. In this document, John Anderson is protesting about the charges held against student James Wilson, believing he was doing nothing but his duty to the college. Wilson's expulsion was strongly opposed by Anderson.
University of Glasgow Archive Services, GB248 GUA26692., p.257.

began, with thirteen students including Muir (viewed as one of the ringleaders), being banned from lectures and called to disciplinary hearings. Although the students requested legal representation at their hearings, this was denied. Students began to be expelled, and some, such as Alexander Humphreys and William Clydesdale, were also deprived of their degrees.[13] Interestingly, Muir the nascent lawyer opted for voluntary removal from the university, rather than suffer exposure to proceedings at which he believed he would not be fairly represented or treated. Although not recorded in Faculty or Senate minutes of the time, it has been widely held by scholars that Muir acted pre-emptively in order to prevent the Faculty from stripping him of his MA degree, as they did to others.

John Anderson's dispute with the University. Anderson delivered papers entitled 'Protests and Reasons of Protests' to the College. These were frowned upon by Principal Leechman and others, who decided that the 'said papers contain many misrepresentations and falsehoods highly indecent and unconnected with the subject of complaint, and improper to be recorded in the Books of the College'. The college therefore rejected the papers, and this subsequently led to Anderson establishing the Andersonian College in revenge.
University of Glasgow Archive Services, GB248 GUA26692, p.355.

on

The most thorough history of the institution, James Coutts' *A History of the University of Glasgow* (1909) mentions the travails of James Arbuckle but surprisingly fails to note those of his successor student-activist, Thomas Muir. It does, however, deal at some length with the Anderson affair, providing fine-grained detail that, along with the Faculty minutes and other documents drawn upon below, is useful as background to a closer focus on Muir's activity in the fierce staff-student politics at Glasgow in the period 1783-4. Muir had become a close ally of Professor John Anderson, the serial litigator who for more than a quarter of a century fought court battles with colleagues, most famously the Principal, William Leechman (1706-85) but also Muir's mentor John Millar, among others. Anderson, seemingly a gifted and charismatic teacher, had the nickname 'Jolly Jack Phosphorous' bestowed upon him by students.[14] Anderson quarrelled with James Moor (c.1712-79), Professor of Greek (apparently the two brawled in a tavern), and with the Reverend Hugh Macleod (d.1794), a contretemps that even Anderson's hugely sympathetic biographer, James Muir, describes as 'a deplorable, almost an incredible [...] waste of time and temper'.[15] Anderson was also admonished by the University Faculty even as it was forced to drop a case that it sought to bring before it for the professor's alleged dangerous assault of a student named James Prosser. Anderson effectively collapsed the Faculty's attempts here by taking the case to the Court of Session and the whole episode seems to have fizzled out.[16] After his death his educational legacy, 'Anderson's Institution', was known by that name until 1828, thereafter going through a number of other iterations until in 1964 it became Strathclyde University. The modern university makes much of Anderson's desire that it be a place of 'useful learning', but this phrase was also collocated more fully among the founder's desire that his institution 'become a Seminary of Sound Religion; Useful Learning; and Liberality of

(Opposite) Expulsion of Alexander Humphreys. This document records the expulsion of Alexander Humphries, a student in Anatomy. He requested the support of a witness, but this request was refused. In turn, Humphreys ignored his summons, and was expelled for contumacy and deprived of his Master of Arts Degree.
University of Glasgow Archive Services, GB248 GUA26693, p.52.

52.

College Records.

[margin: W. Rowland, Auditor or Comp. 1783 given in]

College Revenue for the year 1783. were given in to the Meeting and Doctor Findlay Mr Cumin Mr Clow and Doctor Reid are appointed a Committee to examine the said accompts and to report

Jas Clow praeses
Patk Wilson Vice Coll

Glasgow College April 15th 1783.

Sederunt The Revd Doctr Robert Findlay S.S.T.P.
Mr James Clow G.P. Dr Alexander Wilson L.L.P.
Mr John Millar J.C.P. Mr Patrick Cumin L.L.P.
Dr James Williamson M.D. Dr Thomas Reid P.M.P.
Dr Alexander Stevenson M.D. Mr William Richardson
L.H.P. Mr John Young L.G.P. Doctor
Hugh McLeod H.E.P. Mr William Hamilton
A. et B.P.
A Meeting of Faculty being duly
Summoned and Convened

[margin: Alexr Humphreys summoned before the Meeting]

Alexr Humphreys Master of Arts and Student of Anatomy in this University being duly summoned with Intimation in writing that he was to answer to the Faculty for his Conduct in subscribing certain Publications injurious to this University And being called in he refused to appear before the Meeting unless permitted to bring along with him such persons as he chose. The Meeting upon this sent the Clerk of Faculty and Mr Jardine to inform him that the Faculty required his immediate attendance; That his desire of having other persons along with him could not be complied with, Another message was immediately after carried from the Faculty by the same persons, to the same effect, And also informing Alexr Humphreys that upon his Refusal to appear he would be held Contumacious and proceeded against accordingly

The Meeting having thereafter deliberated upon the above behaviour of Alexander Humphreys who still refused to appear unattended, were unanimously of Opinion that the said Alexr Humphreys ought to be Expelled from this University for his **Contumacy** and that he ought to be deprived of his Degree of Master of Arts. —

53.

15.th April 1785.

The Meeting therefore did and hereby do Unanimously Expel the said Alexander Humphreys from this University and deprive him of his Degree of Master of Arts therein and order his name to be erased from the Matriculation Books and, from the list of Masters of Arts in this University. And the Meeting order this sentence to be intimated to him by the Bedellus, and they further order that no Professor or Lecturer shall admit him to attend his Lectures: And they appoint Mr Hamilton to publish this Sentence in the Anatomy Class.

[margin: Alexander Humphreys Expelled the University for Contumacy]

William Clydsdale Student in Divinity, having also been served with a written summons to answer to the Faculty for his conduct in subscribing certain publications injurious to this University, was called in. The Rev.d Doctor Findlay having previously gone out and conversed with him apart upon the subject of the Complaint against him: And the said William Clydsdale having refused to appear before the meeting unless permitted to bring along with him a number of his friends. He was informed by the Clerk and Mr Jardine, that his desire of bringing in his friends along with him was Contrary to the Rules of College procedure in such Cases, and that if he should not appear before the Meeting he would be held as <u>Con= tumacious</u> and must stand to the Consequences, Notwith= standing of which he still refused to appear.

[margin: William Clydsdale also Summoned]

The Meeting having, thereafter deliberated upon the above behaviour of the said William Clydsdale Un= animously did and hereby do expel him from this Uni= versity and order his name to be erased from the Ma= triculation Books.— They Order this sentence to be inti= mated to the said William Clydsdale by the Bedellus.— They further order that no Professor shall admit him to attend his Lectures— And that this sentence shall be published by Doctor Findlay in the Divinity Hall.

[margin: And Expelled the University for his Contumacy]

Sic Clenn process
W.t t. Wilson Cler: Coll.

Sentiment'.[17] It may be inferred that Anderson did not fully believe that Glasgow University could be characterised in these terms. In spite of Anderson's expressed desire for 'liberality of sentiment', Tom Devine has pointed to Anderson's rather militant, illiberal Protestantism, with its strong intolerance of Catholicism.[18] Such an attitude contrasted, for instance, with Anderson's Glasgow colleague (and erstwhile ally who was eventually also to fall out with him), Thomas Reid (1710-96), Professor of Moral Philosophy at Glasgow until 1781 and Vice-Rector of the university until 1785. Reid, a liberal in a very wide cultural and ecumenical sense was, for instance, the enabler of the Catholic priest, Alexander Geddes (1737-1802), gaining access to the university library as he pursued his pioneering biblical studies. Anderson's proclaimed hope that the new institute would become a 'seminary of sound religion' is also clearly suggestive of his jaundiced view on the 'Moderate' Presbyterian outlook at the University of Glasgow at this time. His actions at Glasgow, leaving aside his explosive personality, exemplified by a persistent opposition to the ruling Moderate party there, would seem to be of a piece with his theological temper. These Moderates included Leechman himself, Professor of Divinity from 1744 and Principal from 1761. Much admired by Francis Hutcheson, Leechman like his admirer was accused by the presbytery of Glasgow of unsound doctrine.[19] In a way that resonates with Hutcheson's arraignment earlier and with the William McGill case in which Thomas Muir was later to be intensely involved, Leechman's published sermon, 'On the Nature, Reasonableness and Advantages of Prayer' (1743) was believed by the presbytery to be heterodox in placing too little emphasis upon Christ's bringing of salvation into the world. From 1784, Anderson was ferociously on the attack against Leechman and also, as part of the same dispute, engaged in enmity with the Reverend William Taylor (1744-1823), who had been awarded a Doctor of Divinity degree in 1783 (with Muir's later ecclesiastical enemy, another Moderate William McGill, being awarded the same degree by

(Opposite) Expulsion of William Clydesdale. This page minutes the expulsion of William Clydesdale. Clydesdale was a student of Divinity alongside Muir. He also refused to appear at his summons, and was therefore considered to be contumacious and expelled.
University of Glasgow Archive Services. GB248 GUA26693, p.53.

the same institution in 1785). We see, then, the Moderate party authorities at Glasgow rewarding individuals in this period who were anathema to the Calvinist Popular Party grouping, which had its own distinctive strengths within the city. Although never given the professorship which he coveted, Taylor became Moderator of the General Assembly of the Church of Scotland in 1798 and was made Principal of Glasgow University in 1803, serving in this role until 1823. He was also, from 1791, Librarian of Glasgow's Stirling Library, an institution that Anderson sneered at in his will. Leaving aside certain undoubted talents, Taylor owed advancement to some extent to the approval of Henry Dundas, Scottish Lord Advocate from 1775, Rector of Glasgow University from 1781-83 and British Home Secretary from 1791. In his own way Dundas was a man of the Enlightenment, encouraging theological and intellectual liberalism to some extent. He was also, as the events of the 1790s especially were to show, fearful of more radical political thinking, associated often with Whigs and also the Popular Party. However, we need to be careful here as, for instance, William Peebles (1753-1826) was an ally of Thomas Muir's in the pursuit through the ecclesiastical courts of William McGill, but was also – like Dundas – a staunchly conservative, loyalist in the period following the French Revolution. Investigating the intellectual, political, ecclesiastical connections around Muir, beginning with those orbiting around the University of Glasgow, opens up an 'enlightened' world that is much more nuanced, and cross-grained even, than is typically drawn upon in Muir Studies and elsewhere.

In 1784 when John Anderson accused William Leechman and the senior management at Glasgow University of financial irregularity, this charge was also bound up with a culture of patronage disliked by the Principal's accuser. Roger L Emerson has shown a complex pattern of patronage at Glasgow during the eighteenth century, but – broadly speaking – the Squadrone Volante party, which had played an important part in the Treaty of Union in 1707, had dominance until the late 1720s, and thereafter there was a varied mixture of aristocratic and church patronage, with the family of the Duke of Montrose exercising large influence (through four generations as Chancellors of the university with the 3rd Duke also a ministerial colleague of Dundas's in the government of William Pitt). In the period of reform, and the time of the Pitt-Dundas administration in Britain, there is a strong suggestion of Anderson's radical

The Reverend William Taylor (1744-1823). Taylor was Moderator of the General Assembly of the Church of Scotland in 1798 and Principal of Glasgow University from 1803 umtil 1823. In 1784 he became involved in a dispute between Leechman and Anderson. This image has been digitised from a small original photograph.
Mitchell Library Photographic Department TGSA03568.

political sympathies. In an episode that may have found an echo in the fabricated nineteenth-century story of Robert Burns sending carronades to the French revolutionaries, Anderson sent a self-designed canon to the French nation in 1791, albeit two years before Britain and France came to all-out war in 1793.[20] Was Anderson politically progressive and also more staunchly Calvinist than most of his colleagues at the University of Glasgow? This seems very likely from the hints we have, and albeit with the possible complication of a head-strong, combative personality which the evidence does indeed suggest, also we see perhaps a Whiggish Anderson opposed to the often – though not exclusively – Tory, Moderate party dominance of Glasgow University.

The case of the slandering of the Reverend William Taylor amid Anderson's attacks on Glasgow University is particularly revealing. On the face of it, a minor part of the Anderson affair, when investigated it casts interesting light not only on Anderson himself, but also on the rather nasty situation into which his acolyte Thomas Muir had wandered, whether willingly or naively and innocently. An advertisement preceding publication of a printed letter appeared in the *Glasgow Journal* of 17 March 1785 with the clear intent of publicly shaming Taylor. James Coutts sums up the outcome of the incident:

> Dr. Taylor having raised an action in the Court of Session against Anderson as the real author of the paper of the defamatory paper issued in the name of Humphreys, recovered £250 by way of damages from Peter Tait, proprietor of the *Glasgow Journal*, in respect of a paragraph which appeared in that paper, and of which Tait refused to disclose the author's name.[21]

Both of these documents, advertisement and published letter, can be retrieved from the papers that form the Court of Session legal process, *State of the Process, The Rev Dr William Taylor against Mr John Anderson*, where they are recorded verbatim. The advertisement ran:

> Will soon be published (not anonymous), A Letter to the Rev. Dr Taylor, one of the Ordinary Visitors of the College

of Glasgow, inscribed to the Ministers of the Session of the
Inner High-Church of Glasgow.
    'Thou lovest lying rather than righteousness, *Psal.* Iii.3.
    'Let the lying lips be put to silence, *Psal.* Xxxi.18.
    'Lying lips are an abomination to the Lord, *Prov.* Xii.22.[22]

The letter itself on the printed bill ran as follows:

Rev. Sir,
Satan has surely got footing in the House of God, when
such preachers as you are permitted to instruct the
people. Those virtues that constitute a Man, and are the
distinguished characteristics of a Christian, are entirely
unknown to you. Vice and Folly, though detested by every
great and good man, seem to be courted by you; and it
would be injustice to conceal your real character to future
ages. Sawney Bean, with all his cruelty and barbarity, was
not to be more dreaded than you, who under the mask of
Religion, commit such crimes as you have done.[23]

That there was an insidious, underhand and sinister campaign
against Taylor is in no doubt, and the legal records also exhibit an
anonymous letter that he received with a postmark from Ireland:

Rev Sir,
Perhaps a greater villain never appeared in the Church.
Your late conduct shows at once the knave and fool; the
knave in joining the Faculty to rob the College of its funds;
the fool by commencing a suit at their instance, who, to
please your vanity promised to get you made Principal [...]
You ought to be afraid of just revenge, for I assure you, you
will meet it when you least suspect it.[24]

Among numerous sworn witness statements made while Taylor
pursued Anderson through the court was the following, dated 3
May 1786:

James Muir Hop-merchant in Glasgow, aged 50 years
and upwards, married solemnly sworn, &c. depones, That

upwards of a year ago, as the deponent thinks, a printed
paper, consisting of a number of sheets, came addressed
to his son, Thomas Muir, under cover, from the Glasgow
post-office: That the deponent read about two pages of the
said paper. And the printed Letter referred to in former
depositions, addressed to the Pursuer [ie William Taylor],
being shewn him [ie James Muir], depones, That he thinks,
and is very certain, that the title-page of the printed paper
sent his son, and part of the first paragraph of the printed
Letter now shewn, and the size and form were as he thinks
also the same: That the said printed paper was seen by the
deponent's wife and son; but whether they read it or not,
he cannot say. *Causa Scientiae pate:* And this is truth he
shall answer to God. Upon the Pursuer's again questioning
him, depones, that he was an Elder of the College-Church
Session at the time the foresaid printed paper was
received.[25]

This evidence is both interesting and strange. We see, as later in
the Cadder Kirk case, that the Muirs, father and son, are involving
themselves in a dispute with ecclesiastical and other dimensions.
James Muir, as an Elder of the university church is closer to the
affairs of the 1783-6 University of Glasgow/Anderson dispute
than Thomas Muir's biographers have hitherto realised. It is also
frustrating, but possibly in its own way suggestive that Thomas
Muir should not be called to give evidence but that his father,
James, should be. Is the father shielding the son? He does not
attempt to deny a connection with the letter-document attacking
Taylor, and, indeed, admits that it has been sent to Thomas. But
he, James, has opened it, and – rather awkwardly – it might be
thought, he does not know that either his son or his own wife (is
she brought in as part of an attempt to further obfuscate?) has
read it though both have certainly seen it, he declares. There is in
the statement provided by James the distinct whiff of sophistry.
Has the father offered to give evidence to take the heat off of his
son, who is by now (in the spring of 1786 as James's evidence is
recorded) pursuing studies at the University of Edinburgh, and
best not to be dragged back into the affair? Alternatively, it might
be conjectured that James Muir was disgusted by the Taylor

affair and willingly appeared in court to make a statement about the offensive letter; further work is needed to clarify motivation in this intriguing episode. Remaining in speculative mode, it is known that John Millar had helped smooth Thomas's entry to Edinburgh after the student's exit from Glasgow and Millar is someone who is increasingly wary of Anderson and the effect of his actions during this same period. Essentially simultaneous to the action of the Taylor case, as we see in a document dated 20 April 1787 though raised seemingly during 1785 (while Edmund Burke was still Rector), the University of Glasgow goes on the offensive against Anderson. The papers for this case are gathered together under the title, *Information for the Most Honorable The Marquis of Graham* [the Duke of Montrose]; *Chancellor, The Right Honorable Edmund Burke, Rector, The Reverend Dr Meek, Dean of Faculties, the Rev. Dr Taylor, Minister of Glasgow, one of the Ordinary Visitors of the University of Glasgow etc.* As well as these most senior officers of the university, are also named a list of Glasgow academics, two of whom are Thomas Reid, an ally of Anderson's in his earlier complaints about Glasgow finances during the 1770s and John Millar.[26] This document rehearses Anderson's actions during the 1770s and 1780s and also narrates a great deal of the technical fiscal history of the University of Glasgow going all the way back to the 1720s and the period of James Arbuckle's complaints (we shall see below why such a long time-frame was felt needed as context to the action against Anderson). What we also find mentioned in *State of the Process, The Rev Dr William Taylor against Mr John Anderson* is the petition against Taylor and the management of the university which sees the Glasgow Trades, Merchants and Manufacturers siding with Anderson and the students.[27] Given the appearance of 'Hop-merchant', James Muir as sworn witness in the Taylor slander affair we glimpse the Muir family almost certainly in its closeness to the centre of this network, as well as the Popular Party interest in and around the university and in the city more widely.

Earlier in evidence there had been a statement by James Gibson, student of Divinity at Glasgow about a meeting at the Tontine Tavern where mischief against Taylor seems to have been planned, and where the name of Thomas Muir had occurred. Part of Gibson's evidence runs that '[...] the deponent went in company with Alexander Humphrays' and that also 'present [were] Mr Anderson, Defender, Messrs Thomas Muir, Robert Edmond, David McIndoe, James Robertson, John Wilson' and 'others, in all about eight or ten'.[28] Clearly, Muir is prominent here as the affair is unfolding and action is being planned. Among other sworn statements about the 'abusive' document (the letter against Taylor), Dugald Stewart, 'Professor of Moral Philosophy in the College of Edinburgh' recollects that he has been sent it in the post.[29] Dr James Gregory, 'Physician in Edinburgh' has also seen it, as has the Rev. John Burns, Minister of the Barony-parish of Glasgow.[30] What emerges here, clearly, is a concerted campaign that seeks to influence ecclesiastical opinion in Glasgow and, to some extent also, the great and the good of Edinburgh. Further research might be able to demonstrate whether or not there is a discernible pattern here (which if there is might be one that shows, for instance, a particular set of Anderson's acquaintances).

The printer, Peter Tait, appears in the proceedings and swears that he does not know who sent to him the advertisement for publication and that he cannot find the original manuscript (which, on the face of it, is a different version of events than that provided by James Coutts above).[31] David McIndoe swears that he was given a copy of the (printed) letter by Anderson himself. But it would seem to be on his evidence that Humphrays was fixed upon as the main culprit in the authorship and broadcasting of the letter. McIndoe relates:

> That he was at a meeting with Alexander Humphrays, late student at the University of Glasgow, and several other Students, in the house of Mrs Shedd vintner in Glasgow, upon Wednesday evening, immediately preceding the Spring Sacrament, which he understands was convened for the purpose of suppressing the said letter.[32]

The contretemps between Anderson and the students against the authorities of the University of Glasgow had long roots going back to the 1770s. It involved not only university finances, but the proportion of students appropriately graduating, rectorial voting rights (in an echo of the days of Arbuckle) and was to involve not only a network of Scottish students such as Muir, McIndoe *et al* but

Professor Dugald Stewart (1753-1828). Stewart was educated at Edinburgh and Glasgow and was appointed Professor of Moral Philosophy at Edinburgh University in 1785; he was a disciple of Thomas Reid and claimed that he had been sent the 'abusive' letter against Taylor in the post. This portrait was painted by Sir Henry Raeburn.
National Galleries of Scotland, PG 821.

also a large network of Anderson-supportive Irish students (which would seem to explain the significance of the Taylor's letter's Irish postmark). As a prelude to his main actions of 1784, however, Anderson had busied himself being supportive of an article by the Unitarian minister John Disney (1746-1816) in the *Gentleman's Magazine* for September 1783. Interestingly, this sought to emphasise the long-standing fiscal mal-administration of Glasgow University going back to at least 1727. Disney's article drew on material from manuscript memoirs of a William Robertson who had graduated in 1724 (but who was expelled in 1725 and later reinstated). Via Robertson, the claim was made that Principal Stirling had embezzled thousands of pounds 'which it was said the Commission of 1727 had obliged him to refund'.[33] In fact the Commission recorded no such events, though it did identify the university accounts as being disorganised and badly ledgered.[34] In general, from the 1720s to the 1780s, for all that accounts of Thomas Muir's life tend to see fiscal corruption at Glasgow University in fairly face-value fashion, the biggest problem seems to have been a sluggish, unprofessional attitude to funds. Likely, it would take the forensic skills of a historian of eighteenth-century accounting to make sense of what precisely was going on in University of Glasgow finances through the eighteenth century, and even then such an examiner would probably not have enough material to reach definitive conclusions about any possible wrong-doing by Stirling, Leechman or others. In response to Disney's article, Principal Leechman raised the issue at Faculty and a letter was written to Disney to disabuse him of his essentially unfounded account of Stirling's 'embezzlement'. Anderson, on the other hand, as Disney was later to attest in a letter to the university authorities, visited Disney and sought to persuade him of the essential truth of Robertson's memoir. What comes into view, then, is the strong possibility that Anderson's charge of financial corruption, among his other complaints in 1784, are inspired by the events of sixty years before and, indeed, are reiterations of these 'myths', albeit myths based on the undoubted financial chaos at Glasgow. Similarly, Anderson's appeal for a Royal Commission in the present of the 1780s may well have been inspired by the visitation of 1727. Whether Anderson had any real trust that such a visitation might be accomplished in the 1780s, with powerful men like Henry

Dundas and Edmund Burke opposing such a move, might be open to some doubt. The present authors are tempted to speculate that Anderson's appeals for a Commission arose out of his habitual reflex of demanding official, legislative scrutiny and also, perhaps, with the intention of creating a situation where people might believe there could be no smoke without fire. Anderson is one of those individuals whose petulance makes it quite difficult to judge of the merits of his (highly frequent) complaints. However, this has not been the place to analyse the affairs of Anderson and the University of Glasgow with some closeness for their own sake, but rather to set their context, their mood even, in which we might begin to locate Thomas Muir a bit more sharply than in previous accounts of his time at Glasgow University. Future consideration of Anderson's actions at Glasgow and also the Taylor case will almost certainly cast even sharper light on Muir. For the moment it is difficult to determine exactly whether Anderson was the main agent in the slandering of Taylor and whether it was arranged for Humphreys and eventually Peter Tait to carry the can.

What we see in the events of 1784-5, whatever the precise rights and wrongs of the situation, is a battle between Moderates, perhaps in the minority but firmly in control of Glasgow University, and Popular Party adherents. The latter included Anderson, Thomas Muir, ecclesiastical figures beyond the university and also merchants and members of the trades guilds, such as James Muir who had connection and influence within the institution. Groupings including the students, merchants and tradesmen would seem to have picked their side in the dispute based on a complex combination of theological and political outlook, both of which might well be described as 'anti-patronage'. Much of the fine-grained history of Glasgow, its university, its church, and its powerful lay groupings has settled into convenient generalities about Glasgow in the eighteenth century. When we begin even merely to scratch the surface of the affairs of the University of Glasgow in the period, via contemporary sources, a fascinating ideological struggle begins to come into view, and in that view much food for thought begins to be provided about the location of Thomas Muir as a student at the University of Glasgow.

Notes and References

1 Arbuckle, 1722, p.3. In this pamphlet Arbuckle is referred to in the third person.
2 Arbuckle, 1722, p.3.
3 Arbuckle, 1722, p.5.
4 Arbuckle, 1722, p.5.
5 Bewley, 1981, p.3.
6 Donnelly, 1975, p.2.
7 Donnelly, 1975, p.2.
8 For Anderson's complaint of financial misappropriation see, Faculty Minutes of the University of Glasgow, Volume 77, 19 December 1781; for his reiterated charge of corruption see, for instance, Faculty Minutes of the University of Glasgow, Volume 77, 5 April 1783.
9 Faculty Minutes of the University of Glasgow, Volume 77, 17 September 1784.
10 Biography of John Anderson (1726-1796) by Paul Wood, 2004, in *Oxford Dictionary of National Biography*, Oxford University Press: http://www.oxforddnb.com/view/article/481.
11 Biography of John Anderson. http://www.oxforddnb.com/view/article/481.
12 Donnelly, 1975, p.5.
13 Faculty Minutes of the University of Glasgow, Volume 79, 15 April 1785.
14 Muir, 1950, p.4.
15 Muir, 1950, p.18.
16 Emerson, 1993, pp.21-39.
17 Muir, 1950, p.142.
18 Devine, 2006, p.80.
19 Kennedy, 1995, p.58.
20 Biography of John Anderson. http://www.oxforddnb.com/view/article/481.
21 Coutts, 1909, p.294.
22 *State of the Process, The Rev Dr William Taylor against Mr John Anderson* (11 February 1786), p.1.[Legal gatherings from the Court of Session, collected together with other related documents in a volume in the University of Glasgow Special Collections (Mu Add q 16).]
23 *State of the Process*, 1786, p.147.
24 *State of the Process*, 1786, p.155.
25 *State of the Process*, 1786, p107.
26 *Information for the Most Honorable The Marquis of Graham* [the Duke of Montrose]; *Chancellor, The Right Honorable Edmund Burke, Rector, The Reverend Dr Meek, Dean of Faculties, the Rev. Dr Taylor, Minister of Glasgow, one of the Ordinary Visitors of the*

University of Glasgow etc. (1787); in a volume in University Glasgow Special Collections (Mu Add q 16).

27 *State of the Process*, 1786, p.155.

28 *State of the Process*, 1786, p.75.

29 *State of the Process*, 1786, p.90.

30 *State of the Process*, 1786, p.91; p.95.

31 *State of the Process*, 1786, p.105.

32 *State of the Process*, 1786, pp.110-11.

33 Coutts, 1909, p.286.

34 See Coutts, 1909, pp.286-7 for the basic facts of the Anderson-Disney episode.

Thomas Muir at Glasgow: John Millar and the University

Ronnie Young

Thomas Muir's career at Glasgow University has been viewed by many as a key influence upon his subsequent career and central in shaping his later role as reformer and 'father of Scottish democracy'. Much of that influence has been attributed to the charismatic teaching of John Millar (1735-1801), the leading Enlightenment thinker, protégé of Adam Smith, and Professor of Civil Law at Glasgow College from 1761 until 1800. Millar's lectures are often cited as the reason that Muir, who was originally planning to study Divinity, changed to become a lawyer, and Millar's political outlook – as constitutional Whig, champion of meritocracy, and active political player in the late Enlightenment public sphere – has also been considered a shaping context for Muir's own politics and the reformist-over-radical direction of the Society of the Friends of the People, of which Millar and Muir were members alongside Millar's own son John Millar Jr. In this essay, I will look at Muir's Glasgow career from his early years as 'gowned' student through his studies in Law with Millar, until the events that led to his withdrawal in 1785.

Early years at Glasgow College

Although biographers have agreed on the importance of Muir's time at University, not all concur on the dates of his attendance. The first published account of Muir's time at Glasgow by William Marshall in the *Glasgow Magazine* of 1795 records that Muir entered 'the gowned classes of Glasgow college, on the 10th October 1775, being then little older than ten years of age'.[1] Peter Mackenzie followed suit in his influential life of Muir in 1831, placing the year of entry at 1775.[2] In her biography, Christina Bewley notes that Muir entered the junior section of the University in 1777, that he turned to Divinity at his parents' urging two years later, and that he finally set his eye on the Bar 'after matriculating in April 1782'[3] – dates followed in the Dictionary of National Biography.[4] Michael Donnelly, for his part, claims that Muir entered University and attended the junior classes for five sessions before matriculating in 1777, after which he is said to have graduated in 1782 and then gained admittance to Millar's Law and Government class in 1783.[5]

Some of these details require clarification. That Muir started attending classes at the University at the young age of 10 is a reasonable proposition given that the entry age for University was much lower in the eighteenth century. Muir's own mentor John Millar was 11 when he first attended Glasgow College as student in 1746.[6] Moreover, it was common for students to take classes before matriculating or not to matriculate at all, as matriculation was only a requirement for students in the Faculty of Arts who intended to graduate MA or those who wished to vote in the election of rectors.[7] Matriculation did not have to take place in the first year of study, as attested by the records of students matriculating in classes other than Latin. While it would be possible for Muir to have studied at Glasgow for some two years before matriculating, University records show that Muir did in fact matriculate in 1777. The matriculation album for that year lists Muir under the heading 'Nomina Discipulorum qui hoc anno intrarunt sub Praesidio Gul[ielmus]: Richardson L.H.P',[8] meaning that the student named entered this year under the supervision of William Richardson, Professor of Humanity, who taught the first year class in Latin. Muir's entry consists of his signature in ink on parchment followed by the hand of the Clerk of Faculty[9] detailing in Latin that he is the only son of James, merchant in the City of Glasgow: 'Thomas Muir filius unicus Jacobi Mercatoris in urbe Glasguensis'.[10] (illustrated on p.114)

Muir is also listed, alongside his nationality, on the graduation rolls of the University for 24 April 1782[11] (page 115), confirming that he did graduate Master of Arts that year.

To graduate MA in 1782, Muir would have undertaken five years of study from 1777. The normal pattern of study over the course of these five years was Latin for the first year, Greek for the second, in third year Logic, followed by Ethics and then Physics or Natural Philosophy in the final year, followed by examination

Muir's entry in the Matriculation Album, 1777.
Glasgow University Archives, GUA 26678.

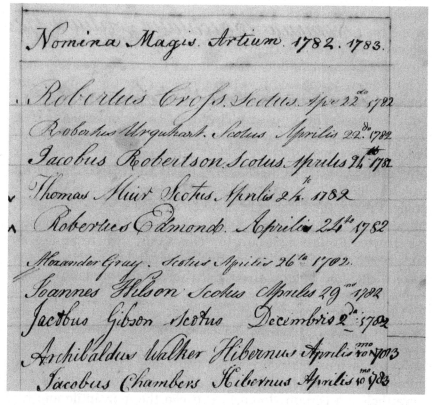

Muir listed Master of Arts in the graduation roll for 1782.
Glasgow University Archives, GUA 26676.

in these subjects in order to graduate.[12] From 1777 to 1782, Muir would have studied in turn under Richardson, John Young, George Jardine, the renowned 'common sense' moral philosopher Thomas Reid, and, in his final year, John Anderson, the divisive Professor of Natural Philosophy whose actions against the University would later lead to Muir's eventual withdrawal as a student.

For Muir, entry to the University in the late 1770s would not exactly be entry to an unfamiliar world. The College was then situated on Glasgow's High Street just up the street from the property in which Muir's family lived at the time. In the late eighteenth century, the High Street was still very much the heart of an expanding mercantile centre, although the colonial trade in such commodities as tobacco that had increased the City's prosperity throughout the century was about to take a significant downturn with the onset of hostilities with the American colonies.[13] As a civic space, it was dominated by the Cathedral and the University, which stood on the junction where College Street (completed nine years after Muir withdrew from Glasgow) meets High Street. As shown in John McArthur's map of Glasgow dating from the time Muir was student there, the University stood on extensive grounds, where, in addition to the College building itself, there was the newly constructed Professor's Court (or 'New Court') where professors such as John Millar lived, a 'physick' garden linked to the teaching of medicine and botany, Blackfriar church, and gardens leading out to the east towards an observatory.

Though there was a traditional civic distinction in Glasgow between 'town' and 'gown', made flesh by the requirement that students in Arts such as Muir wear a distinctive scarlet gown,[14] and though tensions between the two often surfaced, as in the John Anderson affair that led to Muir's withdrawal, there was nevertheless a certain closeness between the mercantile and the scholarly spheres.[15] Merchants such as James Muir sent their sons to the College to complete their education. Muir entered the College of Glasgow as a fairly typical student and matriculated for a first-year class in which he was just another of the thirty-seven sons of Glasgow City and surrounding areas. The fifty-two students

Opposite: Detail from John McArthur's 1778 Plan of the City of Glasgow, showing the Old College and grounds off the High Street.
Glasgow University Library, C18:45 GLA1.

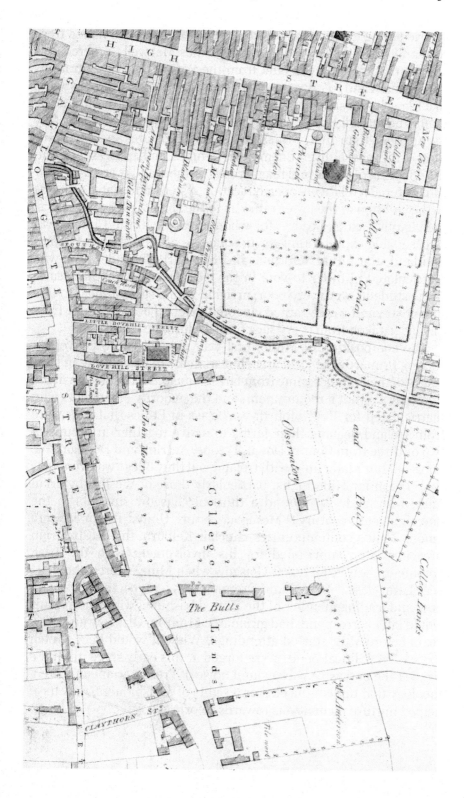

matriculating for Richardson's Latin class that year all hailed from Scotland (with the exception of one James Maxwell, a merchant's son from Maryland), the bulk from the West, with concentrations from Lanark and Ayr. By far the majority of Muir's classmates were, like himself, the sons of merchants or of fathers involved in trades, crafts and manufactures, again with a large proportion from the City itself; other than that, Muir's first-year classmates included four 'sons of the manse', five from military families, and, to a lesser extent, the offspring of clerks and magistrates, farmers and weavers.[16] Muir thus entered a relatively open education system, affordable as it was to the children of the lower ranks as to the sons of prosperous local merchants such as Muir – for whom a career in the Church was a reasonable expectation – or to someone of the stature of James Maitland, the future reformer and 8th Earl of Lauderdale, who matriculated in order to vote in the election of rector that year.[17] Some students were very poor, arriving with a sack of meal to tide them over, and were granted customs relief by being exempt from 'the ladel' taken from every sack brought into the burgh.[18]

The composition of Muir's first-year class sees the University serving primarily the local area, but students matriculating in later stages of their studies came from farther afield. Matriculation in the first year was not a requirement, and the majority of students who matriculated for Reid's fourth-year class in Ethics that year were from Ireland, leaving their farms to arrive together in groups of two or three from County Down, Tyrone, Antrim, and Donegal. We know of Muir's later links with Ireland, but the College was a popular destination for Hibernians, particularly those of the Presbyterian faith, who made up around a third of Glasgow students in the late eighteenth century.[19] Moreover, future United Irishmen were among Muir's contemporaries. Sinclair Kelburn, the Presbyterian preacher later imprisoned for his involvement with the Irish volunteers, was studying at Glasgow when Muir entered the first-year Latin class.[20] Dr William Drennan (1754-1820), the physician, poet and leading member of the United Irishmen with whom Muir would later correspond, had graduated MA from Glasgow just a few years before Muir started attending.[21] While it would be a stretch to say that political bonds were forged at this early stage in Muir's life, yet the pervasive background noise of Presbyterianism, with a theology that upheld the electoral rights of parishioners, may have helped nurture inclinations towards reform.

Most commentators note that Muir's early years at University were relatively undistinguished, and little record of this time exists. He gains a minor mention in connection with the College prize-giving ceremony of May 1779, where he was awarded a prize 'for good behaviour during an attendance of two Sessions in the public Class' for Humanity – a meagre honour, far below the prizes for essays and for elocution, and a laurel he had to share with another seven students.[22] Yet, if his early years were marked only by mediocrity, the education offered to him at Glasgow was anything but. The University was in many ways dynamic and forward looking. The 'regent' system, whereby students were taught by the same individual across subjects, had been abolished following visitation by a royal commission in 1726 and a series of specialist chairs had been instituted in philosophy for teaching logic, ethics and physics. One such 'specialist' professor, Adam Smith, who was Glasgow's Professor of Moral Philosophy from 1752 to 1764, later wrote about the benefits to productivity arising from the simple division of labour in his pioneering analysis of political economy, *The Wealth of Nations* (1776). Lectures in Latin were being phased out in favour of a precise modern English in such areas as Moral Philosophy, firstly by the great Francis Hutcheson, who had taught Smith, and later in subjects such as Law, which Muir went on to study. With reform, came a forward-looking curriculum that taught 'experimental philosophy', or science on the Newtonian model, and a version of 'moral' thought that under Hutcheson, Smith, and in turn Millar, offered a strikingly modern vision of the individual as a self-sufficient yet socially-grounded moral agent, guided by their intrinsic sentiments, sympathies, and sense of justice, within a commercial public sphere.

Glasgow itself was one of the main centres of the 'Scottish Enlightenment', a key part of a wider Enlightenment in which intellectuals were engaged in a systematic re-examination of the natural and social order, probing into the nature of the human species and its various relations: moral, social, economic, political, and legal. In America and France, Enlightenment produced the revolutionary establishment of new representative political systems; Scots intellectuals, though inclined towards a comparatively settled constitution, fed into the intellectual ferment of ideas for political change. Enlightenment culture in Scotland was centred around the University towns of Edinburgh, Aberdeen, and

Glasgow itself, and the clubs, societies and publishing networks that sprang up in and around places of learning. In Glasgow, the famous Literary Society and the Foulis press were based in the University. By the time Muir reached Glasgow, its contribution to the Enlightenment had been marked. Former staff and students included the 'father of the Scottish Enlightenment' Francis Hutcheson, Professor of Moral Philosophy 1730-46, who taught 'political economist' Adam Smith and was an influence alongside Locke on the founding fathers of America.[23] Adam Smith returned to teach at Glasgow in the chair of Logic in 1751, shifting over to Moral Philosophy the following year. He was succeeded in 1764 by Thomas Reid, one of the main exponents of Scottish 'common sense' philosophy in opposition to the scepticism of David Hume. In science, pioneering chemist Joseph Black had been Professor of Medicine from 1757 until 1766, and engineer James Watt had worked for Black as an instrument maker at the University.[24]

Studying law with John Millar

No mention of Glasgow's Enlightenment would be complete without mention of John Millar. who made a decisive contribution to the Enlightenment study of 'the natural history of man' with the publication in 1771 of his *Observations concerning the Distinctions of Ranks in Society*, a work which gained him a reputation as one of the founding fathers of sociology.[25] Millar was Regius Chair of Civil Law at Glasgow from 1761 to 1800, during which time he invigorated the teaching of law, expanding the subject with a series of innovative and popular lectures on law and government that turned the young Muir's head. After graduating Master of Arts in 1782, Muir shifted from a planned career in divinity, towards Law. The catalyst for this change was Millar, whose lectures Muir had started attending. Muir, who had by this means developed an interest in the subject, then applied for the classes in Law and Government for session 1783-84.[26]

Glasgow was at this time acquiring a reputation in the teaching of Law, largely through the efforts of Millar, who had succeeded Hercules Lindsay as Regius Professor of Civil Law in 1761. Craig estimates that where hitherto only four or five students had studied Law at Glasgow, distanced inconveniently as it was from the courts in Edinburgh, the school increased as much as tenfold under the

Professor's watch.[27] As Robert Heron remarked in the 1790s: 'It is to hear his Lectures on the first elements of Jurisprudence and Government, – on the Roman or Civil, – on the Scotch, – and on the English Law, that students resort, from all quarters of Britain, Glasgow is, in short, famous, as a school for Law, as Edinburgh as a school for medicine'.[28] Such praise Heron did not extend to Muir, whom he went on to allude to as a 'a young man who had studied law' and who 'had taken it upon him to act as the great apostle of Reform in this neighbourhood'.[29]

Millar's success has been attributed to such factors as his expansion of the curriculum, the content of his lectures, and his personal lecturing style. In addition to statutory 'public' classes on Roman Law, Millar was by the 1770s delivering lectures on Scots Law and also a series of Lectures on Government.[30] Millar had also altered the classes in Roman Law, covering the Justinian Institutes in the first term, and supplementing this with a modern course of Lectures on Jurisprudence on the model of Adam Smith.[31] Millar was a popular professor, famed for his style of lecturing, which he chose to carry out in English rather than Latin.[32] Although unscripted to a degree, his lectures seem to have been remarkably well organised, as shown by existing lecture notes taken by students.[33] The poet Thomas Campbell (1777–1844), who attended Millar's classes in the early 1790s, later noted the Professor's statuesque appeal:

> Such was the truth, cheerfulness and courage that seemed
> to give erectness to his shapely bust, he might have stood
> to the statuary for a Roman orator; but he was too much in
> earnest with his duty, and, too manly to affect the orator;
> but keeping close to his subject, he gave it a seriousness
> that was never tiresome, and a gaiety that never seemed for
> a moment unillustrative or unnecessary. His cheerfulness
> appeared as indispensable as his gravity, and his humour
> was as light as his seriousness was intensive [...] His
> students were always in the class before him waiting as for
> a treat.[34]

In his *Life of Lord Jeffrey*, Cockburn records Millar's powers as teacher during the 1780s, the decade when Muir attended his classes:

Professor John Millar, whose subject was Law and
Government, was then in his zenith. His lectures were
admirable; and so was his conversation; and his evening
parties; and his boxing (gloved) with his favourite pupils.
No young man admitted to his house ever forgot him; and
the ablest used to say that the discussions into which he led
them, domestically and convivially, were the most exciting
and the most instructive exercises in which they ever took
a part. Jeffrey says that his books excellent though they
be, 'reveal nothing of that magical vivacity which made
his conversation and his lectures still more full of delight
than of instruction; of that frankness and fearlessness
which led him to engage, without preparation, in every fair
contention, and neither to dread nor disdain the powers of
any opponent; and still less, perhaps, of that remarkable
and unique talent, by which he was enabled to clothe, in
concise and familiar expressions, the most profound and
original views of the most complicated questions.[35]

Although noting that Millar's written works capture little of his
brilliance as lecturer,[36] Cockburn's account shows the reputation
Millar had acquired in person among students both inside and
outside the lecture hall. Millar lived in the spacious residence
at No.1 Professor's Court which faced the High Street, with his
large family and also student boarders. It was a common practice
for Professors to take in students: when Muir matriculated
at Glasgow, Lord Maitland and David Hume, nephew of the
philosopher, and one other were boarding with the Professor.[37]
Millar also entertained at this house. Edmund Burke dined there
on the event of his inauguration as rector, along with Adam Smith
and philosopher Dugald Stewart from Edinburgh.[38] Bewley notes
that Muir was among the favourite students who were invited to
Millar's house for discussions.[39] Professor and student had much
in common. Like Muir, Millar had studied MA at Glasgow (1746-
1751), and, had switched from a planned career in the ministry
to the law. He had also moved between Glasgow and Edinburgh,
where he had practiced as advocate briefly before taking up the
professorship in Civil Law. Muir also became acquainted with

John Millar junior, who was like him studying law at this time, and who later died in America after emigrating to avoid punishment for his activities alongside Muir in the Friends of the People.[40]

Extra-curricular links extended to the Glasgow Literary Society, on whose membership roster Muir appeared[41] and of which Professor Millar was already an active member. Founded in 1752 and based in the University, the Society was one of the main improving societies that were to characterise Scotland's convivial Enlightenment, alongside the Select Society of Edinburgh and the Aberdeen Philosophical Society, with which Glasgow had shared some members (notably Adam Smith, David Hume, and Thomas Reid).[42] It also shared a broad 'philosophical' outlook with its cousins in other University Towns. Here its 'Literary' title should be understood in the expansive eighteenth-century sense of 'polite learning', as it discussed topics ranging from Moral and Natural Philosophy through to Economics and Education, and was as comfortable discussing constitutional matters as questions restricted to belle lettres. The Society was based in the College itself, and normally met at 5.30pm on Fridays during term time from the start of November until early May of the following year.[43] There is little to note the impact the Glasgow Literary Society had on Muir, and nothing to suggest that it was a reputed 'hotbed of radicalism' like the Speculative Club of Edinburgh,[44] but active members included Professors who later sympathised with the French Revolution – Reid, Anderson, and Millar himself – and questions on Government had been a favourite topic of discussion, as we know from the minute books of the society.[45]

Beyond personal attachment and influence, there were the law classes themselves. A fuller outline of Millar's thinking (much of which has been covered in detail by WC Lehmann and by John Cairns) is beyond the scope of the present chapter, but we can make some general remarks. Millar had taken much of the inspiration for his lectures from his friend Adam Smith, whose lectures on jurisprudence he had originally heard in Edinburgh.[46] This approach can be described as a combination of historical and sociological enquiry, one which looks not at 'law', *per se,* but also at the general 'laws' by which societies progress; at the derivation of rights related to person and property as social formations evolve; and the mechanisms by which such laws, created as they are by a species with relatively uniform inclinations, diversify over time and across national frontiers. From Smith, Millar took a 'theoretical' (or 'conjectural') and 'stadial' approach to human history. 'Conjectural' history involved 'informed' conjectures about human history on the known and uniform principles of human nature.[47] Craig, for example, called Millar's lectures a 'general system of laws founded on the principle of justice', wherein he 'began by investigating the origin and foundation of each right in the natural principle of justice; and afterwards traced its progress through the different conditions of mankind'.[48] In other words, Millar exposed students such as Muir to the view that rights are founded on an inbuilt sense of justice which is uniform throughout the species, and that those rights become diversified over time according to the different circumstances of different nations. 'Stadial' history was a key mode of Scottish Enlightenment historiography which viewed human history on a sliding scale of progress from savagery to civilisation, famously mapped out by Smith into key stages of human societal development – hunter-gatherer, pastoral, agrarian, commercial – each of which gives rise to different and ever more complex forms of law and government.[49] In his writing, Millar acknowledged there is 'in human society, a natural progress from ignorance to knowledge, and from rude to civilised manners, the several stages of which are usually accompanied with peculiar laws and customs'.[50] His lectures took a similarly historical view of institutions as they progressed through set stages. Although in such histories, pre-democratic, constitutionally unreformed and not-quite-fully-extricated-from-the-slave-trade Britain sat at the apex of 'civilisation', stadialism helped shape the ideology of reform and could be embraced by Millar as a progressive thinker with abolitionist sympathies. In general terms, Scottish historiography offered a dynamic view of human history with a core underlying assumption that 'progress', in the sense of meaningful, positive change, is possible and in many respects inexorable. Such a 'teleology of civility', as Murray Pittock shows, underpinned the development of the Whig school of history, 'the analysis of the past not on its own terms, but in the light of what it could contribute to an account of progress towards the present'.[51] We see something of this Whig historiography in Mackenzie's 1831 life of Muir, which subordinates Muir's story to the contemporary purposes of the

1832 Representation of the People Act, and fits that story within a grand narrative of human liberation against tyranny and the progressive triumph of justice.[52]

From advertisements in the Glasgow newspapers we know the specific classes Millar was teaching when Muir turned to Law. In October 1782, he advertised his 'Prelections on JUSTINIAN'S INSTITUTES and PANDECTS' and 'Lectures on PUBLIC LAW' commencing that November.[53] The following session, 1783-84, when Muir formally signed up for classes, Millar had placed the following advert in the *Glasgow Mercury*:

JOHN MILLAR, Professor of Law in the University
of Glasgow, begins his Prelections on JUSTINIAN'S
INSTITUTES and PANDECTS, upon Monday the third day
of November next. Also
A course on PUBLIC LAW, on Monday the tenth. And,
A course of Lectures on the LAW OF SCOTLAND, on
Tuesday the eleventh day of that month.[54]

Student notes outlining Millar's teaching in Roman and Scots law exist for a considerable number of sessions and are too extensive to cover here; however a copy of notes from his Lectures on Government were written out by Alexander Campbell for the sessions Muir attended, giving us a valuable insight into the kind of education in matters of Law and Politics that Muir received from Millar. These notes show that Millar began with a customary introduction in which he outlined the 'General principles of Government, and different Systems which have been adopted with regard to those principles', offering a 'stadial' history of the progress of government through the four stages of 'savage', pastoral, agricultural, and commercial society. Millar then moved on to the 'Modern States of Europe' before focussing in on: France from the Franks to the present time; Germany from Charlemagne to the present; England, taking in Britons, Romans, Saxons, Normans and again continuing to the present; the Government of Scotland from the departure of the Romans to post-Union; and finally a historical survey of Government in Ireland. The historical sweep is continued in series of lectures on Ecclesiastical government since the establishment of Christendom. Finally, in

Part III of the lecture series, Millar enquired into 'the Present
State of Great Britain'. These outline the powers of the constituent
members of the British Parliament, of King, Lords, and Commons,
before concluding with a review of the judicial establishments in
Britain and the ecclesiastical courts of Scotland.[55]

During the final part of the lecture series there are intriguing
detours, such as remarks upon inequality in representation
between England and Scotland, in which Millar reminds students
of the principles of representative government and free election
(361-2), revealing his characteristic wariness of universal suffrage
(instead, he was said to prefer a franchise based on merit).[56] Millar
also offers some remarks on the state of the royal prerogative which
perhaps exemplify the political views he was willing to express in
lectures:

> The Powers invested in the Crown were at the Revolution
> ascertained and reduced into moderate bounds.
> Since the Revolution however the great increase of
> the revenue has tended considerable [sic] to extend the
> indirect influence of the Crown – The effects produced by
> the increase of the Crown Revenue are discernible in many
> Particulars especially in those which now come before the
> Parliament.
> It was ascertained that the Crown would not interfere in
> any measure but in the last resort. But instead of this it is
> by the influence of the Crown that the most important Bills
> are introduced into Parliament, by the Ministry and those
> persons who do depend upon it, and such is their weight
> that these measures are also carried through – If this was
> universally the case and no check could be put upon it, the
> Crown would be altogether absolute. And a Government of
> this kind would be even worse than for the King avowedly
> and openly to exercise all the Powers of Government
> for then it would be known with precision from whom
> oppression came. Whereas in the other case the King after
> he has got Parliament to adopt a measure unfavourable for
> the interests of the People, skreens himself under it, and
> makes the Parliament blameable in the first instance by
> making it stand between him and the people. If this indirect

influence of the Crown was without a check the government would long ere have lost its original balance (442-43).

Millar was opposed to 'secret influence' or the indirect extension of royal power through patronage and favour. Here, such influence is said to be exerted insidiously by the Crown in order to push legislation favourable to its own interest, for which Parliament becomes scapegoat. The encroachment of executive powers upon the Revolution settlement was a key concern of Millar, which he also voiced in his published works, particularly his *Historical View of the English Government*, a Whig response to Hume's 'Tory' *History of England*.[57]

Millar's work reveals his orientation towards constitutional Whiggism and an abiding belief in the Revolution settlement and the mixed or balanced constitution. It is possible that views on the abuses of aristocratic patronage chimed with the 'Popular' views Muir would have held on the Church of Scotland, but one can see how Millar's thinking may have shaped Muir's politics, inculcating Fox-ite inflections pro-constitutional reform over revolutionary Paine-ite radicalism. Glasgow had its Tory traditions – Millar's own chair, for example, was a Regius chair and thus subject to the kind of royal influence he opposed.[58] Yet, for all its Tory leanings, the University contained reformist energies, and Millar helped shape a number of leading reformers, such as the Earl of Lauderdale, who with other Glasgow-educated Edinburgh lawyers helped usher in the great reform of 1832.[59]

Millar's lecturing did cause some concern among the Tory establishment. Francis Jeffrey never attended Millar's law classes while at Glasgow due to his father's distrust of Millar's Whig principles, liberal reputation and 'free doctrine'.[60] Alexander 'Jupiter' Carlyle called Millar's pro-teaching poisonous for its pro-democratic views.[61] Alexander Fraser Tytler, Lord Woodhouselee, offered censure of principles along with praise of talents:

> [...] although the republican prejudices of Mr Millar gave to his Lectures on Politics and Government, a character justly considered as repugnant to the well-attempered frame and equal balance of our improved constitution, there were few who attended those lectures, without at least an increase of knowledge.

Establishment idolisers of a perfectly balanced constitution such as Tytler rallied against Millar's belief that the 'liberties of the subject are in perpetual danger from an increase of the influence of the Crown', which Tytler characterises as 'unreasonable alarm' at 'chimerical' fears,[62] yet it might be too much to suggest that students like Muir were indoctrinated in Whig ideology. Millar's reputation had not stopped other Tories such as philosopher David Hume from sending his nephew and namesake to study with him at Glasgow. Indeed, during Muir's time as student of law, we see Millar offered a passionate defence of his teaching:[63]

> If we are charged with *lecturing* upon politicks, I am afraid the charge must fall principally upon myself, as in lecturing upon public law I certainly am guilty of endeavouring to explain the principles of our own government. I know that I have been accused of inculcating Republican doctrines, but I am not conscious of having given any just ground for such an imputation. It has always been my endeavour to recommend that system of limited monarchy which was introduced at the Revolution, an acquaintance with which I conceived to be as useful to young men of fortune as many other branches of science. I should think it petulance, if, in the capacity of a public lecturer, I was to meddle with the local and partial politicks of the day; and in order to avoid the suspicion of intending any thing of that message, I have, in some lectures, been careful to pass over in a more slight and general manner certain subjects which I used formerly to treat at more length.[64]

That said, Millar's defence here appeared in the context of charges made by John Anderson against colleagues at the University rather than as a riposte to Tory concerns, even if it does appear to answer the latter. It is also slightly disingenuous. As a 'private citizen' at least, as Lehmann points out, Millar did in fact more than meddle in the politics of his day.[65] He was a committed supporter of the Rockingham Whigs led by Charles Fox. He became active in the abolitionist movement in Glasgow.[66] Millar also pinned considerable hope on the French Revolution, albeit with reservations about the confiscation of Church property and other actions of the Assembly.[67] In 1791, he presided over a dinner in Glasgow to commemorate the fall of the Bastille.[68] He authored the republican *Letters of Crito*, sent anonymously to the editor of the *Scots Chronicle* in 1796, on the prosecution of the war with France, and was said to have authored an earlier Glasgow petition against the war.[69] In Muir's time at Glasgow, Millar had led an assemblage of citizens who voiced opposition to the Pitt's accession to office by disrupting a public meeting in Glasgow on 28 February 1784, intended as a loyal address.[70] Despite the professor's protestations about the impartiality of his teaching, Millar had well-founded Whig credentials and was a well-known progressive in Glasgow circles and beyond. Although there has been some debate about the level of his participation in the Society of the Friends of the People – over whether he was a 'zealous member' as Craig claimed or simply gave it 'moral support' – Millar likely acted as inspiration to members Muir and his own son John.[71]

Muir's withdrawal from University

That Millar's teaching was a formative influence on Muir is not in doubt. Yet beyond the professional mentorship and the shared membership of the Society of the Friends of the People, there are complexities which suggest that their sympathies did not always perfectly coincide. The events leading up to Muir's withdrawal from the University show that Millar held quite different views to Muir with regard to John Anderson and the 'crisis' of 1783-84, commonly held to be the reason for Muir's 'self-expulsion' from the University in 1785.

Anderson, who had been Professor of Natural Philosophy at the University from 1757 was a difficult and divisive colleague who had involved the University and fellow professors in a series of law suits prior to the crisis of session 1783-84. Though a thorn in the side of colleagues, Anderson, or 'Jolly Jack Phosphorous' as he was known, was popular with students. It was their support for moves to reform the University that helped fuel the crisis, a brief account of which is as follows. Anderson's activities finally got him suspended from Senate, an event that raised much student indignation. The students contacted Rector Edmund Burke to step in, but he refused, leading to a problematic re-election as Rector for the statesman, when re-election for a second year had hitherto been a matter of course, and the worsening of relations between University and students. Anderson petitioned the Home Office for a royal commission to visit in order to sort out the University's affairs, for which he canvassed support among the townspeople of Glasgow and within the student body.[72] This move was finally defeated, leaving Anderson alienated. Leading student reformers were ordered to apologise: some did, while others refused and were expelled; Muir, as the story goes, refused to submit to the University's terms and withdrew, moving instead to Edinburgh to complete his studies.

The account of Anderson and student politics by Carruthers and Kaur in this volume not only reveals the central ideological and theological tensions behind the crisis, but also provides much needed evidence regarding Muir's role, and indeed that of his father, in events. Such evidence helps us to address the uncertainty regarding Muir's actual activities, particularly when biographers have (quite understandably) tended to emphasise Muir's role, seeing it as his first emergence as a leader of reform. In accounts of the events by those involved, Muir is often not mentioned at all. The Reverend James Smith, for example, later claimed to have been a 'prominent reformer' while at the University, and recounted how he himself became one of the leaders of 'certain students of reform principles' who attempted 'a thorough reform of the University', petitioning the King and Parliament for a royal commission to examine management of University finances, the library and compulsory library fees. These actions invoked the hostility of the majority of professors, with the sole exception of Anderson, who 'joined the party of reform students', inviting them to breakfast in his house to discuss strategy. Where others focus on Anderson as the prime mover, Smith emphasizes the students' role in initiating calls for reform. In order to quash this 'reform movement', the university 'selected a few of the leading reform movement, and, *interrorem*, expelled them from the university', including Smith himself, who was then forced to apologise in order to continue his studies in Divinity. No mention is made of Muir.[73]

A second eyewitness account appeared in the short-lived radical monthly *The Glasgow Magazine* of July 1795.[74] Written a year after the trial of Muir as the first part of a projected life by William

Marshall, a Glasgow lawyer and one of the magazine's editors, this account appears to have been the major source of information for Muir's student politics followed by later biographers. This outline, Marshall says, is intended to do justice to Muir, that is to quash rumours circulating at the time that Muir was expelled, a task for which the editors 'are enabled from a perfect knowledge of the circumstances attending it'. Marshall was in fact one of the students involved. According to him, Anderson's suspension from office as 'member of the *jurisdictio ordinaria*' during session 1783-84 so offended students that they sought redress the following session. For his sanctioning of such injustice they attempted to block Burke's re-election as rector for his second year, but, despite forming a 'formidable faction' they were defeated by the powerful professorship. This action, Marshall claims, was carried out by students alone, without Anderson's backing. The College's attempts to intimidate students backfired, prompting reformers to turn to the more serious action of procuring the royal visitation, 'to correct the abuses which had crept into the university'; this was with a view to preserving long-standing student rights in the election of rector, against which professors had been asserting their better qualification over pubescent students to choose an appropriate rector. There are echoes here of wider electoral battles regarding constitutional reform, and Marshall's account makes explicit the parallels between the crisis and other struggles: 'The university acted on this occasion as every other corporation would have done in the same situation. Tenacious of its power, it opposed to popular clamour its ancient usage'.[75] It is at this stage that Muir emerges as a central figure:

Mr. Muir, from the beginning, considered an application for a royal visitation as the right and privilege of the students, and the grievances complained of as warranting that measure, and incompatible with the character of freemen. He therefore exerted his talents in promoting the cause [...] and by his prudent counsel tempered [...] the fervent enthusiasm of the youths who co-operated with him. After their undertaking had totally failed, and at the commencement of the next session, a circular letter was issued from the faculty to all the professors, enjoining them not to admit into their classes Mr Muir, nor twelve others, who were named in it, as it was alleged that those so excluded, had been concerned in certain publications injurious to the characters of the professors. Mr Muir could easily have vindicated himself from this charge, but finding that it was only the ostensible cause for their proceeding, and that the most humiliating and ignominious concessions were required, he turned from Glasgow college with indignation and disgust, and went to Edinburgh [...][76]

Marshall was keen to vindicate Muir against rumour-mongering, but already in this account there is the kind of shaping of events to prefigure the later Muir as leading reformer that is taken up by later biographers. Peter Mackenzie's account followed Marshall with little to add other than the significant alteration that at this time Muir 'threw off' his habitual reserve and emerged one of the students 'most enthusiastic leaders'. This small change may be significant in enhancing Muir's role. Indeed, a 1946 pamphlet in 'The Fight for Freedom Series' based on what it calls 'data' from Mackenzie, proudly headlined this episode 'THOMAS MUIR LEADS STUDENT PROTESTS'.[77] Bewley likewise held Muir up as 'one of the most energetic and admired student leaders [...] one of the deputation who presented the students' resolution to Burke, and the convenor of a meeting of senior students which decided to publish a pamphlet ridiculing Leechman and his supporters'.[78]

Other commentators have been sceptical about Muir's student leadership. George Pratt Insh went so far as to question the foundation of claims about Muir being obliged to leave Glasgow because he found no evidence in University records that Muir had led anything other than a 'blameless life'.[79] That said, there is no reason to discount Marshall's account of Muir's involvement, as Marshall himself was directly implicated in events and was censored by the University for his conduct in January 1785 while a student in Anderson's class.[80] Though Muir, unlike Marshall, is not mentioned in College minutes, as Bewley recognised those records are 'incomplete'.[81] Moreover, the students identified by name in Faculty records are either those expelled for 'contumacy', viz. David McIndoe for petitioning for the royal visitation, and Alexander Humphreys and William Clydesdale for authoring pamphlets attacking the University, or those students who apologised to the University for attending a meeting which authorised publication of the student pamphlets.[82] That Muir does not appear among these names would actually lend support to the idea that he refused to submit to the University's terms, and instead withdrew to Edinburgh. Muir is, as Carruthers and Kaur reveal in this volume, linked directly to the student campaign in Court papers, and in a defamation case between Anderson and plaintiff Dr William Taylor – who had been the particular target of student reformers in their slanderous pamphlets – Muir's own father testified regarding his son's entanglement.

Millar's role in the crisis

There is a certain romance to accounts of student politics in so far as they show the emergence of Muir the rebel against unjust authority, wherein events become an apprenticeship in martyrdom in which, in the words of AH Millar, Muir 'suffered for vindicating the principle of representation'.[83] History has sided in this affair with Muir, with fellow student reformers, and, to an extent, with Anderson as beneficent pioneer of technical education and founder of Anderson's Institute, yet the actions of other Professors show a quite different side to events.

Muir's mentor seems to have taken the side of the University against this incipient reform movement. Millar attended the meetings at which students were expelled, and wrote to rector Burke against student reform on a number of occasions. On 16 August 1784 he addressed reports spread by Anderson, such as the accusations of meddling in politics in his lectures mentioned above, noting his distance, and that of colleagues from Anderson. Anderson, he says, is 'never happy but when engaged in some dispute, generally about a frivolous matter, which by his trifling head, is magnified into an affair of importance and which after spinning it out as long as he can in our College meetings, he carries it at length, if possible, before the civil courts'.[84] In a letter to Burke of 19 January 1785, Millar reported that student support for the petition for a royal visitation started by divinity student David McIndoe had not been unanimous, and that students Thomas Kennedy and John Hamilton[85] had brought the petition to the notice of Faculty after repenting their signing of it. It had also emerged that students as young as eleven had been 'inveigled, without knowledge of parents and guardians, to subscribe this paper, but have been refused the liberty of withdrawing their subscriptions', leading to McIndoe being called before Faculty and, after failing to appear, expelled.[86] Millar then wrote again in April to thank the Rector for his intervention, hinting that a letter from the Secretary of State disapproving of the late actions against the University and attempts to 'excite the younger students, and the tradesmen of Glasgow', were it to be made public would 'be very effectual in putting an end to the disorders which have taken place, and in re-establishing our authority'.[87] What is striking about this letter are the terms used by Millar to describe student action: 'I formerly acquainted you,' he reminds Burke, 'that we *expelled* one of our students, who was the ringleader of the sedition'. Perhaps not the terms we would expect a future Friend of the People to use, but confirmation that Millar was on the other side of Muir's early reform activities.

Principal William Leechman's letters to Burke go further than those of Millar, outlining some of the wider popular reform networks in Glasgow involved in the crisis. Leechman accuses Anderson of having held 'Cabals with Students at Taverns and other places in the town', with consorting with 'certain of the Masters of Arts' – which likely included Muir – to gain support for his cause, and raising the 'interest the Lowest and Classes of Mechanics and Manufacturers here', publishing advertisements and 'defamatory Handbills' in order to encourage 'all Classes of People' to sign the petition in favour of his 'pretended Grievances'. Matters are exacerbated by Kirk politics and the Moderate position from which Leechman attacks Auld Licht Anderson, yet even from such partisan attacks we gain some insight into the strangely popular support for the Professor of Natural Philosophy. '[I]t was the more easy', he says, 'for Mr Anderson to procure a promiscuous multitude of such names both on account of the Active part he took among them in the disturbances about the Popish Bill, as it was called, and of the constant support he gives to the Fanatical Party, as an Elder in the General Assembly of this Church'.[88] Though hardly impartial, there may be some grounds for Leechman's claims against 'Fanatical' support: opposition to the Catholic Relief Bill of 1778 had been widespread,[89] and the anti-patronage protest of the Popular Party had also begun to take on pro-reform characteristics (in fact, both may have fed into the later reform movement of the 1790s).[90] Not long before 'Andersongate', the trades and corporations of Glasgow had been active in popular opposition to the 'Popish Bill'. Groups were formed such as 'The Friends of the Protestant Interest in Glasgow' and the 'Committee of Correspondence', who set up as networks of intelligence and a means of canvassing subscriptions against repeal of the penal statutes against Catholics. The 'self-defence' of Protestantism was also, as figured by the Burgesses of Glasgow, a stated defence of constitutional liberties set out in Reformation, Glorious Revolution, and Union 'which freed us against Popery, slavery, and arbitrary power'.[91] One John Anderson of Lanarkshire appears on the list of subscribers to the anti-Popish petition of the 'Eighty Three Societies in Glasgow'.[92] It is possible, then, that Anderson was able to harness such energies that would later feed into networks for popular political participation, albeit in this case on a very limited, localised scale. Leechman suggests that the expulsion of student petitioner David McIndoe had been used to draw additional support due to McIndoe 'being the Son of a Low Fanatick'. Certainly, it seems that Anderson had the ability to mobilise popular support: Coutts records that the Professor left petitions in shops, that porters were sent out to solicit signatures from passers-by, and that his followers even indulged in house to house canvassing. Anderson also appears to have made particular attempts to gain the support of Masters of Arts within the College, a group to which Muir belonged.[93]

Anderson printed a handbill to the Masters of Arts of the University, undertaking to set out to London with no less than fifteen petitions to the King signed by the Masters of Arts of the University, from 'most of the Irish students', the Trades House and corporations of Glasgow, and 'merchants, traders, manufacturers', totalling in all, he claimed, 'three-fourths of the students that were at the University last year and from more than two-thirds of the inhabitants of the city'.[94] Reporting Anderson's departure for London, Leechman wrote again to Burke, and charged Anderson with having met 'with certain of the Lowest of the Scotch & Irish students' in taverns and in his own house, which led to 'defamatory publications', circulated privately among students.[95] Besides the expulsions, Leechman remarked that a number of other students who had supported Anderson and signed petitions had applied for Degrees and Certificates, but had been refused them until they made acknowledgement of their undutiful conduct, which the students had refused to do. Such students, Leechman claimed, had been openly aided and abetted by Anderson, 'and indeed have been his constant companions during the Winter in Open Defiance of all academical order and authority'. Though Muir is not named directly in any of these letters, he would have been among this group.

It is difficult to side with the University when one sees its efforts to squash a student reform movement and its introduction of repressive measures which included the monitoring of the membership and activities of student literary societies.[96] Yet should we also suspend our sympathies for Millar? Bewley notes that during this crisis Millar had defended student rights, and indeed was instrumental in getting Muir a place at Edinburgh.[97] Millar's response to the crisis complicates his relationship with Muir, and though that relationship did not apparently suffer in the longer term, it would be wrong perhaps to see their relationship as a straightforward, uncomplicated transference of reform principles from Professor to student. The professors at Glasgow University certainly had a formative influence upon Muir, and Millar more so than others, but the way in which Glasgow shaped the young Muir was not simply the outcome of his Law classes.

Notes and References

1 Marshall, 1795, p.41.
2 Mackenzie, 1831, p.1
3 Bewley, 1981, p.3.
4 Biography of Thomas Muir (1765-1799) by HT Dickinson. In: *Oxford Dictionary of National Biography*. Oxford: Oxford University Press, 2004 [Online 2010]. Available from http://www.oxforddnb.com/view/article/19498 [Accessed 31 August 2016].
5 Donnelly, 1975, p.2.
6 Craig, 1806, p.ii.
7 Addison, 1913, p.xi.
8 Addison, 1913, p.119.
9 For an outline of the matriculation process see Murray, 1927, p.274.
10 Matriculation Album, 1756-1809, GUA2878. Glasgow University Archives.
11 Register of Masters of Arts, 1764-1888, GUA26676. Glasgow University Archives.
12 For a detailed account of the curriculum, see Coutts, 1909, pp.208-9.
13 Mackie, 1954, p.210.
14 For an account of student life at Glasgow College see http://www.universitystory.gla.ac.uk/student-life/ [Accessed 2 August 2016].
15 The relations between town and University are outlined in Sher, 1995-96.
16 Figures compiled from the entries for 1777 transcribed in Addison, 1913, pp.116-20.
17 Addison, 1913, p.119.
18 Eyre-Todd, 1934, p.113.
19 Eyre-Todd, 1934, p.113.
20 Addison, 1913, p.119; Biography of Sinclair Kelburn (1753/4-1802) by T Hamilton. In: *Oxford Dictionary of National Biography*. Oxford: Oxford University Press [Online]. Available from http://www.oxforddnb.com/view/article/15280 [Accessed 31 August 2016].
21 Addison, 1898, p.165; Biography of William Drennan (1754–1820) by IR McBride. In: *Oxford Dictionary of National Biography*. Oxford: Oxford University Press, 2004 [Online 2008]. Available from http://www.oxforddnb.com/view/article/8046 [Accessed 31 August 2016].
22 Addison, 1902, p.6.
23 Fleischacker, 2003, pp.316-7.
24 Biography of James Watt (1736–1819) by J Tann. In: *Oxford Dictionary of National Biography*. Oxford: Oxford University Press, 2004 [Online]. Available from http://www.oxforddnb.com/view/article/28880 [Accessed 31 August 2016].

25 On this reputation, see Lehmann, 1960.
26 Donnelly 1975, p.2.
27 Craig, 1806, p.xi.
28 Heron, 1799, vol.2 p.418.
29 Heron, 1799, vol.2:p.420.
30 Cairns, 1995, pp.134-9.
31 Craig, 1806, pp.xix-xx.
32 Craig, 1806, p.xii; Cairns, 1995, p.134.
33 Notes of Millar's lectures are held at Glasgow University Special Collections, at Glasgow's Mitchell Library, and the National Library of Scotland and the University Library in Edinburgh.
34 Cited in Lehmann, 1960, p.31.
35 Cockburn, 2004, vol.1, pp.10-11.
36 See Murray, 1927, p.224.
37 Murray, 1927, p.397.
38 Lehmann, 1960, p.51.
39 Bewley, 1981, p.5.
40 Meikle, 1912, p.157.
41 Lehmann, 1960, p.53n, cf. Bewley, 1981, p.8.
42 For a standard overview of club culture in the Scottish Enlightenment, see McElroy, 1969, especially pp.41-44 for the Glasgow Literary Society.
43 Lehmann, 1960, p.53.
44 Bewley, 1981, p.8.
45 Among questions discussed in this period, those related to government were discussed on twenty-two occasions – more than any other subject: for a breakdown, see Sher, 1995-96, p.338.
46 Scott, 1937, p.56 and p.63.
47 Stewart, 1982, p.293.
48 Craig, 1806, p.xxiii, p.xxvi.
49 An exemplary excerpt from Smith's Lectures on Jurisprudence appears in Smith, 1997, pp.478–87.
50 Millar, 1806, p.4.
51 Pittock, 2003, pp.258-62.
52 See Mackenzie, 1831, pp.45-46.
53 *The Glasgow Mercury*, 10-17 October 1782 [Periodical]. Murray collection, Mu60-f.1-14. Glasgow University Special Collections.
54 *The Glasgow Mercury*, 16-23 October 1783 [Periodical]. Murray collection, Mu60-f.1-14. Glasgow University Special Collections.
55 Lectures on government, delivered in the University of Glasgow by John Millar, written from notes taken by Alexander Campbell, 1783 [Lecture notes]. MS GEN 179. Glasgow: Glasgow University Special Collections. Further references to this text appear in parenthesis.

56 On this point, see Lehmann, 1960, p.67.
57 Millar, 2006, vol.4, pp.699-712.
58 Millar, 1886.
59 Bewley, 1981, p.4.
60 Cockburn, 2004, pp.10-12.
61 Carlyle, 1860, pp.492-4.
62 Tytler, 1807, vol.1, pp.199-201.
63 See Cairns, 1995, p.145.
64 John Millar to Edmund Burke, 16 August 1784 [Facsimile letter].
   MS GEN 520/37. Glasgow University Special Collections.
65 For an overview of this private activity, see Lehmann, 1960,
   pp.64-76 (especially pp.71-2).
66 Craig, 1806, pp.cxi-cxii.
67 Craig, 1806, pp.cxii-xciii.
68 Meikle, 1912, p.49; Lehmann, 1960, p.68.
69 Millar, 1796. Available online from http://oll.libertyfund.org/
   titles/288 [Accessed 31 August 2016]; on the petition, see Meikle,
   1912, p.129.
70 George Pratt-Insh, Unpublished biography of Thomas Muir,
   pp.23-24 [Typescript manuscript]. NLS Dep 344. Edinburgh:
   National Library of Scotland.
71 Craig, 1806, p.cxv; cf. Lehmann, 1960, p.73.
72 For an overview of the whole Anderson affair, see Coutts 1909,
   pp.283-94.
73 'Senex', 1856, pp.372-3.
74 For a recent account of the magazine, see Leask, 2015.
75 *The Glasgow Magazine*, July 1795, p.43 [Periodical]. Murray
   Collection, Mu 24-d.15. Glasgow University Special Collections.
76 *The Glasgow Magazine*, July 1795, p.44.
77 Anon, 1946.
78 Bewley, 1981, p.7.
79 George Pratt-Insh, Unpublished biography of Thomas Muir, p.22n
   [Typescript manuscript]. NLS Dep 344. Edinburgh: National Library
   of Scotland.
80 Records of Glasgow College, 20 January 1785, GUA 26693. Glasgow
   University Archives.
81 Bewley 1961, p.195 (note 3). Indeed, the Faculty records for 4
   November 1785 allude to a previous meeting at which a number
   of students were called to answer for their actions, but the present
   author could find no minute of this earlier meeting.
82 See Records of Glasgow College for 1785 and 1786.
83 Millar, 1886.
84 John Millar to Edmund Burke, 16 August 1784 [Facsimile letter].
   MS GEN 502/37. Glasgow University Special Collections.

85 Identified in Records of Glasgow College, 13 January 1785.
86 Millar to Burke, 19 January 1785 [Facsimile letter]. MS GEN 502/38. Glasgow University Special Collections.
87 Millar to Burke, 17 August 1785 [Facsimile letter]. MS GEN 502/39. Glasgow University Special Collections.
88 William Leechman to Edmund Burke, 16 February 1785 [Facsimile letter]. MS GEN 502/35. Glasgow: Glasgow University Special Collections.
89 See, for example, *Scotland's opposition to the Popish Bill: a collection of all the declarations and resolutions, published by the different counties, cities, towns, parishes, incorporations, and societies, throughout Scotland* (Edinburgh: David Paterson, 1790) [Rare book]. Bdg.s.38. Edinburgh, National Library of Scotland.
90 A recent discussion of the continuity between reform societies and earlier popular movements appears in Honeyman, 2009.
91 *Scotland's opposition to the Popish Bill*, p.56.
92 *Scotland's opposition to the Popish Bill*, p.94.
93 Coutts, 1909, p.290.
94 Cited in Coutts, 1909, p.291; and Muir, 1950, pp.21-2.
95 Leechman to Burke, 1 May 1785 [Facsimile letter]. MS GEN 502/35. Glasgow University Special Collections.
96 See the Records of Glasgow College, 20 October 1786.
97 Bewley, 1981, p.8; cf. Millar, 1886.

Thomas Muir and Kirk Politics

Gerard Carruthers

Having been found guilty of sedition and sentenced to a fourteen-year long transportation to Botany Bay in August 1793, Thomas Muir found himself held in the notorious prison-hulks at Woolwich from late in the year and into the next. From the Thames, he wrote a letter to 'a Gentleman' in Cambridge that appeared in the *Cambridge Intelligencer* and which was reprinted in the London radical periodical, *Politics for the People*. Previously held in the Tolbooth prison in Edinburgh, where he had a room to himself and his own meals brought in, as well as in nicer initial quarters in the British capital, Muir found the hulks an altogether more dreadful place:

> Hurled, as it were in a moment, from some of the most
> polished societies in Edinburgh and London, into one of
> the Hulks upon the Thames, where every mouth is opened
> to blaspheme God, and every hand stretched out to injure
> a Neighbour, I cannot divest myself of the feelings of
> nature; I cannot but lament my situation; and where [sic]
> it not for hope of immortality founded upon our common
> christianity, Alas! I might accuse the father of all Justice
> and of all Mercy with severity. But blessed be God, every
> thing in the great system of nature, every thing in the little
> system of individual man, corresponds with the great
> demonstrations of the gospel, and demonstrates its efficacy.

He continues:

> In *solitary* exile there is dignity, there is a conscious pride,
> which, even independent of Philosophy, may support
> the mind, but I question much, if any of the illustrious of
> ancient ages, could have supported an exile similar to mine,

surrounded by the veriest outcasts of society, without the
aid of religion and of the example of JESUS.[1]

Through his shock at his recent downturn in fortunes, we
hear the religious voice of Thomas Muir (drawing probably on
Job, especially 1:22, 'In all this, Job did not sin by charging God
with wrongdoing'), revealing a religious sensibility that needs
to be better comprehended if we are to obtain the fullest picture
of the man. The following essay, drawing on some startling new
material uncovered in the archives of the Faculty of Advocates in
Edinburgh, considers Muir's religious identity, indeed, his active
ecclesiastical endeavours, in the context of two legal cases that
stretch from 1786 to 1792. On the face of it, Muir's involvement in
these two contretemps represents an engagement as committed as
his secular constitutional endeavours during the 1790s, and indeed
– in certain aspects – we might realise that the two spheres of kirk
and secular politics cohere (including also his student politics,
dealt with elsewhere in this volume).

In 1786 Muir's services as a lawyer were engaged in the case
mounted against William McGill (1732-1807) by those allied to
the Popular Party of the Church of Scotland, broadly speaking the
theologically conservative, 'auld lichts'. McGill, a minister in the
town of Ayr (having charge there of the second oldest Presbyterian
church), had received a doctorate of divinity from the University of
Glasgow in 1785 and was a good friend of the poet, Robert Burns
(1759-96). Like McGill, Burns's own allegiances were clearly to
the Moderate, or 'new licht' tendency in the church opposed to
the Popular interest, and representing in general a more liberal
theology or an outlook less dependent on traditional Scottish
Calvinism.[2] Much of Burns's early career needs to be understood
in this context. His first published collection, *Poems, Chiefly in the
Scottish Dialect* (1786), was subscription-powered, particularly
enabled by fellow Moderates who were pleased that he had
recently picked up the cudgels to oppose what he and they took
to be the forces of Popular Party reaction in the Ayrshire church.
Burns's 'The Holy Tulzie' (1785) and 'Holy Willie's Prayer' (1785)
were both propagandistic, party poems; Burns writes about these
(and also the slightly different text, 'The Holy Fair') in his long
autobiographical letter of August 1787 to Dr John Moore:

The first of my poetic offspring that saw the light was a
burlesque lamentation on a quarrel between two rev^d.
Calvinists, both of them dramatis personae in my Holy
Fair.– I had an idea myself that the piece had some merit;
but to prevent the worst, I gave a copy of it to a friend
who was very fond of these things, and told him I could
not guess who was the Author of it, but that I thought it
pretty clever.– With a certain side of both clergy and laity
it met with a roar of applause.– Holy Willie's Prayer next
made its appearance, and alarmed the kirk-Session so
much that they held three several meetings to look over
their holy artillery, if any of it was pointed against profane
Rhymers.–[3]

The 'session' to which Burns refers was his local one of
Mauchline around a dozen miles from the county town of Ayr.
Among those presumably joining in the 'roar of applause' were
Gavin Hamilton (1751-1805), a man of property and a lawyer in
Mauchline who had been accused at kirk-session level of various
infractions including lax church attendance by the Reverend
William Auld (1709-91), minister for the village. Hamilton,
supported by the lawyer, Robert Aiken (1739-1807), appealed to
the higher authority of the Presbytery at Ayr which threw out the
charges. Consequently, Burns's 'Holy Willie's Prayer' was an act
of poetic revenge lampooning Auld and his allies and celebrating
the victory of Hamilton and Aiken. Not for nothing did Aiken
later take on one hundred and forty-five subscriptions out of six
hundred and twelve for himself and his friends of Burns's *Poems,
Chiefly in the Scottish Dialect*, and the volume itself was dedicated
to Hamilton. In other words, Burns's first publication can be seen
in part, at least, as a production of the late eighteenth-century
enlightened, Moderate church party of Ayrshire, to which the poet
had attached himself.

Hamilton's situation and the provenance of Burns's kirk satires
also have to be read in the context of an even wider Popular/
Moderate power struggle. The central protagonist in the former
party was the Reverend William Peebles (1753-1826), minister at
Newton upon Ayr, who would go on to attack the Scottish bard

in *Burnomania: the celebrity of Robert Burns considered in a Discourse addressed to all real Christians of every Denomination* (1811), a remarkably venomous performance published a decade and a half after the bard's death. For a time in the 1780s and 1790s, the central party-battleground in Ayrshire, as the trading of insulting sermons (at least one of them published) demonstrates, is between the Reverend Peebles and the Reverend McGill.[4] Not only words in church circles but legal salvos were exchanged, and an attempt was mounted to charge McGill with heresy, specifically, as it seemed to his accusers, in that this clergyman was guilty of denying the full divinity of Jesus Christ. We can access something of this protracted case by turning to the pamphlet, *A Memorial and Remonstrance concerning the proceedings of the Synod of Glasgow and Ayr and of the General Assembly in the case of Dr William McGill* (1792). This publication reiterates the main charges which had previously been made against McGill in response to his, *A Practical Essay on the Death of Jesus Christ* (1786). *A Memorial and Remonstrance* seems to be the product of a group of men of similar theological mind-set to, and including, Peebles who attack the 'Socinianism' of McGill.[5] Among other things the originally Polish Socinians paved the way for Unitarian rather than Trinitarian views of God in the eighteenth century. A remarkable number of radical and revolutionary thinkers of the late eighteenth century, including the likes of Joseph Priestley (1733-1804), are Unitarian. The rationalism of Unitarianism, which rejects the doctrine of the Trinity on arguments of theological ingenuity and obscurantism, appealed to the more rationalist, scientific mind-set of Priestley *et al.* However, the evidence that McGill himself was an out and out 'Socinian' or even on the road to Unitarianism is rather thin, and rests largely on the fact that Christ incarnate is pictured by McGill as not having a perfect view of the future; however, there seems little doubt also that elements of Priestley's theology were attractive to the clergyman and so the 'Socinian'/ Unitarian charge had some efficacy in it.[6] In his *Practical Essay* of 1786, McGill had written: 'He (Christ) seems not to have considered his excruciating death, in the manner it happened, as previously fixed by an absolute, divine decree'.[7] The writers of *A Memorial and Remonstrance* drew attention to what seemed to them to be yet more impiety in McGill's disregard for the Crucifixion. McGill had written: 'To suffer many indignities in the world, and to die on the cross, were not the chief and ultimate ends of our Saviour's mission'.[8] Furthermore, McGill's opponents were exercised by the Ayr clergyman seeming to suggest that Christ's blood was in some way transformed by the cross. No, they retorted, the divine blood was the divine blood anyway: simultaneously human and divine, not made *more special* by Christ's sacrifice.[9]

As well as reiterating the charges against McGill, *A Memorial and Remonstrance* protests about the injustice of protracted ecclesiastical proceedings against their heretic that had run from 1788 until 1791, having come to nothing.[10] It is in this context that we find the one reference to Thomas Muir. The pamphleteers complain that when the case was taken to the General Assembly in Edinburgh, the proceedings descended into 'trivial discussion' and the complacent assertion by the Assembly that the case was 'already judged' with no charges for McGill properly to answer.[11] Here we glimpse the liberal character of the presbytery of Ayr that had occasioned Robert Burns earlier in 1785, to write of it in his poem to the Rev John McMath:

O Ayr, my dear, my native ground,
Within thy presbyterial bound,
A candid lib'ral band is found ...'[12]

Actually, the pamphleteers insist, 'with the clearest evidence our counsel, Mr Muir, prov'd the contrary' to the findings of the Assembly that there was no answerable case.[13] Interestingly, when one looks at Muir's speech it is couched much more in terms of the technicalities of the national church's responsibilities than a propos the theology of McGill.[14] Although more research is required on Muir's precise place within the Popular Party grouping that pursued McGill, there is certainly a chiming between his Assembly speech and the fact that *A Memorial and Remonstrance* insists that McGill's heresy has to be seen in its context of being clearly contrary to the Confession of Faith, the Constitution of the Church of Scotland and the Catechisms, larger and shorter.[15] The Church of Scotland, if it will not prosecute McGill, our authors tell us, is now suffering a complete failure of authority. They are clearly frustrated that not only has the Presbytery of Ayr dismissed the case but so too the General Assembly. The pamphlet declares: 'Ichabod, the glory is departed, may be very justly written upon all the courts of our church, especially upon her General Assembly'.[16] The mention of Ichabod references the loss of the ark of the covenant of the Jews to the philistines and here, as elsewhere, we see the mentality of our authors writ large where they believe that true Protestantism in Scotland is being largely betrayed; and especially, as they see it, with the major motor here (implicitly) being the Patronage Act, to which we will return below.

A Memorial and Remonstrance provides us with a strong glimpse of Muir's theological associations from the 1780s to the 1790s. As an important aside, it is worth pointing out that this grouping's activities, certainly by the time these came to the notice of the General Assembly in 1791, would have led to Muir being on the radar of the political as well as the theological authorities of Edinburgh some time before his political trial of 1793. These were authorities which often overlapped in the culturally compact Scottish capital of the late eighteenth century (to say nothing of a crucial hinge-point among such groupings being also the legal profession), and this is an area in which more connective research needs to be done in future. Earlier than *A Memorial & Remonstrance* is published a pamphlet entitled, *The Group, A Letter Containing Articles Exhibited Against Dr William McGill* (1790), attributed to 'Decius' (after the Roman emperor, Trajan Decius, c.201-251, among whose endeavours, tellingly, was an attempt to promote public piety). *The Group* pamphlet is both an attack on McGill and, like *A Memorial and Remonstrance*, is about wider principle, especially the 'Tory Law of Patronage' with which the Moderates are associated – not unreasonably, since moderates like McGill and Burns believed in Patronage, or ministers chosen not by congregations but rather by the local propertied class.[17] *The Group* claims of McGill that '[h]e alledges that no inconvenience would arise from patronage, nor has arisen, where parishes submitted peaceably to it. Just so Doctor, there would be no rapes if the ladies were all sufficiently condescending'.[18] The acidic tone of the pamphlet continues to wrap itself around trenchant complaints as *The Group* opines that Patronage as supported by McGill can be characterised as relying upon by what it calls 'Cock Lairds' defined as '[T]he landlord or proprietor of only one or two small farms, though with a cock's voice' who can appoint the local minister without any say from the congregation.[19] What we might quite clearly see here is how Thomas Muir would easily have made connections between the situation of ecclesiastical Patronage and the secular democratic deficit – the rotten burghs and so on – in the British Isles. For *The Group* church and constitutional politics are, indeed, intertwined. The text goes on to argue that while the Union of 1707 does not materially change the ecclesiastical situation in England (since its Bishops are still represented in the House of Lords), in Scotland something transformational has happened.[20] *The Group* contends that the Union of 1707 allows the Patronage Act of 1711, which empowers minority selection of parish ministers, and that this weakens ecclesiastical authority within Scotland. The direct consequences are that there are fewer true ministers called forth by the people, and also fewer excommunications which attests how lax the Church of Scotland has become.[21] Once upon a time the proud national church in Scotland would not have been embarrassed, so we can infer, to excommunicate the likes of William McGill.

A number of things come clearly into view in the McGill case. These include Muir's strong commitment to the cause of the Popular Party, something we will see further as we turn to his lawyerly actions in the parish of Cadder, overlapping in time to some extent with the McGill controversy. As noted above, it is probably safe to assume that Muir's visible presence in Scottish kirk politics is being noted in political circles in Edinburgh (especially if the direct claims in *The Group* about ecclesiastical and national politics is a note being strongly bruited about, as it certainly must be in the context of the fraught Patronage issue throughout the eighteenth century). The affairs of the General Assembly of the church, the secular legal cases and burgh and parliamentary politics involved often the same individuals from a fairly small class of the powerful in Scotland (often jurists), especially around its capital (see also Don Martin's essay in this volume for links between Muir's arch-foe, James Lapslie, and the Dundas family). As dealt with elsewhere also in this volume, in the essay on Muir and student politics, we also might note the presence of another metropolitan power-struggle, specifically centred round the University of Glasgow. McGill had received his doctorate from Glasgow in 1785, the year Muir removed himself from the institution to avoid actual expulsion. As detailed in the student politics chapter by Satinder Kaur and the present author, Muir was close to John Anderson (1726-96) who eventually had such enmity with another of Muir's mentors, John Millar (1735-1801) that the two were to face one another in court. Moreover, Millar's son John junior (1760-95), like Muir and Millar senior was also a lawyer, and he also represented the opposing side to Muir in the case to which we will now turn. All of these personal and ideological transactions are intimate and also complex. The clear difference in kirk politics here between Muir and Millar junior is, for instance, complicated by a similar political outlook following the French revolution since 'for fear of reprisals for his radical politics' the latter was eventually driven 'to migrate to America'.[22] It might also be noted that fraught theological and legal entanglements notwithstanding, Muir in political exile retained what was clearly a strong friendship with Millar junior.[23]

If the McGill case is suggestive of the theological temperature of Muir, so too to some extent is the Cadder case even as this much more clearly relates to church governance rather than to the scriptural basis of faith. As in the McGill case, some light is thrown at Cadder upon the ideas about the status of the national Scottish church that Muir was representing. There is, however, future work to be done in drawing together the McGill and Cadder cases and, indeed, Muir's activities at the University of Glasgow to bring into sharper focus a description of Muir the Presbyterian and Calvinist. The present essay, however, has had to restrict itself to disinterring something of a basic descriptive narrative, with some initial suggestiveness analysis in the case of both McGill and Cadder. The Cadder case is often depicted as a dispute between the congregation (especially the elders) and the heritors at Cadder Kirk (located between Glasgow and Kirkintilloch) during the period 1790-92 over the ministerial vacancy that had arisen upon the death of the minister, Alexander Dun. It is also often stated or assumed that Muir was the victor in the protracted legal proceedings that went from the church to the Court of Session. As we shall see, these are assumptions on which there can now be intriguing new light. Some sets of papers, residing in the Faculty of Advocates in Edinburgh, have informed no previous, modern account of Muir's career and are drawn upon extensively here for the first time.[24] It should also be noted that only one set of central proceedings is drawn upon in the present essay, as compared with a much wider set of Court of Session documents that are being prepared within the context of a longer essay on Muir's Cadder case by Martyn Jones and the present author.

The part of the Cadder case dealt with here is principally detailed in three Edinburgh legal printings, following from legal action raised at the Court of Session by James Dunlop (1741-1816) and others, against Thomas Muir and others, with a reply by the Muir party, and a subsequent reply by the Dunlop party:

Bill of Suspension (James Dunlop of Garnkirk, Esq, and others against Thomas Muir, Esq; Advocate, and others) [appointed 14 December 1790], compiled by John Millar junior. This document is also printed and filed with 'Answers for Thomas Muir', dated 12 December 1790, by his agent, James Keay, though clearly compiled from Muir's arguments and, indeed, words. It also includes, 'Replies for James Dunlop' and 'Extract of the Minutes of the Meetings of the Heritors and Elders of the Parish of Cadder'. (illustrated on page 166)

Information for James Muir & others against James Dunlop (supplied in printed form at 13 October 1791), compiled by George Wallace.

Information for James Dunlop, Esq. & others against Thomas Muir & others [printed from 17 November 1791], compiled by John Millar junior.[25] (illustrated on page 151)

This extremely detailed and important set of documents (with some other sets) requires extensive analysis beyond what can be offered in this essay. In some initial close focus in the limited space here, however, Thomas Muir's activity in the Cadder case can be exhumed and we can begin to see its significant place in the history of eighteenth-century Scottish church Patronage history. The Patronage controversy raged throughout the eighteenth-century,

82

Upon the Bill of Suspension for James Dunlop, Esq; of Garnkirk, and others, against Thomas Muir, Esq; and others, the Lord Hailes, as Ordinary, officiating on the Bills, pronounced the following interlocutor:

LORD HAILES.   " EDIN. DEC. 14. 1790.

" The Lord Ordinary appoints this Bill, Answers, and Replies, to
" be printed and put into the Lords Boxes against Friday next, that
" the Cause may be reported.   (Signed) DA. DALRYMPLE."

In obedience to this Interlocutor, the Bill Answers, Replies, and Extracts of the Minutes of the Meetings of the Heritors and Elders of the Parish of Cadder, founded on by both parties, are now printed and boxed, that the Cause may be reported by the Lord Ordinary.

BILL OF SUSPENSION,

JAMES DUNLOP of Garnkirk, Esq; and others,

AGAINST

THOMAS MUIR, Esq; Advocate, and others.

MY LORDS, &c. Shew your servitors, James Dunlop, Esq; of Garnkirk, John Kincaid, Esq; younger of Kincaid, Patrick Baird, Esq; of Auchinloch, John Purdon-Gray, Esq; of Chryston, and David Muir, Esq; of Gartferry: That, in consequence of the present vacancy in the parish-church of Calder, a meeting of the heritors of the parish was held upon the 19th August last, for the purpose of taking into consideration the measures necessary to be adopted for supplying the present vacancy in the parish, which meeting was adjourned till the 4th day of November, when a number of the heritors and elders convened—Thomas Muir, Esq; Advocate, was chosen preses of this meeting—That gentleman, it may be proper to observe in passing, is not an heritor, though he has been appointed one of the elders. Among other proceedings of this meeting, Cornelius Tod of Adamswall made a motion,

Court of Session: 'Bill of Suspension' document, 14 December 1790. Reproduced by kind permission of the Keeper of the Faculty of Advocates Library, Mungo Bovey QC, and the Faculty of Advocates.

NOVEMBER 17. 1791.

INFORMATION
FOR
JAMES DUNLOP, Esq.

L. HILL, W. S. Agent.

H. Clerk.

53

[LORD JUSTICE CLERK Reporter.]

INFORMATION

FOR

JAMES DUNDOP, Esq. of Garnkirk, one of the Heritors of the
Parish of Calder, Pursuer; with the concurrence of John
Kincaid, Esq. of Auchinairn; John Pendon-Gray, Esq. of
Chryston; James Baird of Auchinloch; Patrick Baird of
Auchinloch; John Muir of Gartferrie; William Drew of
Westquarter; John Tenant in Gartinqueen; and Robert
Marshall of Auchinairn, and others, being a Majority of
the Heritors;

AGAINST

THOMAS MUIR, Esq. Advocate, CORNELIUS TOD, Esq. of Adams-
well, and others, Elders and Heritors of that Parish, Defenders.

THE present question has arisen in an action of declarator
raised by the pursuer, in relation to the right and title
which certain persons, calling themselves heritors and
elders of the parish of Calder, have to deliberate and vote
in conducting the business of that parish. The subject
of dispute has been already before your Lordships in different shapes.
The point now at issue, relates to the validity of certain preliminary
objections

Court of Session: 'Information for James Dunlop, Esq. Of Garnkirk [...]'
document, 17 November 1791.
Reproduced by kind permission of the Keeper of the Faculty of Advocates
Library, Mungo Bovey QC, and the Faculty of Advocates.

with different specific impetuses in different decades, and involving the ecclesiastical courts in protracted debate and judgement. This included, most famously, the opposition of Ebenezer Erskine, from the time of the act itself down to the 1730s and the Inverkeithing Case of the 1750s. One of the best modern historians of Patronage, Andrew Herron, has opined, 'From the time when it was re-enacted in 1712 until it was repealed in 1874, the Law of Patronage hung like a great black cloud over the Kirk, and to its baneful influence can be traced, at second if not at first hand, most of the ills that afflicted her during that century and a half'.[26] Herron's account is one of fervent and stressed conscience on the side of those who opposed the act, and implicitly again provides context for the mentality of Muir that was to inform his entire public career. By 1781 the Popular Party in Glasgow was campaigning strongly for the abolition of patronage. And, as well as this noticeable west-of-Scotland agitation, it is also in a context of increasing power by the Moderates in the nation that the Cadder case of 1790 probably ought to be seen. There may have been added impetus too in that Cadder Kirk was strongly associated with the University of Glasgow, the institution which had so honoured William McGill and which had often been seen previously as a powerful cradle of the 'New Licht' or Moderate sensibility. Famously, the Professor of Moral Philosophy at Glasgow, Ulsterman Francis Hutcheson, had been accused and acquitted of heresy within the Glasgow Presbytery for his liberal attitudes to 'heathens'. In the contemporary case of John Simson, Professor of Divinity at Glasgow, the accused was not so lucky, being suspended in 1729 from teaching for the rest of his life, in effect for placing too much emphasis in his classes upon reason and not enough on the divine intervention of Christ.[27] Again in the Simson – as in the McGill – case we can see Popular Party principle at work: intent on maintaining sound scriptural emphasis upon the incarnation and the centrality of Christ's salvific mission, and the attempted policing of sound doctrine in both church and university. Though the 'College of Glasgow' had in 1695 ceded its right of ministerial appointment at Cadder to the heritors and parishioners, it 'drew the teinds of the parish' down to 1821.[28] That is to say, the university drew a tenth of the produce of the parish (the teind traditionally going to the upkeep of the clergy). In Cadder, a manifestation of this duty-collection was the

Teind barn used for storing part of the harvest, which stood until the early twentieth century. That Cadder kirk had bought out the right to patronage from Glasgow College in 1695 was also part of the fairly recent history of the parish on its way to a fuller parochial independence just prior to the Patronage Act controversies of the eighteenth century.

Cottage opposite Cadder Church that was destroyed by fire in 1928. According to local tradition this had at one time served as a 'teind barn' for the church.
Reproduced by kind permission of East Dunbartonshire Archives & Local Studies (East Dunbartonshire Leisure & Culture Trust).

Like any number of kirks by the late eighteenth century, Cadder Kirk in 1790 was ripe for a contest between the elders and heritors, or at least elders and larger landowners of the heritor class, over patronage. What seems to have marked Cadder out particularly, one can infer, is an intellectually powerful will in this otherwise fairly quiet location (including the agency of both Thomas and his father, James Muir), and also, most likely, a background of university politics, as mentioned already. The parishioners for the most part, it would seem, wished the appointment of the Reverend Archibald Provan to the Cadder vacancy, and this was opposed by a group of heritors led by James Dunlop of Garnkirk. Accounts of the case often identify it as revolving around 'Parchment Barons', that is to say, individuals who had 'superiority' even if not necessarily property or land in a particular geographical location. In the first instance, this term related to secular politics in a practice that had become established by the late eighteenth century in Scotland and wielded by powerful men such as the Duke of Hamilton, in the words of David Allan:

> where electoral qualification was predicated not on the occupation or even on the actual ownership of a given quantity of land but on the formal possession of the legal rights of feudal superiority. Ever-obliging lawyers duly invented conveyances bestowing upon dependant voters the requisite title to appropriate-sized sub-divisions of their clients' vast estates. These 'liferent' or 'faggot' votes, and the phalanx of so-called parchment barons wielding them in the service of larger landowners, could easily prove decisive in view of the limited size of real electorates.[29]

The fact that the idea of the 'parchment baron' was soon wielded as a term in the Cadder controversy, should make us take note yet again of the intertwining of, or in the popular mentality of the day, the non-separation even of secular and religious politics.

Dunlop's *Bill of Suspension* (and other documents from the library of the Faculty of Advocates) cast fascinating, detailed new light on the democratic wrestling over enfranchisement, both in church and in state. It narrates that a meeting of the heritors had been held on 19 August 1790 to make arrangements for the selection of a new minister at Cadder, following the death of the Reverend Alexander Dun (the parish minister for forty four years), with a subsequent convocation on 4 November of both heritors and elders at which latter gathering, 'Thomas Muir, esq, Advocate was chosen Preses of this meeting'.[30] However, as we know from 'Answers for Muir', a prior meeting involving elders had been held on 22 July 1790 to discuss the vacancy, at which Thomas's father, James Muir, was appointed Preses and William Stuart, writer in Glasgow, Clerk.[31] Further, a committee of James Muir, James Dunlop, Thomas Ferrie, David Muir and Thomas Muir (three being a quorum) was appointed to meet on Wednesday 1 August 1790. The minutes of this meeting show that it drew up a list of those (including the Muir-favoured, Archibald Provan) who should be invited to preach at Cadder during the vacancy.[32] However, in 'Answers for Muir', Muir stated that:

> The meeting proceeded to make up a list of the different
> candidates, who were proposed for the office of minister:
> and appointed the committee, which they had chosen, to
> present any four of these gentlemen to the Presbytery,
> for the purpose of receiving its permission to allow them
> to preach successively, in order that the electors and the
> congregation might be enabled to form an opinion of their
> suitableness for the office, to which any one of them might
> be called.[33]

This retrospective recalling of events appears to go beyond the terms of the *original minute*, but maybe includes in good faith what the James Muir-led committee tacitly understood to be the case about the trying-out of preachers in the interregnum. At the 22 July meeting the committee had selected four persons, not including Archibald Provan about whom the dispute was to arise.[34] Furthermore, the committee clearly did not put the chosen names, William Richardson, William Pollock, James Robertson and John Hendry, to Presbytery. The reason for this lack of due protocol remains opaque, 'Muir's Answers' referring mysteriously to 'some peculiar circumstances'.[35]

The meeting also decided to adjourn for four weeks, at which time a meeting of heritors and elders would be held in Cadder Church to determine 'what persons have the right to vote at the election of a Minister'. Notice of that meeting was to be given on Sunday first (25 July 1790) from the precentor's desk at Cadder, and at Chryston. The meeting also requested that those who claimed the right to vote upon this election give their names to the clerk. These minutes were signed by James Muir, Preses, and William Stuart, Clerk.[36] On Wednesday 28 July 1790, three of the 22 July committee, James Muir, Thomas Muir and Thomas Ferrie met to decide that James Muir and Ferrie would present the petition to Presbytery asking for appointment of supply.[37] They compiled a list of four preachers requested for this purpose. However, for reasons unknown the presbytery supplied a list of three different names altogether and the committee as a consequence believed that the heritors and elders should be consulted yet again.[38]

The presbytery's action on supply preachers would seem to be a moment when the James Muir committee began to suspect, surely correctly, some behind-the-scenes machinations. In the following month, on Thursday 19 August, open conflict broke out between two emerging factions at Cadder. Either Thomas's father had had enough, or he genuinely had to prioritise his business affairs. His son states the following:

> Before they proceeded to business, Mr James Muir resigned
> the chair as Preses, as his affairs requiring his presence
> about two months in England, could not permit him to
> pay that attention to the interest of the parish, which his
> inclination otherwise led him to do.[39]

In Muir Senior's place, James Dunlop was appointed preses, with the Minute stating that the appointment was unanimous.[40] Thomas Muir, James Muir and their ally Cornelius Todd and others later contested this view, contending, 'Mr Dunlop [...] was elected as his successor, but in a way extremely irregular'.[41] Thomas Muir *et al* complained particularly that some were voting at this meeting before their titles had been properly examined. Muir's account is that as 'an expedient' he proposed that all should be allowed to vote but that thereafter heritor titles should be scrutinised.[42] At the meeting, James Dunlop countered that the list of names were taken from the books of the collector of the cess [land-tax rolls], 'which he maintained to be the only legal evidence the meeting could have, in the first instance, of those who were heritors'.[43] Muir immediately realised that the evidence was inadequate because it contained names of those who 'were denuded of their lands', omitted the names of their successors, included the names of those who had died, included the names of tenants who did not have property in the parish, and also included the names of others 'who were heritors, and whose title-deeds expressly subjected them to the payment of the cess, of public and private burdens'.[44] That is to say, these latter men were minor title-holders who held their titles under larger ones to whom they would in all likelihood be answerable. This presumably is the point at which the controversy over 'parchment barons' arose. In his 'Answers', Muir alleged 'that Mr Dunlop and his friends obtained their object, rather by the violence of their behaviour than by the force of their arguments'.[45] Most likely, this alludes to some kind of shouting match having taken place. Registering a protest, Muir, his father and Todd walked out of the meeting.[46]

The background here a propos the 22 July meeting is that it had been agreed that those claiming the right to vote should give their names to William Stuart, the clerk. Those so proffering their names were to be inserted into the minutes of 19 August and the resulting list comprised the following individuals:

> Robert Hervie, feuar in Chrystone, David Colquhoun, feuar there, Robert Smith, feuar there, Walter Baiton, feuar, Chrystone, Alexander Wilson, feuar in Chrystone, William Scott in Brownknows, Robert Rankine, there, William Jarvey in Auchinloch, Robert Graham in Auchinloch, Robert Stevenson in Boghead, Robert Stevenson, younger there, John Miller in Myriemailling, Cornelius Todd in Annathill, James Anderson in Auchinairn and John Scott in Brownknows.[47]

After that list had been read over, 'the said feuars [a tenant who holds land in feu, with their rent paid in money and/or grain], by a majority of voices, approved of the foresaid election; and the preses intimated to such of them as were present that they should lodge with the clerk their title-deeds within fourteen days, in order that their right to vote may be considered by the committee after named'.[48] Three important points arise. It is not clear how many of those on this list were present. Secondly, they were required to prove their titles. Thirdly, it was stated that the fact that feuars had voted at this meeting of 19 August did not imply a right to vote in the election of a minister.

At this same meeting a committee was appointed to examine these titles, as Muir had wanted, but having left the meeting with his father and Todd, none of the three could be on the committee, which was led by James Dunlop. A subsequent meeting on Wednesday, 25 August in the Tontine Tavern, with Dunlop as preses, failed to investigate titles though waffled on about these at some length.[49] The new Dunlop-led committee intended to investigate those:

> who it shall appear are burdened by their writs to free and
> relieve their superior or others, from whom they derive
> right, of a proportional part, according to the valuation
> of their lands, of the whole public and parish burdens
> imposed or to be imposed thereon, and to free such person
> upon the roll accordingly.[50]

Rather ambiguous as this is, it seems to imply that the criterion of voting legitimacy was that the person's title, derived from a superior, imposed on the feuar an obligation to relieve the superior of a proportion of the public and parish burdens. Again, then, the idea of parchment barons raises its head, with the feuar here seeming to be independent in their vote but actually locked into the wishes of their superior. The *Gentleman's Magazine* for 1795 provides illuminating background to the kind of 'parchment baron' technique being applied here citing the following from the secular, political sphere:

> [...] at the end of the "History of the Boroughs of
> Great Britain" as to the "Method of framing fictitious
> Qualifications" in Scotland, "The most usual way was, for
> a proprietor to convey the whole lands, both property and
> superiority, to a friend, which friend first re-conveyed
> the property to the owner, and then parcelled out the
> superiorities, and conveyed them to the persons who were
> meant to have votes; this way was preferred, as avoiding
> any direct transaction betwixt the owner and the new
> voter." The superiority, it is to be understood, is much like
> the manorial rights in England, which, it is well known,
> a man may have over an estate, with scarce a shilling of
> pecuniary emoluments then arising. Another mode is as
> follows: "A proprietor first feud out the lands, upon which

he meant to make the qualification, to some friend; he
then alienated the superiorities in fee, life-rent, or wadset
(something like an English mortgage), to the persons whom
he wished to entitle to vote; after which, the friends to
whom he had feud out the lands, re-disposed them to him,
and thus he gave away the bare superiority only. This act
was legal in appearance, because the law of Scotland allows
a man to alienate the superiority, provided he retains the
property in his lands; and it entitles the person holding
the superiority to a right to vote. But in this respect it was
illegal, because the persons who received such superiorities
were understood, in honour, to restore the qualifications
when required, which transaction is done in a way so as not
to make it possible for a voter to disturb the titles of the real
proprietor, and to vote under his influence".[51]

A meeting of the Dunlop-headed committee was held on 1
September and again on 6 October 1790 to deal with the interim
supply of the minister in the ongoing vacancy, with the clerk
appointed at the first meeting to report on those who claimed
the right to vote on the permanent appointment.[52] At the second
of these meetings adjournment was made until a meeting on
20 October in the Tontine Tavern, when the committee would
consider 'whether or not the feuars, and such other persons as are
not upon the cess roll, and who have or may claim to vote at the
election of a minister, can be entitled to that privilege'.[53] At this
next meeting the committee would also, it was minuted, decide
upon whom exactly could vote.[54] However, at this next meeting
no such decision was taken, several members being of the opinion
'that they had not legally any proper power to judge on that head'.[55]
In the 'Information for James Muir and others' more information
is given on this point: 'But doubts arising among some of the
members, particularly in the mind of Mr Dunlop, who began to
suspect that he would be in a minority, concerning their power to
make up a roll, no report was made by them'.[56] It seems likely, in
the light of this statement, that Thomas Muir and his allies were
being made aware of the machinations of the Dunlop camp from
meeting to meeting, and they were influencing and persuading
some members of Dunlop's committee to act contrary to their

preses wishes. In some disarray, but with Dunlop remaining dominant, his committee agreed that he would convene a meeting of both heritors and elders at Cadder on 4 November 1790. This meeting was to fix a date for the election of a new minister.[57]

Dramatically, at the November meeting, Muir wrestled back control of the situation.[58] He was able to have himself elected preses with William Stuart continuing as Clerk. Dunlop urged that an election-day be chosen and that the issue of voting-rights be left undetermined until that time.[59] On the practical side of Dunlop's motion was the fact that the parish had delayed in the matter so long that right of appointment would be taken over by the presbytery, if it were not decided by 27 December. On the strategic side, once the election was a *fait accompli*, it would be protractedly difficult to challenge both the appointment and the legitimacy of the titles of all of those who had voted. Muir's ally, Todd, moved a counter motion, '[t]hat the meeting should, previous to the election, make up a qualified roll of the electors'.[60] The procedure adopted was that those who sided with Dunlop would use (or call) the word 'Election' and those who sided with Todd would use the words 'Qualified roll', indicating that they wished the names of those entitled to vote to be read through. The roll of the meeting was then called and votes marked. The majority voted 'Qualified roll'. Dunlop then protested that he did not believe the meeting had the power to make up a qualified roll, but a committee was formed anyway to draw up this roll. The members were William Stirling, who does not appear to have been at the meeting, Thomas Muir, William Gray of Auchengeech, William Drew of Burnbrae, Cornelius Todd, James Muir, Robert Hunter, David Gray, James Carse, Robert Stevenson feuar, William Gray of Wester Muchroft, George Moncrieff, Alexander Baxter, John Barclay, Thomas Ferrie, Thomas Young and James Angus. Any five would be a quorum with Thomas Muir, as preses, being one of the five and also convener.[61]

This new committee was appointed to meet on 9 November 1790 at Cadder Church to begin work on the qualified roll. Those who wished to be listed on the roll would be required to bring forward their title deeds, or lodge these with the clerk. The committee was licensed to take note of the important points of these titles and judge their merits. Presbytery was also to be petitioned by the committee to fix an election day to appoint a new minister for the parish.[62] Unfortunately, however, there are no minutes or records for the 9 November meeting, though the following day, Thomas Muir and members of the committee went to Presbytery to request their election date. Again, at this point, the Patronage Act issue emerged as Presbytery advanced the view that the heritors and elders should have been proceeding under the 1711-12 Act (of Patronage) and not under the 1690 Act of the Scottish Parliament which gave congregations and their elders electoral priority.[63] Here again, as in the McGill case, we find a tension for Muir in the entangled legislation of Scotland and Britain, which was having the unintended consequence of damaging what was for Muir and others who thought like him, the unassailable national (Scottish) reality of the Presbyterian Church. Nonetheless, Muir went ahead with the plan agreed prior to Presbytery's intervention and called a general meeting of Cadder heritors and elders for 26 November to continue examining titles.[64] By 24 November, James Dunlop mounted a legal intervention in the civil courts, and at the highest level. He raised his Bill of Suspension at the Court of Session in Edinburgh. Among several grounds of Dunlop objection, the most central, perhaps, was found in the statement that:

It is contrary to every principle of reason and expediency, that the elders of this parish, who have not a foot of property in it, should be named members of a committee, whare to inspect the title-deeds of the heritors, and decide upon their validity. The complainers were not disposed to submit themselves even to the judgment of one of the elders, a Gentleman well skilled in the law of the land.[65]

Here, clearly, was a reference to Thomas Muir. Dunlop's 'Bill' also stated, possibly with entire truth, that many of those who voted for the committee were neither heritors or elders.[66] The remedies sought were that Thomas Muir and the others should be inhibited and discharged from making up the Qualified roll, and that the meeting of the heritors and elders for electing the minister, ought not be held till after intimation from the pulpit of a ministerial election (since this had not been properly done either), as well as after circular letters to the heritors had been sent. Dunlop and his allies sought letters of suspension and interdict.[67]

Nonetheless, the meeting of 26 November at Cadder went ahead, with the Bill of Suspension raised and the decision made that Thomas Muir was to employ an agent to answer it and advance counter-legal measures, especially with the aim of staying the hand of any action by the Presbytery until the Court of Session had reached final judgement.[68] Muir's agent, James Keay, signed the 'Answers of Muir' [to Dunlop's 'Bill of Suspension'] dated 12 December 1790, but a note tells us that these are Muir's work. Muir's 'Answer' comprises seventeen pages and contains many fairly minor quibbles about the process that had been undertaken in the Cadder vacancy, particularly about Dunlop's 'Bill of Suspension' not being fully honest about the walkout at the meeting of 19 August.[69] Its major points included the claim, already alluded to, that since 1695 the election of a minister at Cadder had proceeded under the 1690 Act.[70] He argued that the 'feuars' at the 19 August meeting were all heritors, and not only some as Dunlop's case relied upon, under the Heritable Jurisdictions (Scotland) Act 1746, which is a rather nice manoeuvre in that it allows this post-Union act to become interpreter of the pre-Union concept of the heritor (which Muir *et al* were reliant in their insistence of the foundational election-voting criteria of 1690).[71] To Dunlop's argument that Muir's committee had some non-heritor elders on it, Muir retorted that Dunlop's committee had an equal number of elders and heritors.[72] Muir outlined the meetings of Dunlop's committee, noting for its meeting of 20 October 'if the vote had been put, upon that proposition, as some of the members wanted it to be, the resolution entered into, would have been directly opposite to that which now stands in the minute'.[73] In other words, Dunlop at that point would have been stopped dead in his tracks of carrying on the business of preparing to elect a minister, as this meeting clearly felt that Muir's proposed course of action of thoroughly examining the deeds was the correct course, rather than the cursory examining of these on 20 October as Dunlop proposed. The effective collapse of Dunlop's meeting on that date conceded the moral victory to Muir.

'Replies for Dunlop' and others were much shorter (fewer than four full pages compared to Muir's seventeen), but they contain a surprising statement from Dunlop's counsel, John Millar junior. He claimed that it was the respondents, that is Muir and others, who were trying to increase their votes by including small feuars who did not pay the cess.[74] Was Muir attempting to include parchment barons that he thought would favour his candidate? More research is here necessary. Millar maintained that the cess roll should rule and that if there were any omissions, one could refer to the collecting roll of the parish (that is the extant roll of those who were actually paying taxes directly).[75] In support of his case, Millar cited the practice of two churches, Canongate and St Cuthbert's Parish, in support of Dunlop's view of the correct test and procedure. These precedents most likely carried weight in the case.[76] In concluding the 'Replies for Dunlop', Millar emphasised the necessity of relying upon the cess roll and, as Muir had likewise urged, that time now was pressing.[77]

So, how did this case end? The usual biographical accounts maintain that Thomas Muir won the Cadder contretemps. This is not surprising since in time Archibald Provan, the preferred candidate of Muir and his allies, succeeded to the vacant pulpit in the parish. However, in the 'Information for James Dunlop', Miller stated: 'The bill was sisted by Lord Hailes, and an interdict granted; and after answers and replies were lodged, his Lordship took the case to report, when the court unanimously passed the bill of suspension'.[78] So, what the papers in the Faculty of Advocates show is that Muir lost the case, at least initially. As with controversy he had previously entered into at the University of Glasgow and in the McGill case, and as a little later in his political trial, Muir's legal efforts at Cadder were tenacious, to a large degree morally courageous but containing murky elements. The idea that 'parchment barons' featured very largely in the case seems to be belied by the paucity of such creatures on the ground, and it was James Dunlop in fact who was attempting to strike down votes rather than Thomas Muir (albeit on rather different grounds). Both sides seem at points to be accusing the other of relying on cooked votes, and work beyond the scope of this chapter which can only set out a basic narrative, needs to be done. Specifically, much deeper, more forensic investigation is warranted into the status of feuars and heritors in Cadder during this case. What we can say with most certainty, is that the kirk voting situation at Cadder was a mess, much as was similarly the case in secular politics in constituencies throughout the land. No doubt the Court of Session's decision to grant an interdict to Dunlop confirmed his view that the authorities were on the side of the status quo (particularly where it concerned a powerful landowner) and had little interest in investigating the franchise in any deep sense, being content rather to serve the practical, functional reality of late eighteenth-century Scotland where voting rights in both church and state were poorly sanctioned. This chapter has merely begun the job of bringing into focus Muir's activities as an activist and legal practitioner in the ecclesiastical sphere. It has also attempted to provide something of a close-up view of the Muir-Dunlop Cadder contretemps for the first time in print since it happened two and a quarter centuries ago. Much remains to be discovered and narrated. However, as we see also in the McGill case, the Cadder case highlights the centrality of the Patronage issue to Muir and his contemporaries and around it we notice swirling large ideas about the Church of Scotland, in terms of its voice and its democracy, including the complicated matter of its pre and post 1707, as well as pre and post 1711-12, constitution. Such ideas are fuel, clearly, for interpretations of how Muir thought about his church and his country. In a number of ways, generally however, we might see that in his Kirk politics, the stage was being set for Thomas Muir's most public trial yet, either because he was set on a collision course with authority or it was set on a collision course with him.

Notes and References

1   *Politics for the People*, No.XI, 1794, pp.156-7.
2   For a sensible approach to the potentially slippery terms 'new licht', 'auld licht', 'moderate' and 'popular party' see Sher, 1985 [& 2015], especially in the first instance, pp.16-18.
3   Roy, ed, 1985, vol.1, 1780-1789, p.144.
4   See, for instance, the William Peebles sermon (Peebles, 1788) for its ad hominem remarks about McGill from the pulpit.
5   Anon, 1792b, p.79.
6   See Robert Richard, 'An Examination of the life and career of William McGill (1737-1807), controversial Ayr theologian'. Unpublished PhD thesis, University of Glasgow, 2009, pp.161-5 & 202-31.
7   McGill, 1786, p.22.
8   McGill, 1786, p.244.
9   See Anon, 1792b, p.57.
10 For a very nice narrative account, especially of the theological issues, see R Richard, unpublished PhD thesis, pp.254-72.
11 Anon, 1792b, p.69.
12 Burns, 1968, vol.1, p.126.
13 See Anon, 1792b, p.69.
14 Muir's summation of the case can be found, however, largely verbatim in his speech to the General Assembly in 1791 as the case came to an end, to be found in *The Procedure of our Church Courts in the Case of Dr William McGill of Ayr* (Anon, 1792a), pp.131-50, with additional response also likely to be Muir, pp.154-70. I am grateful to Don Martin for drawing my attention to this pamphlet.
15 Anon, 1792b, pp.78-9.
16 Anon, 1792b, p.70.
17 Anon, 1790, p.3.
18 Anon, 1790, p.3.
19 Anon, 1790, p.4.
20 Anon, 1790, pp.4-5.
21 Anon, 1790, pp.5-6.
22 Biography of John Millar by K Haakonssen and JW Cairns in the *Oxford Dictionary of National Biography* (2004); see online edition: http://www.oxforddnb.com/view/article/18716?docPos=2.
23 See Durey, 1990, p.41, for details of Muir's correspondence with Millar junior in 1796.
24 I am extremely grateful to Mr Martyn Jones and legal colleagues of his for making me aware of these papers. Likewise, I express thanks to The Keeper of the Faculty of Advocates Library, Mungo Bovey QC, and the Senior Librarian, Andrea Longson for granting me access to and permission to cite and quote from these papers.

25 For *Bill of Suspension* (James Dunlop of Garnkirk, Esq, and others
    against Thomas Muir, Esq; Advocate, and others), see Faculty of
    Advocates, *Campbell 59*; for *Information for James Muir* & others
    against James Dunlop, see *Campbell 63*; for *Information for James
    Dunlop, Esq.* & others against Thomas Muir & others, see *Dreghorn 72*.
26 Herron, 1985, p.89.
27 See Scott, 1900, pp.83-4; for Simson, see Steer, 2009, pp.189-92.
28 See Beaumont, 1990. This out-of-print booklet is available at:
    http://www.cadderchurch.org/beaumont%20history.html
29 Allan, 2002, p.21.
30 'Bill of Suspension', p.1
31 'Answers for Muir, p.1.
32 See 'Extract from the Minutes of the Meeting of the Heritors and
    Elders of the Parish of Cadder', pp.1-2.
33 'Answers for Muir' p.2.
34 'Extract of the Minutes', p.3.
35 'Answers for Muir', p.3.
36 'Extract of the Minutes', pp.2-3.
37 'Extract of the Minutes', p.3.
38 'Extract of the Minutes', p.4.
39 'Answers for Muir', p.3.
40 'Extract of the Minutes', p.5.
41 'Answers for Muir', p.3.
42 'Answers for Muir', p.3.
43 'Answers for Muir', p.3.
44 'Answers for Muir', p.3.
45 'Answers for Muir', p.4.
46 Note: the Minutes refer to a protest by 'Todd of Annathill', but in
    later Minutes to 'Todd of Adamswell', although sometimes with Todd
    spelt 'Tod'.
47 'Extracts of the Minutes', p.5.
48 'Extracts of the Minutes', p.5.
49 'Extracts of the Minutes', p.7.
50 'Extracts of the Minutes', p.7.
51 *Gentleman's* Magazine, 1795, Vol.77, p.394.
52 'Extracts of the Minutes', p.8.
53 'Extracts of the Minutes', p.8.
54 'Extracts of the Minutes', p.8.
55 'Extracts of the Minutes', p.9.
56 'Information for James Muir', p.3.
57 'Extracts of the Minutes', p.9.
58 'Extracts of the Minutes', p.10.
59 'Extracts of the Minutes', p.10.

60 'Extracts of the Minutes', p.10.
61 'Extracts of the Minutes', p.10-11.
62 'Extracts of the Minutes', pp.11-12.
63 'Extracts of the Minutes', p.12.
64 'Extracts of the Minutes', pp.13-14.
65 'Bill of Suspension', p.4.
66 'Bill of Suspension', p.4.
67 'Bill of Suspension', p.5.
68 'Extracts of the Minutes', pp.13-15.
69 'Answers for Muir', p.3.
70 'Answers for Muir', p.1.
71 'Answers for Muir', p.4.
72 'Answers for Muir', p.6.
73 'Answers for Muir', p.7-8.
74 'Replies for James Dunlop', p.1.
75 'Replies for James Dunlop', pp.2-3.
76 It had already been decided by the Court what was meant by heritors. It was those who paid the cess. Miller refers to two cases involving the appointment of schoolmasters. The first case reported in Lord Kames's *Selected Decisions*, 257, involved a dispute under Act 26th Parl. 1696 between the Earl of Strathmore with all the considerable heritors and the minister and small feuars. The second case (decided in 1787) involved the opposition of Colonel Sinclair and a number of considerable heritors in Dysart to feuars who did not pay the cess; Lord Stonefield reduced the decision made by a majority comprising such feuars.
77 'Replies for James Dunlop', p.4.
78 'Information for James Dunlop', p.3.

Thomas Muir and the *Edinburgh Gazetteer*

Reporting on the 'Friend of the People'
before and after his trial

Rhona Brown

By the 1790s, Scotland had a busy, if not uniformly thriving, periodicals culture. While some journals, magazines and newspapers stayed the course and stood the test of time – one obvious example is the enduring *Scots Magazine*, which published its first issue in 1739 and is still running today, and which was proudly reporting on the Scottish sedition trials at the end of the eighteenth century – others burst on to the periodicals marketplace, shone their lights into the eyes of their readers and the political status quo, only to die away soon after. Many such short-lived magazines appeared and disappeared throughout eighteenth-century Britain and Europe. Thanks to the expense of establishing, printing and circulating newspapers, as well as to increasing and diversifying taxation in Britain, some journals appeared for only two or three issues before their demise.[1] As a result of this unforgiving marketplace, even the most successful periodicals editors had to reinvent their publications over time. Their strategies for survival included setting up new magazine businesses and fresh editorial and printing collaborations, giving their publications new names and regularly reinventing their reporting and journalistic approaches.[2] These innovations were often necessary in response to threats of ever-heavier regulation of news reporting.[3] Alongside this political restriction, which was a reaction, in part, to the events during and following the French Revolution, the financial importance of advertising was also increasingly recognised.[4]

The *Edinburgh Gazetteer* was one of these short-lived publications. However, despite the fact that it ran only from 16 November 1792 until 29 January 1794, it managed to circulate over ninety issues in that short time. Of those issues, around eighty-four remain extant, and hard copies of the journal are extremely rare. Its timing means that it engages with some of the most explosive moments in eighteenth-century Scottish, British and European history. It refuses to shy away from what its editors and contributors saw as difficult but necessary political truths. Despite the limitations of the term in an eighteenth-century context,[5] the *Edinburgh Gazetteer* has been traditionally seen as a radical newspaper which rode the wave of the British, and particularly the Scottish, and even Edinburgh's, response to the French Revolution. It is no surprise, then, that it was heavily and openly engaged with the cause of political reform and, by extension, with the fate of those deemed to have committed seditious acts. It is also no surprise that, for the *Gazetteer*, the life and actions of Thomas Muir were particularly newsworthy. Although Muir was something of a celebrity in the British periodical press towards the end of 1793 thanks to his notorious and well-documented trial, the *Edinburgh Gazetteer* is unusual in that it engages with and reports on Muir and his actions well in advance of and following August 1793.

According to Bob Harris, the *Edinburgh Gazetteer* was 'the main Scottish radical newspaper' which depicted 'the recent upsurge in radical activity in Edinburgh'.[6] For Murray Armstrong, the *Gazetteer* was 'the official paper of the [reform] movement'.[7] Stephen W Brown argues that the paper holds the 'most dramatic' statement of national identity in a period in which 'declarations of a work's "Scottishness" had resonated through [...] the [book] trade'.[8] Not only did the paper engage with politics at home, as Gordon Pentland outlines, it also provided 'detailed reporting of French events'.[9] These descriptions demonstrate something of the *Gazetteer*'s approach, which remained consistent with the purpose set out by its editor and proprietor, Captain William Johnston, in its first issue. This issue, printed on 16 November 1792, was circulated, according to its title page, 'gratis'.[10] Although the *Gazetteer* would eventually cost fourpence to purchase, the fact that this first issue could be obtained for free demonstrates the paper's approach to both its contents and its readership.

Traditionally, in an argument which stems from theories of the emergence of the 'public sphere' by Jürgen Habermas,[11] the rise of the press in eighteenth-century Britain is often regarded as being 'symptomatic of the rise of the middle class'[12] and, according to Harris, 'three overlapping groups appear to have dominated newspaper readership in Scotland for most of the century, certainly before the 1790s – the gentry, local urban elites and merchants'.[13] Going by readers' contributions to and correspondence with the *Gazetteer* and, indeed, those to/with other eighteenth-century periodicals, it is clear that the Scottish newspaper and magazine audience comes from a well-educated populace. It also seems clear that after the events of the early 1790s the periodical press was seen increasingly as a tool which encouraged, if not enabled, political empowerment: 'the terminus' of the late eighteenth-century press was, for Harris, 'support for political reform'.[14] Indeed, Joseph Danvers, MP for Totness in 1738, stated that, 'I believe the people of Great Britain are governed by a power that was never heard of as a supreme power in any age or country before [...] It is the government of the press'.[15]

Offering a new paper for free was, arguably, a political declaration as well as a shrewd business manoeuvre. By this strategy, the *Gazetteer*'s strident opening political statement could reach beyond the traditional, 'middle-class' periodicals readership to a wider, regular audience. In the absence of circulation figures for eighteenth-century newspaper readership in Scotland, conclusions on this point are conjectural; Johnston's decision to give away his first issue is nonetheless clearly a significant one.

As noted, the paper was edited and owned by Captain William Johnston, and printed initially by WG Moffat and latterly by Simon Drummond in the Scottish capital. Moffat appears in the Scottish Book Trade Index as a 'printer and stationer' in Edinburgh in 1792, responsible for printing the *Gazetteer* in that year;[16] Drummond does not appear at all. This omission is perhaps owing to the fact that Drummond was prosecuted, alongside Johnston himself, in March 1793 for the *Gazetteer*'s report of a political trial at Edinburgh's High Court.[17] Very little is known about Johnston, the paper's initial editor, founder and proprietor. There is no Oxford Dictionary of National Biography entry for him, and although the *Gazetteer* is mentioned here and there in scholarship on the Scottish 1790s, Johnston remains a shadowy figure. As well as appearing on the back page of every issue of the *Gazetteer*, with the information that 'This paper will be regularly filed at Mr. TAYLER's Office, Warwick Square, Newgate Street, London, and may be seen at principal Coffee-houses, &c. throughout the Kingdom', Johnston's name appears in a few 1790s publications thanks to his own particular trial: in, for example, Cobbett's *Complete Collection of State Trials* and in *Answers for Captain William Johnston, to the Petition and Complaint of Robert Dundas of Arniston, His Majesty's Advocate for Scotland* (1794). Unsurprisingly, and as noted, the *Gazetteer* forms the basis of Johnston's charge. The *Edinburgh Magazine, or Literary Miscellany* for March 1793 gives some details of Johnston's misdemeanour:

> Edinburgh, Feb. 23. The Lords Commissioners of Justiciary sentenced Captain Johnston the publisher, and Mr Drummond printer, of "The Edinburgh Gazetteer" to three months imprisonment for contempt of court.[18]

This news piece tells only part of Johnston's story. As Cobbett's *Complete Collection of State Trials* states, Johnston was brought before the High Court on nine occasions in January and February 1793, for contempt of court.[19] According to the *Scots Magazine*, Johnston's crime was 'having published in his newspaper (the *Edinburgh Gazetteer*) an erroneous statement of the trial of Craig and two others, for seditious speeches at Edinburgh Castle, and also for inserting two paragraphs reflecting upon the proceedings of the Court in that trial'. It continues: 'they unanimously agreed that both pannels should be imprisoned for three months, and Mr Johnston to find security to keep the peace, himself and two sureties in 500l. and Mr Drummond, himself and two sureties in 100l. for three years'.[20] Following these setbacks, Johnston was replaced by a new proprietor, Alexander Scott, who managed to keep the paper afloat until its eventual closure in early 1794.[21]

Harris argues that Johnston's trial 'reinforced [his] essentially cautious outlook', and that 'the producers of the *Gazetteer* engaged in significant self-censorship to deflect potential legal repression' by keeping 'several radical addresses [...] out of the paper to prevent furnishing occasion for the authorities to suppress it'.[22] This was true in the long term; however, despite the fact that Johnston's crimes were directly connected with his newspaper, the *Gazetteer* tackles its editor's situation head on in the number dated 26 February 1793 with a somewhat knowing quotation from Shakespeare's *Othello*: 'Nothing extenuate,/Nor set down aught in malice'. In the same issue, the *Gazetteer* gives its own version of its producers' legal troubles, reporting that Johnston and Drummond were imprisoned for their publishing of 'the account of the Trial of the Three Printers'; despite this impediment, they insist, '[...] those that report that the Gazetteer is about to stop, report a falsehood; the Gazetteer will exist, and its *principles* will also exist, in spite of the malice of its enemies'.[23] The trials of Drummond and Johnston reflect the turbulent political context for Scottish periodicals in 1793. Despite having existed for less than three months, the *Gazetteer* was already attracting the attention of legal authority. Rather than dampen the paper's spirits, however, the *Gazetteer* was undeterred and almost spurred on by its early hindrances, and moved from its initial weekly publication to being offered for sale twice a week. Johnston's name appeared as the paper's proprietor on its back cover throughout his trial and until Alexander Scott's replaced it from the issue dated 2 April 1793.

Even a cursory glance at the contents of that first issue of the *Edinburgh Gazetteer* gives a good sense of its aforementioned principles and, further, how these principles interact with and complement those of Thomas Muir. The opening issue of 16 November 1792 introduces itself in bold manner as 'A new attempt to diffuse extensively every branch of useful and interesting information', which 'requires no apology'. This immediate and striking confidence is followed by an account of the periodical as 'at once the most easy and most successful mode of propagating knowledge, of enlightening the people, and of connecting every order of citizens in a great state, however various their ordinary occupations'.[24] Although, as noted above, proven details of the readership of the period's newspapers and periodicals are sparse, partially due to their circulation beyond the point of purchase in coffee-houses, convivial clubs, taverns and other social spaces, Johnston evidently saw his publication as having something to say to readers of all social classes; indeed, they are simply fellow citizens of a 'great state', and implicitly of equal importance. This seemingly small detail is of significance because, as Harris has argued, 'the press was certainly seen at the time as threatening traditional political relationships, and the supremacy of landed influence and landed values in politics'.[25] The *Gazetteer*'s subtly egalitarian opening is followed by bolder remarks which argue that, although 'the attention of Europe is directed to the greatest events, and while the minds of men are deeply engaged and agitated by the consideration of the most important objects', Johnston reminds his readers that there is also pressing political need closer to home:

> In the British Empire more especially, where the bread of
> the poor and the rewards of industry are devoured by an
> imminent taxation, every individual has a right to consider
> himself as a proprietor in the government, and to inquire
> into the means on which his property is expended.[26]

The *Gazetteer* is therefore established as a newspaper of opposition to the political status quo. While some historians have taken issue with John Brewer's argument that the press was a central constituent of what he calls 'an alternative structure of politics',[27] it is certainly the case that Johnston addresses 'those who are interested in the welfare of their country', whether they are fully represented politically or (as was most likely) not. Indeed, Johnston goes further, stating that:

> this publication is undertaken with a design to procure
> a ready opportunity of conveying intelligence of abuses
> before they become deeply rooted, - of interesting people
> at large in the fate of every part of the empire, - of arresting
> bad men in their career, by forcing on them the alternative
> of either doing their duty, or of submitting to immediate
> and universal infamy, - and, lastly, to acquire the power of
> searching out and expressing to the world, the detestable
> and crooked schemes by which corruption underlines the
> bulwarks of freedom.[28]

There is little in the way of compromise here; indeed, Johnston stands alongside the radical London and British press with his implicit argument that information, circulated through newspaper channels, is the saviour of the common reader and the enemy of 'corruption'.

This introduction is followed by the 'Plan' or prospectus for the *Gazetteer*, which outlines the paper's strategies and principles. The first of these is also connected with freedom: 'we account it a proper use of the liberty of the press, to expose to mankind, in the strongest points of view, the malversations of those who are intrusted with the business of the property of their fellow citizens'.[29] With property at the core of his argument, Johnston here begins to make a case for political reform, based on the 'malversations' of those in public office. But more than this, the *Gazetteer* is particularly concerned with events in France, as it vows to:

> rescue the Public from those glaring misrepresentations
> of events upon the Continent with which they have been
> abused; and, in particular, to prevent them from being
> obliged to rest satisfied with those partial statements of
> French affairs that have been hitherto given.[30]

Finally, and significantly, the paper presents itself as 'a source of moral instruction'.[31] In these opening statements, therefore, Johnston engages in political rhetoric, stating while not-quite-stating that the cause of political reform is on the side of moral right.

As he bemoans the shortfalls of Britain's two main political parties, Johnston aligns the *Gazetteer* with a third which is, as he declares,

> unconnected with either of these, which has been hitherto
> too little regarded, that of THE NATION, which can have
> no interest but one, the prosperity of the whole. It is on
> the side of this Party that the Proprietors mean to range
> themselves.[32]

While assuring his readership that, 'We are attached to the British Constitution', 'for which our fathers shed their blood', real peace can only be attained, according to Johnston, by 'freedom and equal laws'.[33] If readers are concerned about the *Gazetteer* fomenting riot and social disorder, Johnston states that it is not the paper's aim 'to inflame the minds of the people, or to facilitate the designs of the factious'. On the contrary, their wish is for 'the lasting happiness of society, by diffusing reason throughout the world, and to aid the progress of good sense by calm investigation'. Despite this assurance, Johnston warns his public that 'no interest in this Kingdom is fairly represented in Parliament – that the public money is squandered in the most infamous manner' and, in a stroke which echoes twenty-first-century concerns, that the enormous national debt, of 'TWO HUNDRED AND FORTY MILLIONS', was amassed because 'the People were destitute of a fair representation to do justice to their interests'.[34] There is little to allow a misunderstanding of the *Gazetteer*'s political stance and journalistic strategy.

The first issue continues with many advertisements, details of a society to help aid those whom they call the 'Industrious Poor', as well as reports from the National Convention in Paris via Maurice Margarot and Thomas Hardy, who were then in attendance. The first report from Paris concludes: 'The universe is free! – tyrants and tyranny are no more! – Peace reigns on the earth, and it is to the French that mankind are indebted for it'.[35] Here, as throughout, the *Gazetteer* sets itself against the anti-French rhetoric that had become common in the British establishment and the establishment press since the zenith, earlier in the century, of Whig politician John Wilkes and his nemesis, Prime Minister Lord Bute, and which would soon come to bear in further conflict with France. Elsewhere, a news report proclaims that, 'The chains forged by superstition and by tyranny are every where dissolving away; and millions of wretches open their eyes and wonder that they were ever slaves'.[36] In the *Gazetteer*'s first and soon to be regular poetry section, a 'Sonnet, on the Tree of Liberty being Planted in Savoy, Written by a Lady' appears, in which that 'symbol of liberty' gifted by 'Gallia', becomes 'the guardian friend of the human race'.[37]

It is perhaps natural, then, that Thomas Muir should find a ready home in the pages of the *Gazetteer*. His name first appears as early as the third issue of the paper, when it forms part of the customary reporting on the actions and meetings of the various Scottish branches of the Friends of the People. In the *Gazetteer* dated 30 November 1792, readers are informed that 'Thomas Muir, Esq. younger of Hunters Hill, was unanimously elected Vice President'.[38] In a foreshadowing of Muir's own trial, in which he was obliged to emphasise, through his witnesses and defence, that he was attached to the British constitution and opposed to violent and riotous measures, the *Gazetteer* outlines the resolutions of the Friends of the People:

1. That the name or names of any person or persons belonging to the Associated Friends of the People, who may be found guilty of rioting, or creating or aiding sedition or tumult, shall be expunged from the books of the Society.
2. That any person acting properly, who may be persecuted and oppressed by the arm of power, shall be protected by the whole Societies.[39]

It is instructive to observe which items bookend this first report on Muir and his association with the Friends of the People. Immediately beforehand is the statement, in 'News from England', that, 'If the real wealthy men of this nation reflected on their true interests, they would every one join in a cordial acquiescence to a Reform'.[40] Immediately following the piece on Muir is a printing of Robert Burns's 'The Rights of Woman' which is, although here anonymous and unattributed, very much in keeping with and echoing the first issue's 'Plan' for the *Gazetteer* with its apparently jocular plea for readers to turn their heads from the 'mighty' events in Europe to a more pressing local concern which is, for Burns, 'the rights of woman'.[41] Here is Muir, then, at the heart of political reform in Scotland in the pages of the *Gazetteer*, as Burns plays with Painite ideology and cries out 'ça ira', through the benefit night speech of Miss Louisa Fontenelle, a well-known contemporary actress currently treading the boards at the theatre in Burns's Dumfries.

The *Gazetteer* for 14 December 1792 offers a transcript of a conversation between Muir and Lord Daer.[42] According to Christina Bewley, Muir and Daer had been introduced by Anna Barbauld in the spring of 1792 thanks to the fact that Daer had 'been at Edinburgh University, then in Paris at the outbreak of the French Revolution. He was a keen reformer, a member of both the Friends of the People and the London Corresponding Society'.[43]

As early as January 1793, the *Gazetteer* begins its very extensive coverage of Muir's trial. This aspect of Muir's life has received broad scholarly treatment. Therefore, the focus of the remainder of this chapter is on the paper's coverage of the run up to and aftermath of Muir's trial in order to consider the *Gazetteer*'s response to what might be called the 'singling out' of Muir and, eventually, other reformers who received heavy coverage in the paper, including William Skirving and Maurice Margarot. In particular, I will consider whether this very real and increasing political danger and repression affected the *Gazetteer*'s political principles and journalistic priorities.

The *Gazetteer* reports the so-called 'Examination of Mr Muir' in great detail in the paper dated 8 January 1793. At this point, Muir had been arrested after having been invited to attend and help defend his friend James Tytler, who was also undergoing trial in the Scottish capital. The *Gazetteer*'s narrative begins with Muir's alighting from his carriage at Holytown, only to be accosted by one Mr Williamson, the king's messenger, who promptly issues Muir with a warrant. After demanding to search Muir's portmanteau and being refused, Williamson insists on travelling with Muir into Edinburgh. On arrival, it is reported, 'Muir was brought before Mr Sheriff Pringle, assisted by Mr Honyman, Sheriff of Lanerkshire'.[44] After being asked a number of questions by Pringle, the *Gazetteer* reports on Muir's stalling of the questioning process as follows, explaining that

> he would, in that place, answer no question whatever; that he considered such examination as utterly inconsistent with the rights of British citizens, instruments of oppression, and pregnant with mischief; that in criminal cases, uniformly, in pleading at the bar, he had reprobated declarations founded on such examination. He appealed to Mr Honyman, if he had not frequently been a witness of such conduct. "I will not then," said Mr Muir, "desert in my own case, a principle which I have invariably applied to the cases of others."[45]

After being challenged by Pringle and Honyman that there is 'material difference between pleading on principle as a counsel, and acting on them as a private character', Muir responds in the negative, stating that: 'If principles are just, they must be applicable to all cases, and all situations'. Here, Muir presents his 'declaration', which is given in full by the *Gazetteer* and in which Muir makes the claims that would characterise his defence in trial. The declaration states that he did not circulate seditious or treasonous materials; that he advised his fellow reformers 'to adopt no other than constitutional measures'; and that the petition was the best mode of agitating for reform. He is then questioned on various topics: about lending and therefore distributing the work of Tom Paine, the Paisley address, Flower's account of the French Revolution and the *Patriot*; about his membership of the Friends of the People. According to the *Gazetteer*, Muir refused to comply or provide information to his questioners: 'To all these interrogatories, on the principle he first stated, Mr Muir declined giving any answer, in the affirmative or negative. The examination was then closed'. Muir now takes his opportunity to opine – as he would later in the trial – that 'certain persons had endeavoured to impress the minds of those who may be called as witnesses against him'. The *Gazetteer* report ends with a statement which echoes its plan to be known as a source of moral instruction: 'It is to be hoped, that the conduct of this Learned Counsel, during his examination, will serve as an invariable example to those who may be placed in a similar situation'.[46] Not only are more arrests such as Muir's and Tytler's inevitable, according to the *Gazetteer*'s editorial insertion-cum-moral judgement, Muir is a paragon and a model worth close emulation for those suffering the same fate.

In the following *Gazetteer*, dated 11 January 1793, Muir is quoted in a report on the war with France, stating 'that we are all loyal to our king, attached to our constitution in its pure and genuine principles, and that is our unalterable resolution to oppose the war system, which has dissolved the world, and destroyed the peace and happiness of the human race'.[47] Again hitting targets at which he would aim during his trial, Muir repeatedly emphasises his attachment to the British constitution, just as did the *Gazetteer*'s prospectus and opening 'plan', and as did many who were arrested and tried for seditious practices in the 1790s.

In the issue dated 26 February 1793, a report from the High Court of Justiciary states that, 'Thomas Muir, Esq. younger of Huntershill, not appearing to stand trial for seditious practices, was outlawed and his bail declared forfeited', before giving details of the Lord Advocate's Complaint against the Reverend William

Dun, minister of Kirkintilloch, for not being able to procure the '"Minutes of the Association of Kirkintilloch", libelled on in the indictment against Muir'. As scholars of Muir's trial are aware, Dun would later be imprisoned for removing pages from the aforementioned Minute Book. As the *Gazetteer* reports, the book was 'at last found in the possession of Mr Dun; but three leaves following the eighth page, which it was believed contained something treasonable, were torn out'.[48]

On 1 March 1793, the *Gazetteer* prints Muir's now well-known letter to 'the Friends of the People in Scotland', in which he explains the difficulties he encountered when attempting to leave France: 'Armed with innocency, I appeal to Justice; and I disdain to supplicant favours'.[49] Perhaps unusually for the *Gazetteer*, but nonetheless explicable thanks to the fact that the paper's editor, Johnston's, own legal troubles were concurrently taking place, Muir's letter is printed without editorial commentary. Muir's words were, presumably, enough, and many of the arguments he makes in the letter would be repeated, distorted and echoed by Muir himself and others during the course of the trial.

At this point, the *Gazetteer* begins its reporting of Muir's trial. This reporting is, perhaps predictably for a paper with established political principles and journalistic rhetoric, regular and detailed. However, equally illuminating is the *Gazetteer*'s reporting of the events following Muir's trial, and its response to his sentence. These reports are taken from the last weeks of the *Gazetteer*'s publishing life, and while there is no surrendering of the paper's originally stated political principles, the tone of its reports on Muir has undergone some significant alteration, evidently in response, not only to Muir's treatment and sentence, but to the many others undergoing trial and investigation for sedition and treason. In the issue of 10 December 1793, the *Gazetteer* prints a piece entitled 'Messrs MUIR and PALMER'. By this time, Muir and his fellow prisoner, Thomas Fyshe-Palmer, were imprisoned on board the hulks at Woolwich. Readers' correspondence on this topic is introduced by the editor as follows:

The unparalleled severity exercised against these Gentlemen, has excited general *indignation*. The putting them on board of the Hulks at Woolwich, which is contrary

to their sentence; and the order from the Secretary of
State's Office for separating them, are measures suggested
by such a spirit of wanton cruelty, as must make every
feeling mind revolt.[50]

Again appealing to morality, sympathy and sensibility,
the paper's position on Muir's sentence is clear, thanks to the
editorial and printing decisions made in its aftermath. However,
its description of the inevitability of 'revolt' in the 'feeling mind'
has many interpretations, from a feeling of disgust to outright
rebellion. This short editor's statement, with its nuanced, open to
interpretation insertions, is followed by an extract from a letter
from London, which gives further details of Muir's imprisonment,
reporting that he and Palmer 'are put on board the hulks, with
irons on, the same as common felons'. The correspondent
confirms that Palmer and Muir have been separated, with Muir
on board the Prudentia, and Palmer on the Stanislaus. According
to the correspondent, 'Mr Muir is slightly indisposed. They are
both obliged to work and fare as the common felons'. After giving
some extracts from the letters of both Muir and Palmer and an
update on Muir's failing health, the *Gazetteer* states that these bits
and pieces of correspondence are 'the only authentic intelligence
received here concerning them'.[51]

Later in the same issue, news from Dublin states that Muir and
Palmer were remembered at a meeting of the Society of United
Irishmen on 3 December. Following these accounts, the *Gazetteer*
publishes letters from concerned and indignant correspondents,
including one report in which the United Irishmen of Dublin
describe Muir as 'the suffering friend and advocate of the People'.
Not content with this symbolic support, their 'honest chairman'
moreover 'offered to the suffering patriot, Muir, the earnings of
a life of labour, amounting to 300l., in order to support him in a
foreign land – declaring, that he was willing to depend upon the
support of his daily exertions, rather than behold the friend of the
people depart without the means of comfort or support'.[52] This
report demonstrates the esteem in which Muir was held beyond
Scotland and, indeed, reveals the radical political networks which
supported him and would begin the construction of Muir, the
political martyr, during Muir's lifetime.

A piece published in the penultimate *Gazetteer* of 15 January 1794 is a fitting place to conclude this analysis of the paper's relationship with Thomas Muir. Here, an anonymous poem entitled 'To Messrs Muir, Palmer, Skirving and Margarot' appears. It begins with an appropriate quotation from John Milton's *Paradise Lost*: 'Among innumerable false, unmoved,/Unshaken, unseduced, unterrified'. The choice of motto is significant in itself, setting, as it does, Muir's cause as the right and morally correct one, while willing him and his fellow 'political martyrs' to stand fast among the faithless. This Biblical echo reflects not only Muir's own Presbyterian faith, but also the *Gazetteer*'s opening pledge to provide a source of 'moral instruction'. In this poem, the 'Friends of the People' become the 'Friends of a slighted people' and, for the author, poetry has the power 'To lift the PATRIOT from the servile throng'. In an allusion to Muir's closing statement after his sentence, this poet professes that right will prevail, and that 'High o'er the wrecks of time *his* fame shall live,/While proud Oppression wastes her idle rage,/His name on history's column shall revive,/And wake the genius of a distant age'.[53] The next issue of the *Edinburgh Gazetteer* would be the last.

With the paper's closure, Muir lost a vital public ally. There are few references to Muir thereafter in the wider British periodical press, but at least two notices of his death can be found, buried in the depths of packed obituary columns. In the *European Magazine and London Review* for February 1799, Muir's death is reported simply: 'At Paris, Thomas Muir, of a wound received on board a Spanish frigate'.[54] The *Caledonian Mercury* for 21 February reports the news thus: 'The Clef du Cabinet states, that Thomas Muir died lately at Paris. The wound he received on board the Spanish frigate, in which he returned to Europe, it is said, never was cured, and to that his death is ascribed'.[55] These largely ambivalent and sparse accounts demonstrate not only the lack of concern for Muir in the national and increasingly conservative periodical press, but also the extent to which the political atmosphere had altered in the five years since his imprisonment. Nonetheless, Muir, the *Edinburgh Gazetteer* and the radical 1790s Scottish press suffered similar fates. Captain William Johnston's trial was followed by that of his successor, Alexander Scott, and the closure of the *Gazetteer* in early 1794. In 1793, a sedition charge was brought against the *Gazetteer*'s west coast radical counterpart, the *Glasgow Advertiser*. This political regulation of the Scottish press reflected the move, in the majority of British periodicals, towards loyalist conservatism and, according to Bob Harris, 'Some London newspapers that had initially espoused radical views became more cautious after 1793'.[56] Although the press was instrumental in the challenging of traditional, propertied political power, Harris argues that it 'also provided a vehicle through which the traditional political classes could renew their hold on political power and revitalize their appeal'.[57] This proved to be true for Thomas Muir and the *Edinburgh Gazetteer*. However, the reciprocal relationship between the two means that the *Gazetteer* allows a clearer understanding of how Muir was received by the Scottish publishing and reading public in the early 1790s, just as Muir's case offers an example of how the Scottish radical press operated in that period. The *Gazetteer*'s focus is not merely on the political example of Muir, but on its wider, moral implications. The *Gazetteer* was one of many newspapers which closed their doors thanks to the pressures of ever stricter regulation, while other radical papers adjusted their stance and amended their political tone. Having said this, the scholarly attention that Muir is receiving at the 250th anniversary of his birth demonstrates that narratives of his life and times, including those contemporaneously produced by publications such as the *Edinburgh Gazetteer*, are indeed able to 'wake' the minds of a 'distant age'.

Notes and References

1   For an analysis of taxation in contemporary England, see Beckett and Turner, 1990, pp.377-407. For specific information on the Scottish situation, see Harris, 2005, p.40.
2   For an analysis of how major Edinburgh publisher Walter Ruddiman dealt with his various periodical publications, see Brown, 2009, pp.21-45.
3   For more on this topic, see Mee, 2015, pp.63-75.
4   See also Brown, 2015, pp.21-33.
5   Some historians have seen the labelling of eighteenth-century politics as, for example, 'radical', as 'anachronistic'. See Clark, 2000, pp.5-10.
6   Harris, 2005a, p.199.
7   Murray Armstrong, 'Thomas Muir and the Radical Movement of the 1790s', p.2. http://www.academia.edu/15357723/Thomas_Muir_and_the_Radical_Movement_of_the_1790s, accessed 5 July 2016.
8   Brown and McDougall, 2012, p.540.
9   Pentland, 2004, p.359.
10 *Edinburgh Gazetteer*, 16 November 1792, p.1.
11 See Habermas, 1962.
12 Harris, 1996, p.4.
13 Harris, 1996, p.22.
14 Harris, 1996, p.29.
15 S Targett, 'Sir Robert Walpole's Newspapers 1722-42: Propaganda and Politics in the Age of Whig Supremacy'. Unpublished DPhil thesis, Cambridge University, 1991, p.6. Also quoted in Harris, 1996, p.1.
16 See the Scottish Book Trade Index, http://www.nls.uk/catalogues/scottish-book-trade-index/miller-moodie, accessed 5 July 2016.
17 See also Harris, 2005, p.52.
18 *The Edinburgh Magazine; or Literary Miscellany*, March 1793, p.242.
19 Howell and Cobbett, 1817, p.44.
20 *Scots Magazine*, 55, March 1793, p.150.
21 John Brims, 'The Scottish Democratic Movement in the Age of the French Revolution'. Unpublished PhD Thesis, University of Edinburgh, 1983, p.520.
22 Harris, 2005, p.52.
23 *Edinburgh Gazetteer*, 26 February 1793, p.1.
24 *Edinburgh Gazetteer*, 16 November 1792, p.1.
25 Harris, 1996, p.108.
26 *Edinburgh Gazetteer*, 16 November 1792, p.1.
27 See Brewer, 1976, pp.219-40.
28 *Edinburgh Gazetteer*, 16 November 1792, p.1.

29 *Edinburgh Gazetteer*, 16 November 1792, p.1.
30 *Edinburgh Gazetteer*, 16 November 1792, p.1.
31 *Edinburgh Gazetteer*, 16 November 1792, p.1.
32 *Edinburgh Gazetteer*, 16 November 1792, p.1.
33 *Edinburgh Gazetteer*, 16 November 1792, p.1.
34 *Edinburgh Gazetteer*, 16 November 1792, p.1.
35 *Edinburgh Gazetteer*, 16 November 1792, p.2.
36 *Edinburgh Gazetteer*, 16 November 1792, p.3.
37 *Edinburgh Gazetteer*, 16 November 1792, p.4.
38 *Edinburgh Gazetteer*, 30 November 1792, p.3.
39 *Edinburgh Gazetteer*, 30 November 1792, p.3.
40 *Edinburgh Gazetteer*, 30 November 1792, p.3.
41 See Irvine, 2016, pp.143-73.
42 *Edinburgh Gazetteer*, 14 December 1792, p.3.
43 Bewley, 1981, p.29.
44 *Edinburgh Gazetteer*, 8 January 1793, p.3.
45 *Edinburgh Gazetteer*, 8 January 1793, p.3.
46 *Edinburgh Gazetteer*, 8 January 1793, p.3.
47 *Edinburgh Gazetteer*, 11 January 1793, p.2.
48 *Edinburgh Gazetteer*, 26 February 1793, p.3.
49 *Edinburgh Gazetteer*, 1 March 1793, p.3.
50 *Edinburgh Gazetteer*, 10 December 1793, p.3.
51 *Edinburgh Gazetteer*, 10 December 1793, p.3.
52 *Edinburgh Gazetteer*, 10 December 1793, p.4.
53 *Edinburgh Gazetteer*, 15 January 1794, p.4.
54 *European Magazine and London Review*, 35, February 1799, p.143.
55 *Caledonian Mercury*, 21 February 1799, p.2.
56 Harris, 1996, p.44.
57 Harris, 1996, p.109.

Thomas Muir and the Constitution

Gordon Pentland

A Man who should have incurred the enmity of the most
powerful men in the State – what do I say! – though he
had, like another Vatinius, drawn upon himself the united
detestation of all parties, might, under the protection of the
Laws, and by keeping within the bounds required by them,
continue to set both his enemies and the whole Nation at
defiance.[1]

The Lord Advocate, Robert Dundas, offered a lengthy quotation,
beginning with the passage above, at the conclusion of his address to
the jury at Thomas Muir's trial. It was taken from the Swiss émigré
Jean de Lolme's popular encomium on the English constitution
and Dundas's point was a simple one. All that subjects had to do
to partake of the manifold advantages of the constitution was to
remain within its laws. Thomas Muir, despite the 'extraordinary
indulgence which is shewn to accused persons of every degree'
and the 'spirit of forbearance and lenity prevailing [...] among all
persons in power' had put himself outside of the constitution.[2]

The constitution was the central character in much of the
political debate of the 1790s and beyond, one whose presence
was magnified further in the context of legal trials. This essay
investigates Thomas Muir's relationship to it. First, it explores
what historians mean when they write about the pervasive
presence of 'constitutionalism' in the political language of the
1790s. Second, it examines, principally through accounts of his
trial, how Muir placed himself in relation to the past and present of
the constitution. Much of Muir's defence, which in the absence of
other sources remains the best (though still problematic) guide to
his thought, was aimed at demonstrating that the constitution had
more elastic boundaries than the prosecution was willing to admit
and that Muir had remained well within them. Third, it indicates

some of the ways in which Muir's trial featured as an important episode in a wider discussion about the nature of the constitution, both in the 1790s and long after his own death.

Part One

'Constitutionalism' as a term denotes the prevailing language of eighteenth-century politics in Britain. With monarchy undermined across the seventeenth century as the sacred centre of political authority and legitimacy, the constitution took its place.[3] Groups and individuals defined and positioned themselves and their arguments broadly in relation to two sets of questions. First, they asked themselves and others questions about the present condition and operation of the constitution and the nature and limits of those rights and duties it conferred. Second, they raised questions and told stories about what the constitution had been and where it had come from. In practice, the separation of the 'past' from the 'present' of the constitution was rarely sustained. Political debate and action in the immediate present were pursued through arguments about history. The seventeenth century was the most important stock of examples and dramatic turning points. It provided a rich cast of virtuous defenders of and martyrs for the constitution (for example, John Hampden and Algernon Sidney) and its enemies and attackers (pre-eminently, the Stuart monarchs and their abettors). The gallery of heroes and villains and victories and defeats was much more commodious than this and so constitutionalist arguments also frequently took in Anglo-Saxon institutions and magna carta, as well as crimes attributed to Norman and to Tudor monarchs.[4]

It was thus an essentially English language, albeit one which could be presented in a Scottish dialect by employing Scottish historical episodes, heroes and villains.[5] It provided the rhetorical rules of the political game in the eighteenth century. To engage in political discussion, contemporaries had to do so by telling their own stories, presenting their aims and defending their actions in constitutional terms. If they failed to do so, they stood outside of the political discussion. This is partly why the challenge represented by first the American, but then much more dramatically by the French Revolution, has been seen as so destabilizing. It was embodied most famously in Thomas Paine's *Rights of Man*, which was sneeringly dismissive of this historical approach to discussing political rights and of the very existence of a constitution:

> Can then Mr Burke produce the English Constitution? If he cannot, we may fairly conclude that though it has been so much talked about, no such thing as a constitution exists, or ever did exist, and consequently the people have yet a constitution to form.[6]

A similar disregard for the pieties of constitutionalist debate was apparent in a popular Scottish radical text, James Thomson Callender's *Political Progress of Britain*:

> What 'our most excellent constitution' may be in theory, I neither know nor care. In practice, it is altogether a CONSPIRACY OF THE RICH AGAINST THE POOR.[7]

Universalist political arguments based on ideas of natural rights not only led to calls for extensive reform of existing institutions. They also threatened to junk the very terms of reference and the mental framework for political debate and action. Elite fears in the mid-1790s clustered around that idea that the popular reform movement was seeking to do exactly what both Paine suggested and the French Revolution exemplified: new-model a constitution and dissolve existing political languages. Hence the panic that conventions held in Edinburgh and then planned for London, were intended as bodies aimed at representing the sovereign people and devising a constitution.[8]

Accordingly, one of the principal areas of concern for historians of popular radicalism has been to ascertain how far the 1790s saw radicals jettison constitutionalist languages. For EP Thompson, rhetoric that depended on the constitution was an obstacle to be circumvented or destroyed, a kind of false consciousness inhibiting the development of a genuinely radical popular politics: 'For a plebeian movement to arise it was essential to escape from these categories altogether and set forward far wider democratic claims'.[9] In the last thirty years or so, historians have done a great deal to rescue the constitutionalist languages of past reformers from the enormous condescension of posterity. There are now extremely good reasons for arguing that, in most cases, the engagement with the kind of ahistorical universalism of Paine's *Rights of Man* was important, but that it was partial, limited and conditional. The constitution remained the anchor for much radical political rhetoric and action into the nineteenth and, indeed, twentieth centuries.

The first reason is that it was tactically more sensible to stick to the language of the constitution. This is most strongly brought through in work that embraces the dynamic and complex nature of political languages in the 1790s. The tumultuous decade did not see a straightforward two-sided debate, to which radicals and loyalists brought their own pre-formed ideological arsenals. Instead, different groups and individuals, in their responses to a rapidly shifting political context, developed a 'logic of confrontation'.[10] In the increasingly heated context from 1792-3, this manifested as a public, tactical and rhetorical battle to claim 'ownership' of the constitution.

The second argument is that viewing constitutionalism as a *constraint* on radical speech and action is increasingly problematic. The scope of what could be discussed and done within its elastic boundaries made it a powerful and flexible resource. If the constitution was a contested field of meanings, it was a very wide and muddy field indeed. Its history and its meaning could be put to quite radical ends and could comfortably accommodate the kinds of suggestions made by Paine and others as well as lessons and aspirations drawn from the developing drama across the channel.[11]

Part Two

How did Muir situate himself within these different ways of talking about politics? His trial represented a key opportunity to do so, not least because the history and the practice of law and of the constitution were intertwined. Trials had been and remained a key venue and mechanism for personalizing issues surrounding the constitution and for drawing attention to the conflict between different understandings of its past and present.[12]

The challenge to the jury, which was the first opportunity for Muir to indicate the tenor of his defence, both set the constitutionalist tone for what followed and continued earlier public efforts by Muir and others to dramatize and contest their exclusion from the constitution by loyalists. The attempt by Muir and other Friends of the People to subscribe to the resolutions of Edinburgh's loyalist Goldsmiths' Hall Association had seen their names expunged by the committee.[13] This furnished Muir with an objection to the jurors: 'I object to these gentlemen, not because they associated in defence of the constitution. I too, as well as they, have associated in defence of the constitution'.[14] In many ways this opening salvo indicated what would follow: Muir's attempt to present himself as a consummately constitutional martyr. Muir defended all of his actions as constitutional, though, as will be demonstrated, it was a distinctive version of the constitution on which his defence rested.

To substantiate the claim for some kind of reverence for the history and present of the constitution did involve at least some rejection of Paine. This helps to explain the emphasis, repeated by a number of witnesses, on Muir's claims that Paine's *Rights of Man* was 'foreign to their purpose' and 'not a constitutional book'.[15] Muir returned to these attested statements a number of times, though it should be noted that he was careful not to take issue directly with the content of what Paine had written. Indeed, a large portion of his address to the jury was a pre-emptive defence of Paine's work (which had not been placed on trial in a Scots court) and closely followed Thomas Erskine's celebrated but failed defence of the *Rights of Man* in December 1792.[16]

Nonetheless, Muir's constant engagement with the constitution cannot simply be seen as tactical posturing intended solely for the court. As he tried to demonstrate, his words in the High Court of Justiciary were of a piece with his earlier public statements and actions. A similar approach is, for example, indicated by the evidence we have from his speeches at the conventions: 'our Great business is to reform not to alter – to hold up our Constitution to the people – to get it restored to its original purity'.[17] Doubtless this might be read as a consciously tactical use of language as well. In the absence, however, of other substantial sources from which to read Muir's 'real' ideas, his public statements are the only ones to which historians have access, however imperfect.

If we accept that the framework in which he worked acknowledged the constitution, we might instead interrogate exactly what Muir sought to do within and with its boundaries. It is possible to read his trial defence as an effort to follow through on his statement at the first convention. First, Muir attempted to hold up the constitution to the people and demonstrate what, in his interpretation, it really allowed them to say and to do. Second, the trial saw intriguing references to the related idea of 'restoration' and to those places where Scots might find the constitution in its 'original purity'.

The first aim was articulated most clearly in Muir's responses to two of the principal charges against him: of making seditious speeches to unlawful assemblies and of circulating seditious writings. On the charge of addressing meetings Muir began with an impeccable and unarguable constitutional right: the subject's right to petition. He placed it in its proper historical context:

> We live, and we act under the British constitution. A
> constitution which, in its genuine principles, has for ages
> consecrated freedom. We live, and we remember the
> glorious revolution of 1688, which banished despotism,
> and placed the family of Hanover upon the throne. We
> remember the Bill of Rights, nor shall we forget one of
> its most sacred clauses, which declared, established, and
> sanctioned the unalienable claim of the citizen to petition
> Parliament.[18]

No one in court would disagree that the subject's right to petition existed.[19] Muir was also some distance from Paine's more hostile attitude towards petitioning as a way of legitimizing corrupt and unequal power relations. In the second part of the *Rights of Man* Paine had been sneeringly dismissive of what he called the 'Bill of Wrongs', but had grudgingly conceded that it at least conveyed 'the right of petitioning'.[20] In the *Letter Addressed to the Addressers* (1792), however, he had arrived at a more uncompromising attitude: 'I confess I have no idea of petitioning for rights. Whatever the rights of people are, they have a right to them, and none have a right either to withhold them, or to grant them'.[21]

Paine was an outlier in this regard, but within the consensus that petitioning was a real and existing right, there remained extremely wide scope for debate as to its precise content. The right was constrained by measures aimed at the prevention of 'tumultuous' petitioning, and from the 1790s the use of inappropriate language or of printed petitions was taken to render petitions illegitimate. Indeed, such objections had recently received extensive parliamentary consideration when reform petitions from Sheffield, Birmingham and many Scottish towns had been discussed.[22]

Muir's approach was to take that perfectly constitutional right of petition and extend it to cover a whole range of political actions. For example, by his account, the forming of associations and societies was required to allow people to petition sensibly and meaningfully. If the point of petitioning was to discuss grievances, how could it be determined which were real and which imaginary: 'how are they then to consult the nation, but by bringing the people together in societies, to deliberate and to resolve?'[23] This took Muir towards the much more radical idea of defending the rights of people to associate freely for political ends and to petition not as individuals or as single communities but 'with united and general deliberation, for redress of general grievances'.[24] Indeed, it is no great distance from that inflated right of petition to Paine's definition of government as *'nothing more than a national association acting on the principles of society'*.[25]

Muir approached the language of Paine and of the French Revolution in another sense as well, by describing this right in a particular vocabulary: 'The Bill of Rights declared the unalienable, imprescriptible right of the people to petition Parliament'.[26] Natural rights terminology of 'unalienable' and 'imprescriptible' rights had a novel and unsettling ring in the 1790s. It was emphatically the language of revolution, in particular of the Declaration of the Rights of Man and Citizen. Indeed, Paine's central importance lay partly in the way in which his writings brought rights into sharp focus for audiences in England and Scotland in the 1790s and made them 'the moral and political centre of gravity' for the emerging radical movement.[27]

It is possible to draw a similar picture for Muir's treatment of the theme of liberty of the press. Contemporary 'constitutional authorities' drew a pretty strict line around this liberty, albeit one which was under constant pressure from the 1760s onwards.[28] William Blackstone, the English judge whose *Commentaries* were cited a number of times during Muir's trial, made the important distinction:

The liberty of the press is indeed essential to the nature of a free state: but this consists in laying no *previous* restraints upon publications, and not in freedom from censure for criminal matter when published. Every free man has an undoubted right to lay what sentiments he pleases before the public: to forbid this, is to destroy the freedom of the press: but if he published what is improper, mischievous, or illegal, he must take the consequences of his own temerity.[29]

Blackstone thus offered what was a conventional distinction between a free and a licentious press. Laws and their enforcement were required constantly to police the boundary between the two.

In addressing the question of the circulation of Paine's *Rights of Man*, Muir acknowledged these limits, albeit again within a language redolent of the French Revolution and radical enlightenment:

What is the precise notion which I affix to the term Liberty of the Press [...] I mean not the power of assassinating the reputation, or torturing the feelings of individuals [...] I mean not the power of degrading, and contaminating the public mind by corruption of public morals [...] not the power of inflaming the minds of men against the constitution, of stimulating the people to insurrection, and of tearing down the barriers of public property [...] BY THE FREEDOM OF THE PRESS, I understand the INALIENABLE RIGHT OF PUBLISHING TRUTH; of presenting to the world, whatever may tend to public good, and may not hurt the feelings of individuals, morals, nor established laws.[30]

Muir moved well beyond this contested constitutional right to make more expansive arguments. Like Thomas Erskine, who had defended Paine's *Rights of Man* at trial in December 1792, Muir presented the liberty of the press within a broad history of the British constitution. He cited the same 'speculative' authors as Erskine, those whose overtly political works had not been deemed worthy of prosecution, a list that included Thomas More, James Harrington and David Hume. In this history, liberty of the press featured as a mechanism for improvement and reform:

You have read the history of the British Constitution; and
what is it, but the history of a continual progress? You
will next ask what has been the compelling cause of this
progress? I answer, the right of the universal diffusion of
information, by means of the Liberty of the Press.[31]

In addressing both petitioning and the liberty of the press,
Muir began with constitutional starting points and ended up
in inalienable, universal, imprescriptible rights. In both cases
also, sticking to the language and historical resources of the
constitution allowed Muir to make another powerful point. He
could attempt to turn the tables on the crown lawyers and argue
that it was his accusers who were undermining and endangering
the constitution. In the case of petitioning, Muir argued, prior
association, discussion and deliberation were essential to public
order. Without them: 'a few factious may presume to speak for the
nation; may impose upon the weak, and may plunge the *many* into
inextricable confusion and misery'.[32]

More seriously, by compromising the freedom of the press, the
Lord Advocate's arguments would condemn the constitution itself,
by removing the only mechanism which ensured its development
and kept it in tune with the affections of the people: 'You have
removed what led to progressive perfection. Evil will proceed to
evil. What originated solely from corrupted men, will be imputed to
the constitution itself'.[33] Muir pursued this point by expanding his
defence of the free circulation of information. Speculative works
such as Paine's, he argued, might tend to public good in one of two
ways. Either they contained some truth and so pointed out defects
that required improvement; or they were false and thus served to
remind people of the merits and virtues of the existing consitution.
It allowed him to condemn the crown lawyers with a final flourish.
In vilifying Paine, they were not simply policing the boundaries of
this constitutional liberty: 'if you say that, by any publication, the
British constitution can be injured, you, yourselves, are guilty of
the crime of libeling its strength'.[34]

It was Muir's own way of saying, like Braxfield, that the British
constitution was 'the best that ever was since the creation of the
world', but at the same time contesting the phlegmatic judge's

claim that 'it is not possible to make it better'.[35] Muir's was necessarily a claim to a particular understanding of the past and future of the constitution. It both had been and could be again the most perfect constitution if it was returned to its proper principles and suffered to develop via the mechanism of free discussion. That both Muir and Braxfield could plausibly annexe the constitution to their own very different ideas of acceptable political language and action gives an indication that the flexible boundaries of constitutional language were being stretched to breaking point in the fraught context of the 1790s. Indeed, in the year following Muir's trial, another Scot and proponent of freedom of the press, the anti-burgher minister, Archibald Bruce, sounded a note of exasperation:

> There are few words more equivocally employed or capable of a more abusive use than the Constitution [...] It has served equally the purpose of all parties; and scarce any two writers or speakers will be found to entertain exactly the same view of it. It is often used apparently with scarce meaning at all.[36]

Part Three

Muir's trial saw him deliver a powerful treatment of the nature of the constitution and its direction of travel. It also offered hints as to his understanding of the history of the constitution and the nature of Scots' claims to share in it. One common narrative was that political union in 1707 had given Scots access to an essentially English tradition. Quite apart from anything that had happened in Scotland's past, Scots could tap into an English history of liberty. That rich myth-history encompassing free Anglo-Saxon assemblies, magna carta, the depredations of the Normans, the Tudors and the Stewarts was now the common property of both Scots and English.[37] And Muir did, of course, appeal to that tradition, in this example to the shades of Locke and Blackstone:

> If I am guilty I have in my guilt many associated, men who now enjoy the repose of eternity, whom your fathers admired while living, and to whom you, their children, have erected statues.[38]

There are tantalizing hints from across his career, however, that Muir did not think of this as solely an English story, as for example in the nature of his support for the address from the United Irishmen.[39] Greater complexity is also indicated by his contribution to an important debate at the first convention in Edinburgh. One delegate, Robert Forsyth, had claimed that the convention should, instead of seeking to 'restore' political rights, seek to 'establish' them. It was exactly the kind of apparently semantic dispute that highlighted the potential chasm between constitutionalist and Paineite approaches to rights.

Another delegate, Alexander Aitchison, argued in response that 'restore' was correct, because what Scots wanted was the restoration of rights eroded since the time of King Alfred, that is, the rights to which they had access via the Union. Muir, however, offered a different interpretation. According to the report:

He went largely into this argument and said that he could prove that both England and Scotland were once possessed of a free constitution. That it was only a restoration of old rights, not an establishment of new ones that was wanted.[40]

Muir's 'blustering vagueness' on this question of the Scottish origins of constitutional freedoms makes a little more sense when seen alongside his defence in court.[41] One book that featured in the trial, but has received limited discussion, was Robert Henry's multi-volume *History of Great Britain*.[42] Two of the witnesses for the crown from the meeting in Kirkintilloch (Robert Weddel and Henry Freeland) agreed that Henry's was the one book that Muir had actually recommended to his audience by name.[43] It was the work of a Church of Scotland clergyman who had died in 1790. An innovative and thematically-organized work, it aimed to provide a history of Great Britain '*from the First Invasion of it by the Romans under Julius Caesar*', but had only reached as far as 1603 by the time of the author's death. It is possible, of course, to read Muir's advocacy of this work as another tactical move. It appears in this guise in Muir's address to the jury, as an effective way of refuting the charge of having recommended dangerous republican literature to unlettered weavers:

... the only book which I recommended to be purchased, was Dr. Henry's History of England [sic]. I am an enemy to the constitution, – and yet I recommended to the people the book best calculated to instruct them in its principles, and in its progress; a book applauded in private and public by the Earl of Mansfield, and upon whose application, the author received an honourable pension from the King.[44]

It is probable, however, that Henry's *History* was Muir's proof, or part of his proof, for his earlier assertion at the convention. The second volume of the history, in particular, discussed the political institutions of the Anglo-Saxons. Especially it dealt with the Witenagemot, the regular assembly of all Saxon men, a key motif in 'ancient constitutionalist' accounts of the English past.[45] Henry's history did not focus on England alone and instead aimed at a blended history of constitutional freedoms to which all British 'nations' had contributed. One of Henry's claims, which may well explain in part why Muir had recommended the work, was that Scotland had an ancient constitution of the same complexion, around the same time as the English: 'chiefly inhabited by Saxons, we may be certain, that its government was the same with that above described'.[46]

Part Four

The 'live event' of Muir's trial thus comes down to us as a sophisticated contest over the meaning and ownership of the constitution. It is an obvious point, but historians do not have access either to the 'live event' or to anything approaching a definitive record of the trial. Participants were clearly aware in speaking in court that they were addressing an audience far more numerous than the judges and jury. This wider audience would consume the trial and its lessons in print and the dispute over the constitution was carried on immediately in the different versions that circulated. In the month following the trial, at least three standalone reports of it appeared, as well as numerous accounts and comments in newspapers and journals.

A comparison of these different sources is revealing. The quotes above are all drawn from Robertson's edition of Muir's trial.

Robertson's was the longest version and the one leant on most heavily for Thomas Howell's later collection of *State Trials* as the 'official record'.[47] It is from Robertson's edition that we derive the most celebrated phrases of Muir himself, but also Lord Braxfield's extreme reactionary epigrams, most notoriously his dismissal of the 'rabble' that constituted Muir's audience:

> What right had they to representation? He could have
> told them that the Parliament would never listen to their
> petition: How could they think of it? A government in
> every country should be just like a corporation; and, in this
> country, it is made up of the landed interest, which alone
> has a right to be represented.[48]

Historians and others have (probably rightly) come to rely on the Robertson edition, though without acknowledging that it was also an edition prepared by a political sympathizer. James Robertson was a printer-publisher with links to the Friends of the People, who was himself serving six months in the Edinburgh tollbooth at the time of publication.[49] While the preface claimed to present 'the faithful record', it also indicated that Robertson had received help in compiling the account from Muir's friend, William Moffat, and also, apparently, from Muir himself.[50] Indeed, Robertson's edition openly acknowledged that it was not as 'faithful' in other respects, only providing, for example, 'the most material parts' of the Lord Advocate's speech.[51] It can be placed next to two other accounts, which preceded it. One of these was prepared by Alexander Scott, the conductor of the *Edinburgh Gazetteer*, another sympathizer, who would himself flee in early 1794, threatened with prosecution for reporting the proceedings of the British convention.[52] The other was prepared by a prominent Edinburgh loyalist, the publisher William Creech, who would also act as one of the jury that condemned Joseph Gerrald after the British convention.[53]

The nineteenth-century editor of the *State Trials*, Thomas Howell, suggested that in arriving at his authoritative version, he navigated 'several accounts, – not however materially differing, and in no instance contradictory'.[54] The different presentation and content of these three texts, however, clearly demonstrates that none was aimed only at capturing an objective and impartial account of the trial. All three were continuing its arguments over the constitution by different means. Their respective frontispieces provided an accurate indication of their political content. Robertson's bore a quote from Tacitus' *The Agricola* (c.AD98), bemoaning attacks on public freedoms by spies and informers. Creech's featured a quotation from William Cowper's epic, *The Task* (1785), damning the kind of alehouse politics that corrupted plebeian minds and led them *'from competence and peace,/ To indigence and rapine'*.[55]

They differed also in the tone of their overtly political prefaces. Scott's, for example, offered a potted history of efforts in pursuit of political reform since the American Revolution.[56] Creech's gave the reader a short dissertation on the crime of sedition and appalled at least one reviewer by its defence of Muir's sentence: 'The whole preface is a libel on the true principles of our government, and one of those performances that breathe the genuine spirit *of passive obedience and non-resistance'*.[57] Indeed, in seeking to persuade parliament to overturn Muir's sentence in early 1794, William Adam deliberately quoted from the Creech edition precisely because 'from the motto on its title page, and from the introduction, is evidently meant to bear against the prisoner, and to be partial to that side which has not mercy for its object'.[58]

Such differences were not restricted to the introductory matter and critics also noticed considerable variety in exactly how speeches were reported or misreported. Robertson's edition gave much greater space to the speech of Muir than to that of the Lord Advocate; Creech's gave much greater space to the speech of the Lord Advocate than to that of Muir. The content and tone of the speeches also read very differently. The words 'constitution' and 'constitutional' appear hundreds of times in Muir's speech in Robertson's edition; in Creech's version they appear a grand total of once each. As indicated above, the intemperate phraseology associated forever with the names of Braxfield comes from Robertson; it is not there in Creech, where 'the judges speeches are *garbled*, and many of the objectionable passages omitted'.[59] Reporters and editors almost immediately transplanted the battle over the ownership of the constitution from the courtroom in Edinburgh to the wider public sphere.

Part Five

Thomas Muir's relationship with the constitution was thus a complex one. His defence in court was resolutely aimed at proving that his actions had lain inside the boundaries of the constitution. In common with other reformers, however, Muir sought to stretch these boundaries to encompass what were, for elites, new and unsettling forms of political mobilization. It would be a mistake to dismiss the prevalence of constitutional arguments as tactical, or at least as *only* tactical. A reliance on the constitution allowed Muir to forward dramatic, emotive and sophisticated arguments. He was able to take a good deal from Paine and other 'revolutionary' writers, without accepting the central charge that the constitution itself was a meaningless even a dangerous fiction. Muir could travel towards some of Paine's conclusions without employing Paine's precise arguments to get there.

As soon as the events in the High Court of Justiciary were complete, accounts of Muir's trial inaugurated an immediate discussion about his relationship to the constitution. In March 1794 Whig parliamentarians, led by William Adam, used Muir's trial and that of Thomas Fyshe Palmer, to illustrate the severity of the assault on public liberty in Scotland and to raise more general concerns around 'the safety of the British Constitution'.[60] For English radicals, the actions against Muir and the other Scottish martyrs were clear evidence of an open and unrestrained attack on the constitution and so the stimulus for efforts to organize a further convention:

> Consider, it is one and the same corrupt and corrupting influence which at this time domineers in Ireland, Scotland, and England. Can you believe that those who send virtuous Irishmen, and Scotchmen fettered with felons to Botany-Bay, do not meditate and will not attempt to seize the first moment to send us after them?[61]

These were the beginnings of a much longer conversation. Over the following centuries subsequent radical, reform, nationalist and conservative movements, which sought to harness Muir to their own causes, raise monuments to him, or vilify him, have all had to place him within or outside of their own particular take on the past, present and future of the constitution.[62]

Notes and References

1 deLolme, 1784, p.534; [Robertson], 1793, p.72.
2 deLolme, 1784, pp.535-6.
3 Vernon, 1996, pp.1-2.
4 Hill, 1954.
5 Kidd, 1996.
6 Philp, 1995, p.123.
7 Callender, 1792, p.22.
8 Pentland, 2004; Parssinen, 1973.
9 Thompson, 1968, p.96.
10 Philp, 2013, pp.11-39.
11 Epstein, 1994.
12 Epstein, 1996; Barrell, 2000; Davis, 2005.
13 Bewley, 1981, p.47.
14 [Robertson], 1793, p.32.
15 [Robertson], 1793, pp.36, 44, 108-9.
16 [Robertson], 1793, pp.102-9; Anon, 1792, pp.14-43.
17 Home Office Correspondence (Scotland), December 1792. National Records of Scotland RH2/4/66, f.354.
18 [Robertson], 1793, p.90.
19 Poole, 2000, pp.9-11.
20 Philp, 1995, p.246.
21 Philp, 1995, p.370.
22 *Parliamentary register*, 2 and 6 May 1793, vol.35, pp.345-60, 372-6; Smith, 1984, pp.30-4.
23 [Robertson], 1793, p.90.
24 [Robertson], 1793, p.91.
25 Philp, 1995, p.218.
26 [Robertson], 1793, p.91.
27 Claeys, 1989, pp.171-3.
28 Hellmuth, 1990.
29 Blackstone, 1769, vol.4, pp.160-1.
30 [Robertson], 1793, pp.102-3.
31 [Robertson], 1793, p.103; Anon, 1792; Hellmuth, 2007.
32 [Robertson], 1793, pp.90-1.
33 [Robertson], 1793, p.104.
34 [Robertson], 1793, pp.104-6.
35 [Robertson], 1793, p.131.
36 Bruce, 1794, p.68; Brims, 1989, pp.54-8.
37 Gerrald, 1794; Pentland, 2004.
38 [Robertson], 1793, pp.81-3.
39 McFarland, 1994, pp.83-8; Brims, 1987.

40 Home Office Correspondence (Scotland), December 1792. National Records of Scotland RH2/4/66, f.356; Pentland, 2004, pp.346-7.
41 Kidd, 1993, p.248.
42 Kidd, 1993, pp.190-1, 238-9.
43 [Robertson], 1793, pp.38, 41.
44 [Robertson], 1793, p.95.
45 Henry, 1771-93, vol.2, pp.262-8.
46 Henry, 1771-93, vol.2, p.268.
47 Howell, ed, 1809-28, vol.23, pp.117-236.
48 [Robertson], 1793, p.132.
49 Howell, ed, 1809-28, vol.23, pp.79-116; Harris, 2008, pp.64-5.
50 [Robertson], 1793, pp.3-4.
51 [Robertson], 1793, p.73.
52 Scott, 1794; Harris, 2008, p.119.
53 [Creech], 1794; Harris, 2008, p.79.
54 Howell, ed, 1809-28, vol. 23, p.117.
55 [Robertson], 1793, p.1; [Creech], 1793, p.ii.
56 [Scott], 1793, pp.iii-xi.
57 [Creech], 1793, pp.iii-vii; *Analytical review*, Sept. 1793, p.108.
58 *Parliamentary register*, 10 March 1794 [appendix], vol. 38, p.492.
59 *Analytical review*, Sept. 1793, p.108.
60 *Parliamentary register*, 10 March 1794, vol.27, p. 514; Goodwin, 1979, pp.289-90.
61 London Corresponding Society, 1794, p.6; Claeys, 1995, pp.41-4.
62 Pentland, 2016, pp.207-23.

Thomas Muir's Short Life and Long Legacy in Australia[1]

Beverley Sherry

On 9 May 2009, the Museum of Australian Democracy was officially opened in Canberra, Australia's federal capital, and visitors that day could see an exhibit on Thomas Muir (1765-1799), honoured as a pioneer of parliamentary reform, freedom of speech, and liberty of the press. At the end of this chapter I will return to the Museum of Australian Democracy and Muir's place in it, but his story in Australia begins more than two hundred years earlier when he arrived in New South Wales as a convict.

Museum of Australian Democracy, Canberra.
Home of Australia's Federal Parliament from 1927 until 1988, this building is now a museum telling the story of Australia's democracy. It was opened in 2009. Courtesy of the Museum of Australian Democracy.

Botany Bay in the 1790s.
A view of Botany Bay as printed on a contemporary handkerchief in
commemoration of Muir and his fellow political martyrs: Margarot,
Palmer, Skirving, and Gerrald. Courtesy of East Dunbartonshire Leisure
& Culture Trust.

After the American colonies gained their independence in 1776,
Britain had to find a new dumping ground for its surplus criminals
and established a penal colony in New South Wales. In 1788, after
a voyage of eight months, the First Fleet, headed by Captain Arthur
Phillip, landed with 775 convicts at Botany Bay. Because of limited
fresh water and lack of security for large ships, the convoy moved
within days to Port Jackson (Sydney Harbour) several miles north.
Phillip reported to Lord Sydney, the Home Secretary, 'we had the
satisfaction of finding the finest harbour in the world, in which a
thousand Sail of the Line may ride in the most perfect Security'.[2]
Within Port Jackson, the settlement was established at Sydney
Cove, although 'Botany Bay' remained in the popular imagination
and parlance in Britain. By 1790 there were more than 2,000
convicts, and transportation continued until 1840. Most were poor
and illiterate, victims of social conditions in Georgian England;
theft was the main offence and seven or fourteen years the period
of sentence. Separate from this mass of common criminals were a
number of political prisoners – Jacobins, United Irishmen, trades-
unionists (the Tolpuddle Martyrs), democrats, and Fenians. The

earliest of the political prisoners were the 'Scottish Martyrs', five men who campaigned for parliamentary reform. Thomas Muir was the most celebrated of them.

Muir in Britain

Other essays in this volume document Muir's political activities in 1792-93. Here I wish only to highlight the calibre and the international renown of a young man the British Government saw fit to exile to the ends of the earth. Muir was a leader in establishing the Edinburgh Society of the Friends of the People in 1792 and became the most inspiring orator of Scotland's fledgling reform movement. A gifted barrister and a young man of principle and polished manners, he fought for the rights of the poor, electoral reform, universal male suffrage, and freedom of speech. Although he shared the reforming zeal of the United Irishmen and the French, he was not a revolutionary but urged reform by constitutional means. However, in a climate of paranoia, when even owning a copy of Thomas Paine's *The Rights of Man* (1791-92) might be deemed sedition, Muir was accused of inciting trouble through inflammatory speeches and circulating seditious writings, including Paine's book.[3]

The members of the jury at his trial (30-31 August 1793) were stunned at the sentence of transportation for fourteen years, imposed by the draconian Lord Braxfield – the first time in the British Empire that transportation had been imposed for sedition. The trial became a *cause célèbre* at home and abroad. It is claimed by some to have inspired Robert Burns's heroic ode to liberty, 'Scots, wha hae wi' Wallace bled', which was written at the end of August 1793. The transcript of the trial was printed in three editions, two of them in New York, and Muir's defence speech was published separately and became a best-selling pamphlet.

Muir languished in a prison hulk on the Thames for eight months and, despite strenuous efforts by Whig members of parliament to have his sentence declared illegal, he was sent to New South Wales on 2 May 1794 on board the transport *Surprize*. With him went three fellow 'Scottish Martyrs': William Skirving, the Reverend Thomas Fyshe Palmer, and Maurice Margarot. They arrived in Sydney on 25 October 1794. The fifth Martyr, Joseph Gerrald, arrived on 5 November 1795. Of the five, Muir and Skirving were in fact the only Scots.

Memorial to Joseph Gerrald, Royal Botanic Gardens, Sydney.
Detail of a sign erected in 1996 on the 200th anniversary of Gerrald's
death. Governor Hunter permitted Gerrald to purchase a small house
and garden at Farm Cove where he is buried. Having arrived in
Sydney in November 1795 in declining health, this eloquent defender of
human rights survived only four months of his fourteen-year sentence.
The Botanic Gardens were established around Farm Cove in 1816.
Photograph by Beverley Sherry.

Muir at Sydney Cove

Muir and his companions brought money with them and were not treated as felons. Coming ashore in November 1794, they were described by Judge-Advocate David Collins as 'the gentlemen who came from Scotland' and were each given a brick hut, not on the west side of Sydney Cove, where the convicts were housed, but 'in a row on the east side of the cove', the area reserved for civil staff.[4]

Sydney Cove, 1794-96, by Thomas Watling.
This painting shows an east view of the Cove, where the Scottish Martyrs were given huts on their arrival in 1794. Watling was from Dumfries, transported to New South Wales for forgery.
Courtesy of the State Library of New South Wales (Digital Order No a928723 – v 1/1794/1).

Two convict servants were assigned to Muir and he was able to purchase land. In a letter of 13 December 1794 to a friend in London he mentions his house 'over the water, a small farm I purchased for £30 sterling', and later offers more detail:

I have a neat little house here [the brick hut at Sydney Cove]. I have another two miles distant, at the farm across the water, which I purchased. A servant of a friend, who has a taste for drawing, has sketched the landscape; I have sent it to my mother; you may see it.[5]

Sydney Harbour 2016, with the Sydney Opera House.
To the right of the Opera House is the entrance to Sydney Cove, site of the first settlement. In 1788 Governor Phillip described Port Jackson as 'the finest harbour in the world, in which a thousand Sail of the Line may ride in the most perfect Security'. Today international liners find easy anchorage at Sydney Cove. Photograph by Edwin Lowe.

The drawing was probably by fellow Scot, Thomas Watling from Dumfries, transported for forgery. Watling was then the most active artist in the colony and a servant to the Surgeon-General John White, who was a friend of the Scottish Martyrs.[6] In his 1831 pamphlet biography, Peter Mackenzie asserts that Muir called his farm *Huntershill* after his father's home in Scotland.[7] Perhaps Mackenzie had heard of a 'Hunters Hill' in the colony and assumed that Muir had named it. In fact the 'district of Hunters Hill', always two words, not 'Huntershill', was named in government documents before Muir arrived and is accepted as honouring Captain (later Governor) Hunter, who charted the harbour.[8] It is marked on maps as the high land on the north side of Sydney Harbour around today's Gore Hill and by 1796 the layout of a settlement was shown there.[9] When the parishes of the colony were formed in the 1830s, the name moved south-west, settling on today's Hunters Hill.

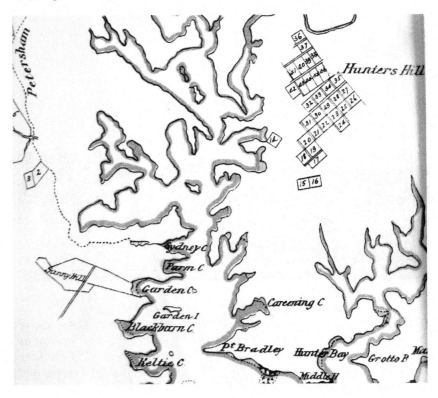

Detail of Deputy Surveyor General's Plan of the Settlements in New South Wales (1796). The settlement of Hunters Hill is marked with 33 farms, numbered 14 to 46. In the complete plan, their size (25 to 30 acres) and owners' names are listed, Thomas Muir not among them. Reproduced from Historical Records of New South Wales, vol. 3, fold-out following title page.

Exactly where 'across the water' Muir's farm was situated is not known. Four different locations have been claimed: Milsons Point, inland from Rozelle Bay, the north shore of the Parramatta River, and between the Lane Cove River and Ball's Head.[10] In fact there are no official records or title deeds for Muir's purchase of his farm. Neither its precise location nor its size, nor its name is recorded. The colony's professional chronicler, Judge-Advocate David Collins, simply states that Muir 'chiefly passed his time in literary ease and retirement, living out of the town at a little spot of ground which he had purchased for the purpose of seclusion'.[11]

Despite their privileges, the Scottish Martyrs were told by Lieutenant-Governor Grose that it was 'absolutely requisite' that they 'avoid on all occasions a recital of those politicks' that had brought them to their present 'unfortunate situation'.[12] There is no evidence that Muir aired his ideas on liberty in Sydney. To be thus forcibly silenced, living on a little patch of bushland, must have been a profound culture shock to the brilliant young orator of Scotland's reform movement. However, Muir was a canny Scot and quickly saw that the 'Rum Corps' was running the place, so began trading. The lengthiest paragraph of his letter to his friend in London is a request that:

> When any money is transmitted, cause a considerable
> part of it to be laid out at the Cape or Rio Janeiro, in rum,
> tobacco, sugar, &c., &c., which are invaluable, and the only
> medium of exchange. [...] In a country like this, where
> money is really of no value and rum everything, you must
> perceive the necessity of my having a constant supply by
> every vessel.

He details the profits he is able to make: 'For a goat I should pay in money £10 sterling; now for less than eight gallons of spirits, at 18d the gallon, I can make the same purchase'.

Although barred from expressing his political views, Muir exercised his legal skills to some extent. The same letter mentions that he was writing a defence of Palmer and Skirving, who had been accused of mutiny on board the *Surprize*. It is likely that the following year Muir also advised his friend John Boston in the first civil law suit in the colony (Boston won against the military).[13] Muir was also deeply religious – he had been an Elder of his local Presbyterian church in Scotland – and reportedly spent time copying passages from the Bible for distribution among the convicts.[14] His true vocation as a political reformer, however, was cut from under him.

The Telegraph

Still, the spectre of Muir worried the Tory establishment in Britain. This is evidenced in an intriguing manuscript held in Sydney's Mitchell Library, *The Telegraph: a Consolatory Epistle from Thomas Muir Esq. of Botany Bay to The Hon. Henry Erskine, late Dean of Faculty*.[15] Erskine was a friend of Muir and was deposed from his position as Dean of the Faculty of Advocates in Edinburgh on 12 January 1796. The poem purports to be by Muir but was actually published anonymously in Edinburgh in January 1796 and is thought to be the work of a Tory clergyman, George Hamilton.[16] The provenance of the manuscript – beautifully handwritten, dated 1796, and water damaged – remains unknown.[17] Someone must have copied it from the printed work and sent it out to Sydney, perhaps to amuse society and certainly to discredit Muir, for it is a full-blown political satire. The Melbourne book-collector and literary patron, JK Moir (1893-1958), knew that *The Telegraph* had been published in Edinburgh but rightly claimed it as 'the first separately printed poem with an Australian background'.[18] Distinctly Australian is the description of an Aborigine setting fire to the bush (pp.8-9), a practice frequently observed by the early settlers. The poem was taken seriously by Robert Hughes as the bona fide work of Muir,[19] but Muir could not possibly have written it, if only because the news of Henry Erskine's fall would not have reached Sydney by sea for at least five months, by which time, as we shall see, Muir had long left the colony.

The speaker of *The Telegraph* is 'Muir', and he lashes himself with the harshest satire in nine pages of heroic couplets. While hardly distinguished as literature, *The Telegraph* is in the mock-heroic manner of works like Pope's *The Dunciad* (1743). By way of consolation, Muir urges Henry to 'come to this sacred shore' (p.5) and bring with him their Whig friends. Interestingly, only their initials appear in the printed version but their full names are written in the manuscript. Ten are named, including leading Scottish reformers Colonel Norman Macleod and the Earl of Lauderdale. The title and opening lines are intended to shock by representing Muir communicating with Henry via the new telegraphic technology:

From this remote, this melancholy shore;
Round whose bleak rocks incessant tempests roar;
. . .
Eager the Telegraphic board I rear (p.1).

Invented by the Frenchman Claude Chappe in 1792, the *télégraphe* was a system of signals that enabled messages to be relayed over long distances and aroused fears of communication between revolutionary France and Britain. Initially startling, the idea of a telegraph from Botany Bay to Edinburgh is a deliberate fiction to ridicule Muir and to rubbish any idea of communication with Henry Erskine. At the same time, the poem is evidence of continuing Tory unease about the circulation of revolutionary information and of Muir's radical ideas about 'the sacred Rights of Man' and 'lov'd democracy' (p.5 and p.9).[20]

At this time, John Milton (1608-1674) occupied a central place in the national consciousness, regardless of political persuasion. A Tory and man of the cloth like the Reverend Dr George Hamilton would have been familiar with *Paradise Lost*, and *The Telegraph* shows that he believed that Muir, like many radicals of the eighteenth century, revered Milton's Satan.[21] A rhetoric of freedom, like Satan's in *Paradise Lost*, runs through the poem: 'Come to these regions, where no Despot reigns, / But freedom revels in her native plains'; 'rather than live in / Courts, in servile state, / To flatter fools and fawn upon the Great'; 'Here no proud title shocks the freeborn mind, / No chief exalted to debase his kind' (pp.5-6). Muir proudly allies himself with Satan, whom he sees as a hero fighting for freedom against a tyrannical king – in *Paradise Lost* Satan rebels against God, the king of heaven, and is thrown with his fellow rebels into hell. So, says Muir, 'we follow cheerful where he [Satan] leads the way [. . .] We act on earth that part which *cost* him heaven' (pp.7-8). *The Telegraph* closes with Muir looking forward to an afterlife in Satan's 'dark abode', where he hopes that he and his Whig companions might raise 'A France in Hell, that rais'd a Hell in France' (p.10). The neat chiasmus recalls Satan's claim to 'make a Heav'n of Hell, a Hell of Heav'n'.[22]

Despite its satirical intent, *The Telegraph* is a reminder of connections between Muir and Milton. Both fought for political liberty and both were passionate defenders of freedom of speech

John Milton from Memoirs of Thomas Hollis *(1780).*
The Memoirs of Thomas Hollis *was a prized possession of Muir. This engraving by Giovanni Batista Cipriani (1727-1785) refers to Milton's* Defensio Pro Populo Anglicano (Defence of the English People) *justifying the execution of Charles I in 1649. It was published in 1651 as a rebuttal to the Frenchman Claudius Salmasius, who is portrayed beneath Milton presumably hanging from his pen. A regicidal axe completes the story. The small owl in the foliage on the lower left is an icon regularly used by Thomas Hollis.*
Courtesy of University of Sydney Rare Book Collection.

and of the press. A particular connection is via Thomas Hollis (1720–1774), a Whig who championed Milton's political ideas and promoted the republic of letters by widely donating books, including to the American colonies.[23] Muir owned a copy of *Memoirs of Thomas Hollis*, a handsome leather-bound folio in two volumes which devotes more space to 'the divine Milton' than anyone else.[24] Hollis's adopted heir, Thomas Brand Hollis (c.1719-1804), commissioned the *Memoirs* and he gave the copy to Muir. Perhaps this was on 13 January 1793, when Brand Hollis attended a meeting in London of the 'Friends of the Liberty of the Press' at which Muir was the speaker. According to the Whig *Morning Post*, it was a powerful address.[25] In his letter of 13 December 1794, Muir writes that the convict ship *Surprize* stopped at Rio de Janeiro, where he visited 'the magnificent library' of the monastery and gave the Abbot some books, including Hollis's *Memoirs*, 'the gift of that excellent man Mr. B. Hollis'.[26] Muir inscribed the book, identifying himself as a 'citizen of the world', as was the habit of Thomas Hollis.[27] Muir was following Thomas Hollis's and Brand Hollis's example of promoting the republic of letters, notably the 'divine Milton'.

View of inner reaches of Sydney Harbour, 1798.
This engraving by James Heath (1757-1834) for David Collins's An Account of the English Colony in New South Wales *(1798) shows the thickly wooded foreshores of the Harbour and in the foreground two members of the Eora people indigenous to the Sydney region. Collins's book is a meticulous month-by-month record of the colony from 1788 to 1796 and includes reports on the Scottish Martyrs as well as detailed accounts and illustrations of the Aboriginal people.*

Muir's escape and journey to Europe

Ironically, when *The Telegraph* was published in Edinburgh in January 1796, Muir was about to escape from New South Wales. The year 1795 had shown him the realities of the place: the new administrator, Captain William Paterson, allowed the army to take the law into their own hands, the mania for spirits continued unabated, bloodshed occurred between the Aborigines and the settlers, criminal courts were regularly called, there were severe shortages of food, and burglaries were rife. Collins reports that in July, 'the house occupied by Mr. Muir was broken into, and all or nearly all that gentleman's property stolen: some of his wearing apparel was laid in his way the next day; but he still remained a considerable sufferer by the visit'.[28]

Muir set to work to draft a legal argument justifying his departure, and as soon as the new Governor, John Hunter – the most eminent Scot in the colony – arrived in September 1795, he prepared to submit it as a petition on behalf of Palmer, Skirving, and himself. Hunter interviewed the Scottish Martyrs individually and they made a good impression upon him. He wrote to a friend in Leith:

> Muir was the first I saw; I thought him a sensible, modest young man, of a very retired turn, which certainly his situation in this country will give him opportunity of indulging; he said nothing of the severity of his fate, but seemed to bear his circumstances with a proper degree of fortitude and resignation.[29]

In fact this 'resigned' young man had his petition all ready, dated 14 October, and he delivered it to Hunter.[30] Drawing on the authority of the Earl of Lauderdale and Sir George Mackenzie, he argued cogently that the extent of their sentences was banishment and that they were within their legal rights to depart from New South Wales, provided they did not return to Great Britain. Hunter was persuaded, and he wrote to the Home Secretary, the Duke of Portland, enclosing the petition: 'I am obliged to confess, my Lord', he wrote, 'that I cannot feel myself justifiable in forcibly detaining them in this country against their consent. [...] Although they have not in their power to return to any part of Great Britain but at the risk of life, they probably might have a desire to pass their time in Ireland'.[31]

As soon as an opportunity arose, Muir absconded from the colony, by means of an American ship, the *Otter*, which had put into Sydney for supplies on 24 January 1796. So, sixteen months after his arrival in Port Jackson, on the night of 17 February 1796, Muir and his two convict servants made their way down the long extent of the harbour and out through Sydney Heads, a daunting feat in a rowing boat and in the dark; 'about the middle of the next day' they were picked up by the *Otter* 'at a considerable distance from land'.[32] Muir left a letter for Governor Hunter explaining that he 'purposed practising at the American bar as an advocate', and Hunter dispassionately reported his departure to the Duke of Portland.[33] In August 1796 the Duke replied to Hunter's original question about Muir's petition. His letter would have arrived in Sydney five to six months later and it set Hunter straight: the Scotsmen were not permitted to go to Ireland, nor could they leave New South Wales until they had served the full term of their sentences.[34] By this time, Muir was on the other side of the world.

After his voyage on the *Otter* across the little-known Pacific to Vancouver Island, Muir transferred to a Spanish ship which took him to Spanish California. He wrote letters from Monterey to his parents and friends and also to Charles Fox and the earls of Lauderdale and Stanhope; he described Port Jackson as 'that remote & horrid region', 'forlorn dismal, & inhospitable'.[35] In a long screed to George Washington he recounted his escape and journey, laying out his plans for life in America and seeking the General's help. None of his letters were delivered; all were confiscated by the Spanish. His journey then became a nightmare. From California he was taken to Mexico, where he came under the Spanish authorities, was transported to Havana and imprisoned there. In March 1797 he was put on another Spanish ship bound for Spain and was caught in a sea battle between England and Spain off Cadiz. His face was badly wounded and he lost his left eye. After being hospitalised in Cadiz he was allowed to go to France in November 1797, where he was given a hero's welcome in Bordeaux. For several months he was fêted in Paris, but his popularity declined and, weakened by his wounds, impoverished, and critically depleted by nearly six years of trauma, he died in obscurity at Chantilly outside Paris on 25 January 1799, aged thirty-three.

One cannot help but wonder, if he had known the dreadful fate in store for him, whether he might not have stayed in Sydney and contributed his skills as a lawyer to the infant colony. A long life in 'that remote & horrid region', though, would doubtless have seemed a fate worse than death. In leaving, he believed he was exercising his legal right to freedom and in reaching France he was able to reanimate, if briefly, his political life and his cosmopolitan identity.

He was ripe for myth-making, and his story proved malleable, as Gordon Pentland has shown, even inspiring historical novels.[36] The first foray, published in Paris in 1798, was entitled *Histoire de la Tyrannie du Gouvernement Anglais Exercée Envers le Célèbre Thomas Muir, Ecossais*. It claimed to be based on conversations Muir had in Bordeaux with a M Mazois. In 1990 it was translated into English by Jonathan Wantrup.[37] It includes a 'Brief Account of Botany Bay' which, the French editor declares, 'word for word and without exaggeration, is what Thomas Muir has related'.[38] In fact much of this account is lifted from Watkin Tench's *Narrative of the Expedition to Botany Bay* (London, 1789), as Wantrup acknowledges. Some details cohere with the known facts but there is added embellishment, such as the story that George Washington sent the *Otter* to rescue Muir.

What is not myth, however, is Muir's work in Scotland, Ireland, and France. He was a radical ahead of his time, a champion of human rights, and a hero of the dispossessed and the downtrodden, people who had no vote. As Michael Donnelly records, he was 'prepared to take on the most unrewarding and difficult cases' in his practice as a lawyer, 'foregoing a fee when petitioned by a destitute client'.[39] His career was savagely cut short but his campaign for parliamentary reform in the early 1790s and the wide publicity over his trial and sentence sowed the seeds of Scottish democracy. With the passing of the Great Reform Bill in 1832, the sacrifice of Muir and his companions was eventually recognised and commemorated. Peter Mackenzie's biography had been published in 1831 and monuments to the Scottish Martyrs were completed in 1846 at Edinburgh's Calton Hill cemetery and in 1852 at Nunhead Cemetery, London.

Captain Cook, Sydney Town Hall, 1889.
This portrayal of Captain Cook, which includes the stars of the Southern
Cross, was designed by Lucien Henry (1850-1896) and exemplifies the
optimism that marked the centenary of British settlement in 1888. A
companion window portrays a female figure representing Australia
replete with national icons. Muir was embraced into Australia's
growing national pride at this time.
Photograph by Douglass Baglin, by kind permission of the Baglin Estate.

Muir's continuing reputation in Australia

From this time, and connected with a growing national pride towards the centenary of European settlement in 1888 and the establishment of the Commonwealth of Australia in 1901, Muir received some glowing recognition. The well-known newspaper proprietor Samuel Bennett (1815-1878), founder of the *Empire* and the *Evening News*, published *The History of Australian Discovery and Colonisation* in 1865, in which he writes that Muir was 'one of the noblest men that ever landed on Australian shores', continuing:

> From the time of his arrival in Sydney he devoted all
> his energies to the good of his fellow-creatures. He took
> pleasure in improving the minds and alleviating the bodily
> sufferings of the wretched criminals around him, and
> applied most of his narrow means to the amelioration
> of human misery. He was a devoutly religious man, and
> wrote out many of the most beautiful passages of the
> Bible for the use of those who were able to read them;
> and after Governor Hunter's arrival, and the setting up by
> his Excellency of a small press, he frequently employed
> himself in printing with his own hand select passages from
> the Holy Scriptures to circulate among the prisoners. The
> effect of such efforts at a time when there was scarcely a
> Bible or a religious book in the colony, and very little care
> taken for the spiritual welfare of prisoners, can hardly be
> overestimated.[40]

Writing in the *Sydney Mail* in 1879, the novelist Marcus Clarke (1846-1881) acknowledged Bennett's work in an article entitled 'The Romance of Thomas Muir', concluding that Muir and his companions 'watered the tree of political liberty with their blood'.[41] Continuing the praise, David Blair, in *The History of Australasia* (1879), describes all 'the Scotch Martyrs' as men of 'peaceable lives and most estimable characters' who 'left behind them in the colony a most favourable impression of their character and conduct'. Deploring their treatment by the British Government, he observes, 'In the present history of Australasia it seems incredible that men could be imprisoned and banished for holding principles which are identical with those that now govern the conduct of all English statesmen'.[42]

The most prolific Australian writer on the Scottish Martyrs in the nineteenth century was George Burnett Barton (1836-1901), journalist and lawyer and elder brother of Australia's first Prime Minister, Sir Edmund Barton. He wrote a series of articles in 1896-1897 (signed G.B.B.) for the Saturday *Evening News* on 'The Scotch Martyrs' as 'Celebrities at Botany Bay'.[43] Enlivened with drawings, they read like an historical novel, with Muir as the hero. On the departure of the *Daedalus* in December 1794, taking letters home, Barton writes: 'After the white sails of the Daedalus had disappeared from view the martyrs returned to their villas in melancholy mood'; and on Muir's opportunity to escape on the *Otter*: 'Muir could hardly believe his own ears; yet there before him sat the stolid American sailor, with an offer of instant liberty, and with it of a new life in a new world. The sensation was overpowering and he burst into tears'.[44] The articles formed the basis of a projected book entitled 'The Scottish Martyrs' and the voluminous draft, dated 1897, is preserved in the Dixon Library.[45] Being a lawyer, Barton was especially interested in the legal aspects of the Scottish Martyrs' trial and defence. His manuscript ends with a description of the memorial erected in Edinburgh in the mid 1840s and his last words are a quotation from the Scottish judge, Lord Cockburn, condemning 'the delinquent judges' who tried the Martyrs.[46]

In the twentieth century, newspaper articles continued to extol Muir. In 1918 Kelso Kelly, writing from Perth (Western Australia), linked Muir's defence speech with Abraham Lincoln's Gettysburg address.[47] In the same year, Queensland MP Charles Collins, urging reform of the franchise, wrote that the Scottish Martyrs were 'the advanced wing of Democracy' and that 'to-day, in Great Britain, the "rabble" mentioned by Lord Braxfield, in his summing up in Muir's case, are still deprived of a vote. Universal suffrage has yet to come in that country. And here in Australia the landed interests and capitalists control our Legislative Councils, and a full-measure of control by the people has yet to be fought for'.[48] In 1934 and 1935 these outbursts appeared in *The Daily Standard* (Brisbane): 'To-day, Braxfield is only remembered to be execrated'; 'The savagery of this sentence kindled resentment throughout the land. Even in the United States and France, where Muir was known as a fighter for freedom, the sentence was regarded as the brutal fear of a ruling class whose rotten system of privilege and reaction ought to be swept out of existence forever'.[49] In 1939, JJ Stewart contributed to *The Queenslander* a long essay on 'Australia's Greatest Martyr: the Remarkable Story of Thomas Muir'.[50]

To a greater or lesser extent, the slippery history of Peter Mackenzie's biography and off-shoots appear in most of the accounts from the nineteenth and twentieth century, but more consistent is the warm praise for Muir as a champion of democracy and vehement indignation at his sentence. The historian John Earnshaw considered him 'perhaps the most celebrated convict ever transported to the shores of Australia';[51] importantly, though, Earnshaw's book *Thomas Muir Scottish Martyr* (1959) eschewed fabrication and was a welcome landmark in sound historical scholarship and archival research.

In the twenty-first century Muir's legacy continued to be malleable. He emerged in a new and personal way in Australia through the Friends of Thomas Muir, a Scottish charity centred in Bishopbriggs, a suburb of Glasgow where Muir's ancestral home, *Huntershill*, still stands.[52] Through an internet search, the Friends contacted the Hunters Hill Historical Society in Sydney in 2009, seeking to establish a link between Muir and the Sydney harbourside suburb of Hunters Hill. Members of the group visited Australia in this cause in 2010. Having written the bicentennial history of Hunters Hill, *Hunter's Hill: Australia's Oldest Garden Suburb*, I was prompted by their visit to further the research I had done on Muir for my book, with the result that I was able to show that there is no historical connection between Sydney's Hunters Hill and Thomas Muir.[53] However, through the visitors from Scotland I became deeply interested in Muir as a pioneer of democracy and consequently visited Bishopbriggs in 2010 and undertook further research on Muir.[54]

Muir and the Museum of Australian Democracy

In concluding this essay, I turn to Muir's place in the Museum of Australian Democracy. During his time in New South Wales, silenced by the government, he was unable to contribute to the advancement of democracy but he is part of Australia's British heritage and the Museum of Australian Democracy rightly has an exhibit on him. A new (iconic) Parliament House opened in Canberra in 1988, Australia's bicentenary, and this left the question of what to do with Old Parliament House (as it is still known). The building itself speaks of democracy and in due course a decision was made to convert it to a museum dedicated to telling the story

Thomas Muir, Museum of Australian Democracy.
Bronze replica of the sculpture by Alexander Stoddart in Bishopbriggs
Library, near Glasgow, cast for the Museum of Australian Democracy
in 2008. Muir escaped from Sydney in February 1796, and in April 1797
was wounded in a sea battle and lost his left eye.
Courtesy of Museum of Australian Democracy.

of Australia's democracy. It opened on 9 May 2009, the same day and month as the opening of Australia's first Federal Parliament in 1901.[55]

The exhibit on Thomas Muir has as its centrepiece a posthumous bust which is a bronze cast of the sculpture made by the Scottish artist Alexander Stoddart for Bishopbriggs Library near Glasgow. The Museum of Australian Democracy approached Professor Stoddart and asked him if he could make a copy. He replied that 'nothing could be more delightful', and the bust arrived in Canberra in September 2008. It portrays Muir as a dignified but shattered hero, with the left side of his face covered with a drape, a reminder of his wounding in the naval battle off Cadiz in 1797. In addition, documentary panels are an important component of the Muir exhibit. One displays stirring lines from *The Telegraph*, concluding with 'The happy fruits of lov'd Democracy'; another reproduces the title page of the 1794 American edition of Muir's defence speech with a picture of Muir addressing the court. Another panel quotes these prophetic words from his speech, 'I have devoted myself to the cause of the people. It shall ultimately prevail, it shall ultimately triumph'. Of particular interest is an interactive panel that honours Muir as a defender of freedom of the press: a portrait of him at his trial in 1793, papers in hand, adjoins a box marked, 'SHOULD A GOVERNMENT BE ALLOWED TO BAN A BOOK? HAVE YOUR SAY'. Below, the visitor is invited to 'CAST YOUR VOTE' by pressing a button for YES or NO. A result immediately appears with the number of votes, for and against received.

The exhibit on Muir forms part of a larger display arranged in a spacious rectangular alcove. Material on Oliver Cromwell, George Washington, Thomas Paine, Mary Wollstonecraft, the Chartists, and Arthur Phillip combine with Muir's story as windows on historical events that link the age of revolutions to the settlement of Australia as a penal colony. Muir is also included in the Museum's 'Milestones in Australian Democracy', which documents the history of democracy in Australia from 1770 to 2016.[56] Finally, Muir is part of a much longer history which goes back to Pericles (c.495-429 BC) and ideas and practices in ancient Greece. Within a month, September-October 2008, two busts arrived at the Museum in Canberra, the one of Muir and another of Pericles – a jesmonite replica cast of the Bust of Pericles in the British Museum.

Bust of Pericles, Museum of Australian Democracy.
The curatorial staff of the British Museum gave permission for this jesmonite replica of the Bust of Pericles to be made in 2008 for the Museum of Australian Democracy.
Courtesy of Museum of Australian Democracy.

Notes and References

1 In this chapter, some material is drawn from my earlier publications: 'Thomas Muir: an Australian Perspective', *Scottish Local History* 92 (Autumn 2015), pp.34-40 and my 2012 essay on Muir in the *Dictionary of Sydney* http://dictionaryofsydney.org/entry/muir_thomas

2 Phillip to Sydney 15 May 1788, *Historical Records of New South Wales*, vol.1, part 2 (Sydney: Government Printer, 1892), p.122.

3 Bewley, 1981, pp.68-9. Bewley's book is the fullest history of Muir and his times. For a general study of the Scottish Martyrs, see Clune, 1969; also Moore, 2010, chapter 1; for Muir particularly, see Earnshaw, 1959. An ABC Radio National Hindsight programme entitled 'The Trials of Thomas Muir' was made in 2011 with speakers from Scotland and Australia. The program is podcast at: http://www.abc.net.au/radionational/programs/hindsight/the-trials-of-thomas-muir/3717128, accessed 29 June 2016.

4 Collins, 1798, p.772. Early drawings and watercolours of Sydney Cove from 1793-96 give a good idea of the arrangement of huts on the east side of the cove: see McCormick, 1987, plates 26, 30, 32 and 34-39. From evidence given in a law suit, John Earnshaw calculates that the Scottish Martyrs 'huts' stood midway along the present day O'Connell Street – Earnshaw, 1959, p.17.

5 Muir to Moffat, *The Monthly Repository of Theology and General Literature* vol.XII (Oct 1817), p.577. Extracts of the letter, with some names blanked out, were published in the London *Morning Chronicle*, 29 July 1795, p.3 and the *Historical Records of New South Wales*, vol 2 (Sydney: Government Printer, 1893), pp.869-70.

6 Earnshaw, 1959, p.19. A letter of Thomas Fyshe Palmer, 15 September 1795, is evidence of Palmer's confidence in White, *Historical Records of New South Wales*, vol.2 (Government Printer, Sydney, 1893), p.880. White was also a naturalist and is almost certainly the unnamed 'most valued friend' described by Palmer in his earlier letter of 15 December 1794, *Historical Records of New South Wales*, vol.2 (Sydney: Government Printer, 1893), p.871.

7 Mackenzie, 1831, p.33. Mackenzie's biography is generally regarded as unreliable. Still, his story that Muir named his farm *Huntershill* was repeated by Bewley (1981, p.122) and Dickinson (2004).

8 Sherry, 2009, pp.3-6: http://huntershilltrust.org.au/wp-content/uploads/2011/03/Vol-47-No-2-Oct-2009-Part-1.pdf; accessed 22 July 2016. In my book published in 1989 I established that the name 'Hunters Hill' predates the arrival of Muir in Sydney but I repeated the assumption that Muir named his farm *Huntershill* (Sherry, 1989, pp.20-1), an assumption corrected in this 2009 article.

9   Deputy Surveyor General's *Plan of the Settlements in New South Wales* (1796), *Historical Records of New South Wales*, vol. 3, fold-out following title page. There are 33 allotments, numbered 14 to 46, and their area (25 to 30 acres) and owners' names are listed. Thomas Muir is not among them, nor is his supposed farm opposite Sydney Cove at Milsons Point marked.

10 John Earnshaw acknowledged that there is no record of Muir's purchase but deduced that his farm must have been at Milsons Point (Earnshaw, 1959, p.18); for the other three locations see Scott, 1960, pp.161-8; Bennett, 1865, p.203; Barton manuscript, 1897, p.287.

11 Collins, 1798, p.457.

12 Letter from Grose to the Reverend TF Palmer, 26 October 1794, *Historical Records of New South Wales*, vol 2, (Sydney: Government Printer, 1893), p.868.

13 Bewley, 1981, p.128. For a record of this protracted case over more than three weeks in December 1795, see Hunter's dispatch, *Historical Records of Australia*, series 1, vol.1 (Sydney: Government Printer, 1914), pp.603-43.

14 Bennett, 1865, p.203. Bennett's history began as weekly chapters in the *Empire* newspaper and the myth that today's suburb of Hunters Hill was named by Muir perhaps began with him. Hunters Hill was established as a municipality in 1861, around the time Bennett was writing, and he states, without documentary evidence, that Muir 'purchased some land on the north shore of the Parramatta River and named the place Hunter's Hill, after his patrimonial estate in Scotland. That locality, now a beautiful and populous suburb of Sydney, still bears the name he conferred' (p.203). George Barton's manuscript 'The Scottish Martyrs' (1897) is based on articles written in the 1890s for the Sydney *Evening News*, a newspaper begun by Bennett. While repeating the myth of Muir and today's suburb of Hunters Hill, he asserted a different location for Muir's farm: 'Muir and Skirving secured adjoining farms, situated on the north shore of the harbor, between the Lane Cove River and Ball's Head, where a village settlement had been laid out by the Major [Grose]' (Barton manuscript, 1897, p.287). The underlining was perhaps intended as a correction to Bennett's earlier claim. Barton was right, however, to report a settlement in that vicinity – see above p.208 and Note 9.

15 Mitchell Library, Sydney, Manuscript Am 9.

16 The catalogues of the Bodleian Library, British Library, and National Library of Scotland all state that the author is George Hamilton, Minister of Gladsmuir. The printed copy I have used, in the Rare Books collection of the University of Sydney library, has been signed on the title page by a John Rutherford Jun, who has also written at

the bottom of the page, 'Supposed to be wrote by Henry Mackenzie Author of The Man of feeling'. Mackenzie was a zealous Tory. The pages are numbered, but there are no lines numbers. My references are to the page numbers.

17 After extensive search, the Mitchell Library (Sydney) has been unable to trace the provenance of the manuscript; it is catalogued as Am 9 and the card states, 'Muir, Thomas Pseudonym'.

18 *Cairns Post* (Queensland), 8 September 1954, p.4. See also John Earnshaw, 'A Sydney Poem from Scotland', *Sydney Morning Herald*, 14 April 1951, p.9; Earnshaw considers that the manuscript 'was probably among the mass of Australiana collected by the late David Scott Mitchell and so came to its present resting place'.

19 Hughes, 1987, pp.178-9.

20 On *The Telegraph* as part of radical cosmopolitanism in 1790s Scotland, see Leask 2007; and for a discussion of the poem, including passages read aloud, listen to the podcast made by Nigel Leask and myself: http://www.abc.net.au/radionational/programs/hindsight/muir-poem-discussion/3731444; accessed 12 July 2016.

21 On 'Satanism' as part of eighteenth-century radicals' reverence for Milton, see Nyquist, 2014.

22 *Paradise Lost* 1.255, in Milton, ed Lawalski.

23 Patterson, 1997, chapter 1. Alluding to Milton's *Paradise Regained*, she sees Hollis's project of promoting the republic of letters as 'deeds of peace'.

24 [Blackburn], 1780. Milton is clearly Hollis's hero, frequently referred to as 'the divine Milton'; the finely illustrated book includes five portraits of Milton, more than anyone else.

25 Bewley, 1981, p.53.

26 Thomas Muir, letter to Mr Moffat, 12 December 1794. *The Monthly Repository of Theology and General Literature*, vol.XII (1817), p.577.

27 Bewley, 1981, pp.114-15; Bond, 1990, p.109.

28 Collins, 1798, p.422.

29 *Historical Records of New South Wales*, vol.2 (Government Printer, Sydney, 1893), p.882.

30 Reproduced in entirety in *Historical Records of New South Wales*, vol 2, pp.883-5.

31 Hunter to Portland, 25 October 1795, *Historical Records of New South Wales*, vol.2, p.883.

32 Collins, 1798, p.457; Cumpston, 1964, p.31. The quotation is from Muir's own account in his letter to General Washington, President of the United States, from Monterey, 15 July 1796, reproduced in Earnshaw, 1959, pp.59-61.

33 Collins, 1798, p.457; Hunter to Portland, 30 April 1796, *Historical Records of New South Wales*, vol.3, p.47.
34 Portland to Hunter, *Historical Records of New South Wales*, vol.3, pp.98-9. In the same volume, see the long letter by Robert Dundas to Portland, 5 September 1796, rebuking Hunter and defending the judgement of the Scottish court. Dundas had conducted the prosecution at Muir's trial in 1793.
35 Earnshaw, 1959, p.64 and p.68. Muir's letters from Monterey, preserved in the Archives of the Indies in Seville, are printed as Appendix 2 of Earnshaw's book
36 Pentland, 2016. George Burnett Barton's unpublished 'The Scottish Martyrs' (1897) is written in the manner of an historical novel. Most recently, Murray Armstrong's *The Liberty Tree: the Stirring Story of Thomas Muir and Scotland's first fight for democracy* (2014) is a markedly hybrid work weaving together fiction with historical detail and appending extensive archival references. EH Strain's book about Muir, *A Prophet's Reward* (1908), is a sophisticated handling of the genre of historical novel.
37 Wantrup, 1990.
38 Wantrup, 1990, p.41.
39 Donnelly, 1975, p.7 and p.13. See also Donnelly's essay on Muir in Baylen and Gossman, 1979, pp.330-4, in which he notes that Muir's trial 'has passed into legal history as a classic example of the abuse of the judicial process for political ends' (p.332).
40 Bennett, 1865, p. 203.
41 'The Romance of Thomas Muir' by Marcus Clarke, in *Sydney Mail, Clarence and Richmond Examiner and New England Advertiser* (Grafton, NSW), Saturday 4 October 1879, p.3. See also *The Colonial Observer* (Sydney), 12 April 1843, p.11, a lengthy article which reports that 'Muir is still remembered by some of the older residents in New South Wales'; *South Australian* (Adelaide), 16 May 1843, p.2; *The Britannia and Trades' Advocate* (Hobart), 25 November 1847, p.4; *The Brisbane Courier* (Queensland), 12 September 1865, p.4; *The Goulburn Herald and Chronicle* (NSW), 25 July 1868, p.7; *The Queenslander* (Brisbane), 24 December 1881, pp.812-3 ('Biography: Thomas Muir' by Peter Joseph McDermott); Bathurst *Free Press and Mining Journal* (NSW), 15 June 1889, p.4; *Truth* (Sydney, NSW), 28 May 1899, p.4 (a scathing Open Letter by John Morton to 'His Excellency the Right Honourable Earl Beauchamp, Governor of New South Wales', praising Australia's political prisoners, including the Scottish Martyrs, as 'Patriots, Reformers, and Radicals' to whom Australia owed a profound debt).
42 Blair, 1879, pp.268-9 and p.274.

43 *Evening News* (Sydney), 15, 22 and 29 August, 5, 12, 19 and 26
    September, 24 October, 5, 19 and 26 December 1896; 2, 23 and 30
    January, 6 February 1897.
44 *Evening News* (Sydney) 26 December 1896, p.2 ('villas' is crossed
    out and replaced with 'farms' in the manuscript, p.287); 23 January
    1897, p.1; and Barton manuscript, p.306.
45 George Burnett Barton papers, State Library of NSW, Dixon Library
    (Sydney), DLMSQ 107.
46 George Burnett Barton papers, State Library of NSW, Dixon Library
    (Sydney), DLMSQ 107, p.374.
47 *The Daily News* (Perth, Western Australia), 29 February 1918, p.7.
48 *Worker* (Brisbane), 15 August 1918, p.6. Charles Collins (1867-1936)
    was writing from the Parliamentary Library and quoted material
    on the Scottish Martyrs from the *Historical Records of New South
    Wales*. He was a Member of the Legislative Assembly, the lower
    house of the state parliament. In 1922 Queensland (uniquely)
    abolished its upper house, the Legislative Council.
49 *Daily Standard* (Brisbane), 20 October 1934, p.5 and 29 October
    1935, p.4.
50 *The Queenslander* (Brisbane), 15 February 1939, p.18. See also
    Newcastle Morning Herald and Miners' Advocate (NSW), 15 July
    1905, p.11 ('A Martyr for the People: Champion of Scottish Rights');
    The Brisbane Courier (Queensland), 14 May 1908, p.4; *Advocate*
    (Melbourne, Victoria), 20 July 1907, p.12; *Watchman* (Sydney), 29
    December 1910, p.7; *The World News* (Sydney), 3 January 1914,
    p.10 ('Five Worthy Scots Banished to Australia For Advocating
    Parliamentary Reform' by E.J.W.); *The Australasian* (Melbourne),
    21 June 1919, p.44; *Sydney Morning Herald* (NSW), 7 June 1913,
    p.5; *The Australasian* (Melbourne), 29 December 1923, p.39;
    Windsor and Richmond Gazette (NSW), 25 January 1927, p.5; *The
    World's News* (Sydney), 31 December 1927, p.10; *The Australasian*
    (Melbourne), 29 September 1928, p.10; *Sydney Morning Herald*,
    25 September 1928, p.11; *The Sun* (Sydney), 1 November 1930,
    p.7; *The World's News* (Sydney) 17 June 1931, p.9 and p.27; *The
    Evening News* (Rockhampton, Queensland), 7 September 1932, p.6;
    Dungog Chronicle Durham and Gloucester Advertiser (NSW), 17
    March 1936, p.6; *The Argus* (Melbourne, Victoria), 10 April 1943,
    p.2; *South Coast Times and Wollongong Argus* (NSW), 5 May 1952,
    p.1 (a lengthy article, 'The Odyssey of Thomas Muir' by K Wallace-
    Crabbe); *Cairns Post* (Queensland), 8 September 1954, p.4; *The
    Argus* (Melbourne), 23 June 1956, p.33 ('Sydney couldn't hold Muir
    [...] He was our Man of Legend. Bill Wannan's Colonial Cavalcade');
    and *The Canberra Times*, 25 November 1989, p.6 ('The Dramatic

Escape of a Scottish Martyr' by Robert Wilson, with a portrait of
Muir captioned 'Persecuted for his democratic views')
51 Earnshaw, 1959, p.4.
52 See the Friends of Thomas Muir website, www.thomasmuir.co.uk.
53 Sherry, 2009; and above, pp.207-9.
54 Sherry, 2011, 2012 and 2015. I am indebted to the family of John
Watson, leaders among the Friends of Thomas Muir, especially for
their generous hospitality when I visited Bishopbriggs.
See http://huntershilltrust.org.au/wp-content/uploads/2011/03/
Vol-49-No-1-April-2011.pdf (accessed 19 September 2016).
55 I am grateful to Libby Stewart, Senior Historian at the Museum
of Australian Democracy, for information on the history of the
Museum.
56 See http://explore.moadoph.gov.au/timelines/milestones-in-
australian-democracy; accessed 16 July 2016.

Thomas Muir: real martyr or merely French propaganda?

Thomas Lemoine

We cannot fully understand the remarkable story of Thomas Muir without considering the fundamental role that France played in his destiny. To what extent did the French Revolution influence this young Scottish lawyer who dreamed of reforms and freedom for Scotland? In what ways did France support him during his struggle and how did France react to the injustice of his treatment? What part did France play in trying to free Thomas Muir from his enemies? Why did France adopt him? And in what way did it make of him a hero of freedom? Why has a man so famous in his time been forgotten by History?

To better understand the link between France and Thomas Muir it is important to remember the political and cultural context of the period. From the beginning of the eighteenth century, France had a special place in the world through its intellectual movement, known as the 'French Enlightenment'. The intellectuals of the French Enlightenment had the will to fight against obscurantism and to try to make knowledge accessible to all. Soon afterwards, from about 1730, the 'Scottish Enlightenment' joined that of the French. This enabled great Scottish intellectuals such as Francis Hutcheson, David Hume, Adam Smith, Thomas Reid and John Millar, to name but a few, to achieve recognition.

The Act of Union of 1707, between Scotland and England, led to many changes in Scotland. These suited some Scottish people better than others. Some of the disaffected suffered after the Battle of Culloden in 1746, when Highland Scots were forbidden the kilt, the tartan, the Gaelic language, the bagpipe and the clarsach; and clans were firmly controlled. Many Scottish people had to come to terms with a changing identity. Against this background Thomas Muir was born on 24 August 1765, in Glasgow.

Despite the progressive development of the Scottish economy since the Act of Union, many Scots remained dissatisfied with their lot. Some were inspired by the Declaration of Independence of the United States of America on 4 July 1776, and the American Constitution of 17 September 1787, to launch a radical movement for the reform of British institutions and a better representation of Scottish people in the British government. The beginning of the French Revolution caused problems for Prime Minister William Pitt. To begin with, the impact of the French Revolution had a positive impact in Scotland, where many were sympathetic to the new political ideas in France proclaimed by its new motto *Liberté, Egalité, Fraternité*. The British government remained careful. At first, Pitt saw a weakening of France, which was good for economic and political interests, but the threat of a revolt in Scotland, even a Revolution there, as well as in Ireland and possibly even parts of England, was taken very seriously. Events escalated during 1792-3, with an increasing number of petitions, riots breaking out, and the creation of new political circles such as the non-revolutionary, reformist 'Association of the Friends of the People', as described by John Brims in his doctoral thesis on the 'Scottish Democratic Movement'.[1] The Scottish radical movement was at its height during 1792-5 before being depressed by the government, forcing its leaders underground to avoid being detained or deported.

Thomas Muir played a significant part in the radical movement. He became one of its leaders. His inspiration came from many sources including the teaching of his former professor at Glasgow University, John Millar. The influence of the French Revolution and its Declaration of the Rights of Man and of the Citizen of 1789, provided Muir with the necessary arguments and examples to convince his compatriots. He went on to deliver many speeches, some inspired by the French Revolution, and to organize conventions of the association of 'Friends of the People in Scotland'. All eyes were on him, including those of the British government. Despite the threats, he continued with his action and recruited more and more partisans. Alongside Muir's activity, other organizations such as the 'Society of the United Scotsmen' were being established.[2] The government's leader in Scotland, Henry Dundas, needed to act fast to avoid a revolution. He decided on a whole series of measures to stop the arrival of information from France and sent spies to identify and stop the leaders. Muir was quickly identified as a danger. Many arrests were made, leading to the trials of the 'Scottish martyrs' during 1793-4. Muir's was held in August 1793 when he was condemned to fourteen years deportation to the colony of Botany Bay in Australia, an extremely severe punishment considered almost the equivalent of a death sentence. It generated a swell of emotion in Scotland, leading to the term 'martyr' being applied. The injustice made an impression on the French government, which had already seen in Thomas Muir a symbol of French revolutionary ideas in Scotland. This sentence was intended to send a very strong message from the British government to its people and also a message of defiance to the French Republic, with which it had been at war since February 1793.[3] The rising of the radical tide, together with the extreme violence in France brought about by the progressive implementation of The Terror from 1792 and then the execution of Louis XVI in January 1793, seriously worried the British government. To counter the radicals, circles of loyal supporters were created and the government succeeded in turning the situation to its advantage by setting the Scots against one another. The radicals were now suspected of planning to assist a future French invasion. Ironically, many of the Scots who felt oppressed by Pitt's government now joined up to participate in the war effort against France.

Thomas Muir's first trip to France

The rise of extreme violence in France did not favour the radicals. Muir decided to intervene to try to persuade the French to renounce plans for the execution of Louis XVI. He also welcomed an opportunity to visit a country he admired. He arrived in Calais on 15 January 1793,[4] but did not reach Paris until the day after the execution of the king, so in this sense his mission was a failure. He found France in an unstable state and under much pressure, seeking to protect its new Republic against a coalition of several European countries. But he was charmed by this apparently free country and even considered settling there. At this time of his life, Muir was neither a hero nor a famous person that people wished to meet. His presence was lost among the forty thousand foreigners, many of them British, who had come to support the French

Revolution and find inspiration for their own countries. During this period it was very difficult for a foreigner to become known in Paris. Great French politicians were numerous; they clashed with each other and monopolized attention. Nevertheless, some foreigners were recognized, such as Thomas Paine the author of *Rights of Man* (1791), a text which had influenced Muir. Thomas Muir and Thomas Paine become friends and Muir was introduced to the 'intellectual salons'. His statements in favour of France, his fight for Scotland and his famous trial distinguished Muir in later years, but at that time the government took little interest in Thomas Muir. However, this first trip to France was a way for him to become known that would save his life in 1797, but this was all in the future.

After a rigged trial, Muir was sentenced to fourteen years of exile on 31 August 1793. The severity of the penalty and its injustice became known throughout Britain, but also in the United States and in France. It was by discovering the unjust circumstances and issues of the trial that France became interested in the fate of Muir. He was seen as a representative victim of British tyranny and the opportunity was too good for the nation of France at war with Britain not to intervene and attempt to rescue him. The French knew that he could be a strong ally in their attempts to influence British public opinion. The French sent boats to try to rescue Muir when he was a prisoner on his way to Botany Bay, but in vain. Only after he escaped from Botany Bay, and crossed half of the planet, over the Pacific Ocean and through Canada and California in New Spain, did Thomas Muir and France get back in touch.

French diplomacy at Thomas Muir's service

In 1796 Muir was in Monterey, California, under Spanish rule; his goal was to reach Philadelphia. During his stay he wrote to his family and friends for the first time in years to give them news and tell them all about his incredible adventures. His letters are more than just travel stories, they are real declarations of faith and show that his commitment to the cause of political reform was still intact. Thomas Muir was back, and he was founding his hopes on the United States. However, the Viceroy Branciforte suspected him of being a British spy and so Muir was imprisoned in Havana, Cuba, waiting to be extradited to Spain. The French government decided to intervene to free Thomas Muir. Victor Hugues, the governor of Guadeloupe, was mandated by the Directory to take appropriate action. He sent a letter to the Viceroy to speak in praise of Thomas Muir and to demand his release. Scrutiny of this letter reveals some interesting information: the Directory has now claimed Thomas Muir as a French citizen deserving of their protection after all he had sacrificed for the Scottish nation with his revolutionary ideas:

> The opportunity that presents itself to be useful and to
> help some of our compatriots, gives us the claim of your
> Excellency to free Thomas Muir held in the dungeons of
> Havana [...]

Victor Hugues was outraged by the unjustified reasons for Muir's detention and the conditions of his imprisonment. In addition to presenting Thomas Muir as a 'good man', Hugues did not hesitate to blame the Viceroy of Mexico:

> We have made known to the Directory and the whole of
> Europe of this event. The act of cruelty and barbarism of
> the Viceroy of Mexico is sure to be marked in the annals of
> the century.[5]

The French did not hesitate to risk a diplomatic incident to save a stranger, even though France could not afford a new armed conflict with Spain following the Basel treaty of 22 July 1795.[6] This action provides proof of the great interest they had in Muir at the time. But this first attempt did not change anything, and Muir was extradited, destined for Cadiz in Spain. This extradition would prove to be near disastrous, with his ship attacked near Cadiz by the English who were trying to capture Muir. After this naval battle, in which Muir fought alongside the Spanish and was seriously wounded in the face, he was released with the other prisoners six days later without being recognized; indeed, the French thought he had been killed in the battle. He received some rudimentary care in Cadiz hospital, but doctors thought he had very little chance of surviving his injuries. The French then discovered that he was still alive, but seriously injured, and so they determined to save him this time. In addition to being a martyr for freedom, he was now seriously injured as a result of British action and his survival was uncertain. It was a great opportunity for the French speedily to use him for their anti-British revolutionary propaganda. The French consul in Spain, Roquesante, paid regular visits to Muir at the hospital. He also arranged for him to receive the best care and tried to negotiate for his treatment at the French Consulate; but the Spaniards refused. Roquesante decided to write to Delacroix, then Minister of Foreign Affairs, to ask for his help. In this letter Roquesante told of the misfortunes of Thomas Muir, his injury in combat and assistance he had given to Muir. He also reminded Delacroix that this was the same Thomas Muir to which

[...] a decree of the National Assembly granted the title of a French citizen and for which the Committee of Public Safety had made so many efforts during his banishment from England [sic] in the care of the Republic.[7]

The minister Delacroix wrote to the Directory to inform them of the situation and to ask for permission to intervene: 'Thomas Muir is too attractive for the Friends of Freedom for me to neglect to inform the Directory of the misfortunes of the famous Scotsman', Delacroix wrote at the beginning of his letter. He told about Muir's adventures since his banishment from Scotland. He asked for permission to help with Muir's medical care and to support him financially. He also pointed out that it was the duty of France to grant him asylum especially as France was 'his country'.[8] The Directory approved Delacroix's requests and granted asylum to Thomas Muir by a decree of 10 July 1797.[9] Delacroix then asked Pérignon, Ambassador of France in Madrid, to intervene immediately. In this way French diplomacy organized the highest summit of the French state in order to free Muir. On 24 July 1797 the Ambassador Pérignon wrote a two-page letter to the Prime Minister of Spain – Manuel Godoy. In this cordial letter, Pérignon briefly recalled the history of Thomas Muir and requested his transfer to an apartment rented by the French Government, where his wounds could heal. Pérignon arranged to provide a French passport for Thomas Muir as soon as his wounds were healed, so that he could easily leave the Spanish territory. Pérignon also referred to the keen interest of France concerning Thomas Muir, and did not hesitate to speak about Muir in glowing terms:

> He had fought like a lion in combat on board a frigate
> against the English, and been horribly hurt [and] the
> French Republic is very interested in the fate of this man
> who was sentenced in Edinburgh to be exiled to Botany Bay
> for showing too much attachment to our Republic.[10]

So in addition to recognizing the life of Muir as one of a martyr, the French propaganda of glorification had begun.

On 15 July 1797, Talleyrand became the new minister of Foreign Affairs and therefore responsible for Thomas Muir's situation. Pérignon sent a second letter on 18 August 1797, expressing some impatience over the release of Muir. The situation was delicate for Pérignon,[11] who clearly needed to find a balanced approach – to use tact when complaining about not having received a reply after two months of waiting but nevertheless to convey urgency about the immediate release of Muir: 'My government strongly emphasizes and demands the release of Thomas Muir'. He also continued to praise Thomas Muir, by claiming he had shown courage in 'fighting valiantly on the frigate'[12] and recalling his martyrdom as an 'unfortunate prisoner'. This time Pérignon might have expected a quick and positive response from the Spanish, but in this he was disappointed. The situation became even more complicated when the British learned that Muir was alive and proposed that Spain should exchange him for Spanish ships in their possession.[13] On 11 September 1797 Pérignon sent a new letter of three pages without salutation to express his displeasure. He could not understand the silence of the Spanish Government and the lack of response to his request for the release of Thomas Muir, now held prisoner and monitored without good cause: 'when a man is languishing in slavery, when he experiences prolonged detention he has not deserved, when he also suffers from his local position due to injuries experienced by fighting gloriously'.[14] Pérignon did not understand why such a simple case could begin to take on such significance. He asked the Spanish Government if they were waiting for Muir's death to release him. He also informed them that Muir had written to him to complain about his hospital conditions and his fear of dying there. Pérignon indicated that his wish was for Muir to heal and leave Spanish territory as quickly as possible. He did not understand why a country that was understood to be a 'friend and ally of France' couldn't meet a simple request for the release of one of its citizens. After more than four months, the French diplomatic pressure was finally successful. Muir was released on 16 September 1797 and assigned to French protection. In friendly hands his health soon improved and he arrived in Madrid on 17 October, before travelling to the French border and crossing to Bayonne. After over three years of trekking and journeying across the world, he was finally a free man.

How did the famous Thomas Muir service French propaganda?

In anticipation of Muir's arrival in Paris, the French government began to prepare a propaganda campaign to promote the history of the Scottish martyr who had been saved by France. For this the Directory decided to make use of their most popular and most significant daily newspaper, *Le Moniteur Universel*.[15] Glowing articles in this newspaper were a mark of official recognition, confirming that Thomas Muir was supported and protected by the French government. He became a real celebrity, as shown by his triumphant welcome in Bordeaux at the end of November 1797. For this occasion, the entire city was decorated in the colours of the French republic and thousands of people were there to see the new celebrity. They offered Muir flowers and applauded him as a hero that had returned as an adopted son of France.[16] He was invited to meet the revolutionaries, political men and significant thinkers of the city. He was invited into the Patriotic circle 'Le Cercle de la Grande Quille', where he showed up on a balcony and was given a roaring ovation by the crowd: 'Long live the defenders of freedom'. A huge banquet was organized in his honour and he gave several toasts. Thomas Muir thanked the French for the welcome they had given him and declared that the fight for freedom in his country was not finished. This event is recorded in an article in *Le Moniteur* n°77 of 7 December 1797, page 310:[17]

This party ended with a banquet. We gave the following toasts: 'To the French republic [...] Glory to its founders! Can the wisdom of its law equal the brightness of its weapons!' and also 'To Thomas Muir and to the victims of the English tyranny [...] Can their homeland, finally freed from an oppressor government, award them the price of their dedication' and 'To the army of England [...] Can it, managed by the liberator of Italy, gather soon the Thames to the Seine, and cause to ring on their free banks, and on the rocks of Scotland and Ireland, the beloved airs of the glory and freedom!'

This was the first article clearly to announce the intentions of France and its projected 'Army of England'. During his stay in Bordeaux, Thomas Muir's portrait was engraved 'in the black way, retouched with the burin and the castor, and colored in the watercolor, circulated everywhere'.[18] Muir was honoured with a magnificent engraving that enabled him to be recognized by all.[19] On the engraving, Muir is represented in bust, an eye-mask covering his wound. It is accompanied by a text of some lines recalling his history:

President of the Company of correspondence of Scotland, who defended the right of his homeland against the English Tyranny; Condemned to death; Commuted to that of perpetual banishment to Botany-Bay; Escaped from this hideous exile; On one frail boat through the vast ocean of India; Collected aboard a Spanish ship which under his command pushed away the English in an unequal Fight where he was injured; Pursued by the influence of Saint James's Office which did not hesitate to offer three vessels to Spain in Exchange for his Head; Finally given back his Liberty by the French Republic; His adopted homeland on the month of Brumaire of the year 6.[20]

There is also a poem:

Written by males against the tyranny, from the oppressed Scotland for which he defended the rights. To the most frightful exile, we condemned his life. He knew how to break his chains. He finds a homeland. And his mutilated body paints the kings forfeits.[21]

The French propaganda machine was fearsome and efficient. Muir was aware of it and intended to use it to continue his fight for reform in his own country. His goal was to convince the French to organize a military landing in Scotland.

Thomas Muir was on his way to Paris. To announce his arrival Pierre David, one of the journalists of *Le Moniteur Universel* and a close friend of Talleyrand,[22] prepared a laudatory article recounting Thomas Muir's history over two pages. It was a real 'consecration' for him. David recalled his struggles in Scotland before his trial and until his return to France. He did not hesitate to glorify Muir and to welcome the martyred man who had sacrificed himself for his cause.[23] The following is from the first paragraph:

> The famous Scotsman Thomas Muir, escaped from
> thousands of dangers, is about to arrive in Paris. His
> banishment belongs to the history of revolutions,
> his courage, in adversity, has come to exemplify the
> proselytes of philosophy and the successful outcome of his
> misfortunes to encourage all the martyrs of freedom.

The tone is set in the second paragraph: Thomas Muir is seen to be promoting the freedom of his country and he needs the help of France:

> Scots had not forgotten their ancient independence, the
> massacre of their ancestors, the tragic death of their queen,
> the eviction of Stuarts from the throne of Great-Britain;
> these memories, the feeling of their beggary, the shocking
> contrast that it offers beside the English opulence, perhaps
> finally the example of our revolution, became the cause of
> the insurrectionary movements that manifested in Scotland
> in 1792, and in which Thomas Muir played one of the
> leading roles.

The rest of the article explains his adventures in chronological order. The most extravagant of adjectives are used to describe Muir, and David employs them to honour the sacrifice of this man of freedom: 'famous', 'enlightened philosopher', 'vehement speaker', 'unfortunate philanthropist', 'apostle of philosophy', 'French by adoption' [...] It suggests that no republican reader could remain insensible to the incredible history of this Scottish martyr. David considered it important to prepare plans to celebrate this martyr: 'In Paris, the capital of the republican world, this meeting place of all the escaped victims of despotism'.

A new article in *Le Moniteur* announced Muir's arrival in Paris, in December 1797:

> Thomas Muir is arrived in Paris; the ministry of foreign affairs has welcomed him with the respect due to his great character, to the service he rendered to freedom, and to the evils he endured in defending this sacred cause.[24]

In Paris Thomas Muir finally met the man who was responsible for his freedom and for all of this promotion of his cause. Talleyrand was behind the propaganda and he intended to provide the finance for Muir's stay and to take care of his wellbeing in France. Indeed, at the request of Talleyrand, the Directory adopted an order of 'help to Thomas Muir' on 4 December 1797.[25] This financial 'help' amounting to 8,000 francs was adopted by order of the Directory on 27 January 1798.[26] It was a significant sum, half of which had been given to Muir by the French government before final confirmation of its adoption. Talleyrand wrote to Muir, on 26 March 1798:

> I advise you citizen, that I have just authorized the head of my office-fund to give you the sum of four thousand francs as well as the one which was advanced on the last 22th nivôse [11 January 1798]. I beg you [...] to be convinced by the deep interest which I take in your quick recovery [...][27]

Talleyrand wanted Muir by his side as a symbol of the revolution and of the French republic worldwide. Thanks to the support of one of the most powerful politicians in France, the stay in Paris was intended to be triumphal for Muir. All the most eminent men – the thinkers, the philosophers, the politicians – wanted to meet Muir and to invite him to recount his adventures in their learned societies. Muir appreciated the French welcome, and enjoyed being the focus of attention in Paris over several weeks. In appreciation of a civic banquet organized in his honour by the

Secretary of the General Police, Jean-Marie Sotin de la Coindière, he sent a letter to thank him and confirmed his commitment. The letter was published in *Le Moniteur* on 4 January 1798:

> I am a United-Irishman, I am a Scotsman; I can speak
> in the name of these two nations. Tears of sympathy and
> affections will flow, when they hear the wishes of your heart
> carried to the United-Irish, to the Scottish highlanders and
> to the English patriots who only await the French to break
> their chains. I will answer you, in the name of the Irish and
> the Scots, that we will break our chains on the heads of our
> tyrants. It is not with the whole English nation that there
> is a fight; but only with a thousand scoundrels; if they fall,
> then the peace of the universe will be established! [28]

The celebrity of Thomas Muir was so great that he even took care of some Irish refugees 'running away from the tyranny of the British government' and considered as spies after their capture by the French. *Le Moniteur* of 13 February 1798, tells us that 'on the recommendation of the famous Thomas Muir, they are well cared for'.[29] *Le Moniteur* of 20 February 1798, announced the release of a book with the title of *Histoire de la tyrannie du gouvernement anglais exercée envers le célèbre Thomas Muir, écossais* [...][30] It retold the adventures and the misfortunes of Thomas Muir, written down after a meeting between Muir and a merchant in Bordeaux, citizen Mazois – a text to the glory of Thomas Muir who had been influenced and saved by France, naturally. The book starts by detailing Muir's struggles in Scotland, and the reasons for his deportation. Muir is portrayed as a victim of English tyranny; but thanks to the inspiration of French revolutionary ideas, he finds energy to escape from Botany-Bay. All his adventures are slightly romanticised and even exaggerated, like the episode of his escape where he is said to have been involved in a fight while waiting for the American boat to rescue him. The episode of naval battle off the coast of Cadiz speaks for itself:

> We fought desperately (it is good to notice that his name
> was ignored by the whole crew, except for the captain). He
> was a sailor; the Spanish captain was killed, Muir exhorts
> his companions, takes the command on himself, and he is

in turn suddenly hit, which takes from him his left eye and
a part of the bone [...]³¹

The romanticized description of the battle suggests that Muir
fought as a hero beside the Spanish against the English. Later
in the book, Muir, when hospitalized in Cadiz, is betrayed by a
Spaniard who informs the English government as to his identity
and whereabouts. The English want to capture Muir and they are
ready to exchange boats and Spanish prisoners for him. The French
government, learning of Muir's misfortunes, decides to intervene
and free him from the Spanish: 'here is this brave man finally
extracted from the infernal pursuit of his tyrants'.³² Injured and
disfigured Muir is welcomed as a 'martyr of freedom' in Bordeaux
and 'the government surely consoles him for his misfortunes'. The
book was a huge success. In three months, the French government
had demonstrated that they knew how to present a laudatory
image of Thomas Muir: the narrative draws the conclusion that all
that was needed from Muir was now known,³³ and so an invasion
of Britain could be prepared.

What was the goal of the propaganda surrounding Thomas Muir?

For several years France had been planning an invasion of
the British Isles. The Directory believed that the time had come
to attack; the British had just suffered defeat by the Germans
while general Napoleon Bonaparte had returned from a victorious
campaign against Austria and the Italian kingdoms. Moreover,
since 1793 the situation in France had changed. Paris had become
a violent and dirty city, where poverty reigned because of the
numerous sacrifices made by the French people to finance the
wars against European countries. France had been in a continuous
war since 1789 to preserve the Republic, so it faced enemies both
from without and within. There was a feeling of fear everywhere.
The French were exhausted and it was becoming more and more
complicated for the government to finance and justify its wars.
On the other side of the English Channel, Britain was using every
means of pressure at its disposal against France and welcomed
the undeclared war between France and the United States in July
1798.³⁴ France was fighting on all fronts. Since 1793 it had been at
war with Britain, with no peace treaty in sight. With the projected

success of an invasion of Britain, the Directory hoped to reduce the economic crisis in France and divert public attention from that crisis by highlighting external threats, such as those posed by the English. This is where Thomas Muir was needed, as a martyr to sensitize the French to his fate at the hands of the dastardly British. In addition the Directory needed public support in Britain for the establishment of a Republic there and Thomas Muir's story was useful propaganda in this regard. Muir's celebration as a political martyr in Britain and his heroic travels around the globe provided a useful narrative for French use. In his article of 2 December 1797, in *Le Moniteur*, David emphasized Muir as a symbol of revolutionary hope:

> The Scottish insurrection had given great hope to our revolutionary government; this has vanished; but Republicans in France who saw the members of the Edinburgh Convention as friends of liberty, are very interested in their fate.[35]

France continued to take an interest in ideas that might keep the flame of Revolution burning in other countries.

Thomas Muir, *Le célèbre* – forgotten

Through his spies, Pitt's government knew full well about Muir's celebrity status and its potential for harm. Since his arrival in France, Muir had participated in many meetings, given speeches and written letters in support of his adopted homeland, and had promoted revolutionary projects. For France to be able to produce a British national willing to defend the Republic and its values was a strategic asset. English spies informed Pitt that Muir had become so important that if France was able to establish a Directory in Scotland he would be a vital part of that government.[36] Muir seemed to be back in circulation, supported by the French government, and with one new goal, namely to convince France of the merits of a rapid invasion of Scotland where numerous partisans were waiting to join him. But for Muir everything did not go as planned. On his return to Paris, he contacted his faithful friend Thomas Paine who introduced him to Irish radical circles including one managed by Theobald Wolfe Tone. Wolfe Tone was a strong and influential personality in France. He had been noticed by Talleyrand and General Bonaparte. He was as ambitious as Muir, but he wanted an Irish landing to be accorded priority. The two men were soon rushing to be the first to convince the French government of the merits of their respective plans. Muir composed long letters to the French government with a view to convincing them to support an invasion of Scotland where he believed that thousands of partisans were ready to fight for their freedom.[37] In fact, since his departure from Scotland in 1793 the Scottish radical movement had become much less significant; but Muir did not know this. Moreover, Thomas Muir was not fully recovered from his injuries. Tiredness, pain and his appearance began to have dramatic consequences for his mind and his judgment. Some of his public declarations seemed confused and Wolfe Tone did not hesitate to criticize his invasion plans for Scotland as 'very stupid'.[38] Despite Muir's unwavering perseverance and strong faith in his ideas, Wolfe Tone's arguments convinced the French to organize a landing in Ireland, which was then given priority over Scotland, and this took place during 1798. Muir, exhausted but still agitating, saw his support from the French government gradually weaken. He had rapidly become a famous and important man in France (between November 1797 and April 1798), but his influence was destined to recede just as quickly, during May-September 1798. By 20 May 1798 he was obliged to write a letter to the Directory asking for a loan of 150,000 francs to buy a house (which he offered to reimburse in two years). No reply was ever received.[39]

For almost a year, Muir continued to promote his ideas by means of his speeches and other forms of persuasion. He sent letters to Talleyrand and to other levels of the French government, proposing invasion plans for Scotland with estimates of the kind of support that could be anticipated and narratives of the history of Scotland as context. However, he eventually became aware of an increasing unlikelihood that the French would ever invade Scotland. Indeed, his remaining hopes disappeared after the successive failures of the landings in Ireland (between August and October 1798) with massacres of the French, and the arrest and execution of Wolfe Tone. Within a few months, Thomas Muir fell from his status as an extremely popular man benefiting from the generosity of the French government to an individual laid low by the speed of events in Europe. By this stage he was an ill man who only managed to hang on through the generosity of friends like Thomas Paine. He decided to move away from busy Paris to the village of Chantilly in Picardie, where he sought rest and seclusion. He perhaps also needed to hide from the English spies who quite possibly were continuing to watch for him. He finally died alone, in misery, in the early morning of 25 January 1799, in his small hotel room. The mayor of the village only discovered his identity by means of letters in his possession. A man who had been, just a few months previously, a celebrity and a martyr for freedom fully honoured by the French republic – and who had seen his adventures spread over two pages of *Le Moniteur* – was already forgotten. The same newspaper spared only a few lines to announce his death, on 30 January 1799 – without much praise or sorrow, relegated among the other articles to a small piece of routine news:

> Thomas Muir, this Scotsman so famous for his love of freedom, for his misfortunes, for his deportation to Botany-Bay, for his escape from this exile [...] died following the injuries he had sustained, about three years ago, in his fight.[40]

This was his last act of homage in France. Thomas Muir was buried in the cemetery of Chantilly, in the grounds of the hospital where he had been treated for his injuries. Today the hospital is a hospice for old people and there is a car park above the old cemetery. Thomas Muir's dream had been to return to his native Scotland and to be buried with his family in due course, but this dream remained unfulfilled.

Thomas Muir was born at a time when Europe suffered unprecedented upheaval – a time when men wanted to take control of their own destiny. The Act of Union, the French and Scottish Enlightenments, the Independence of the United States and the French Revolution all had an influence on Muir. As a young man he stood against injustice, and the French revolution was the trigger that gave him the opportunity to play a major role in Scotland and in France. In France today discovering his grave has become a kind of 'quest for the Holy Grail' for some Scots, who hope to see his remains returned one day to his native land to be buried among his own people.

* *Collaborative research by Christiane Lemoine and Dimitri Lemoine; translated into English by Dimitri Lemoine.*

Notes and References

1 John D Brims, The Scottish Democratic Movement in the Age of the French Revolution. Doctoral thesis, University of Edinburgh, 1983.
2 The Society of the United Scotsmen was formed in 1790. The members had been inspired by the events of the American and French revolutions. The purpose of this organisation was to achieve universal suffrage and annual elections to Parliament. After steps were taken by the British government to stop the radical movement, the Company of the Close Scottish People became more radical and worked for a Revolution in Scotland with the support of Holland and France. If successful, the Company planned to set up a temporary Scottish government with Thomas Muir as President.
3 Great Britain and France were not at war only because of the threat of a British radical revolution. Indeed, since 1789, France had wished to export its revolutionary ideas and to free other peoples of the yoke of their sovereigns and aristocracy. It achieved annexation of Belgium and the control of the River Scheldt. London could not accept that the financial centre of Antwerp was now controlled by the French. They feared economic, commercial and colonial competition. The partisans of the war in Great Britain now had enough argument to join the coalition of European powers, already at war since 1792.
4 National Records of Scotland, NRS 02023 JC26-276-8-1-00001.
5 Victor Hugues's letter, reference number ESTADO, 26, N.30. Spain – General Archives of the Indias. Link: http://pares.mcu.es/ParesBusquedas/servlets/ImageServlet?accion=41&txt_id_imagen=9&txt_rotar=0&txt_contraste=0&txt_zoom=10&appOrigen=&cabecera=N
6 Spain had unsuccessfully tried to save Louis XVI and a war had broken out between France and Spain in 1793. France repelled the Spanish assaults and the peace was decreed with the treaty of Basel after several Spanish defeats.
7 Roquesante's letter to the minister Delacroix, le 13 Floréal de l'an 5. National Archives. Pierrefitte-sur-Seine. Reference number: AF/III/62, dossier 246 Volume 1.
8 Roquesante's letter to the Executive Directory. Le 22 Messidor de l'An 5. National Archives. Pierrefitte-sur-Seine. Booking number: AF/III/457, booklet 2730 (n°2).
9 Directory's minutes of 22 messidor year V (July 10th, 1797). National Archives. Pierrefitte-sur-Seine. Booking number: AF/III/7 N°1 (page 22).

10 First letter of Pérignon. Reference number ESTADO, 37, N.32B. Spain – General Archives of the Indias: http://pares.mcu. es/ParesBusquedas/servlets/ImageServlet?accion=41&txt_ id_imagen=13&txt_rotar=0&txt_contraste=0&txt_ zoom=10&appOrigen=&cabecera=N

11 The position was delicate for Pérignon. Indeed, he had responsibility for the Treaty of Basel which reconciled France and Spain, and was in charge of securing the friendly relations that these victories had established, also to conclude an offensive and defensive alliance. This alliance was formalized by the Treaty San Ildefonse of August 1796.

12 Second letter of Pérignon. Reference number ESTADO, 37, N.32B. Spain – General Archives of the Indias: http://pares. mcu.es/ParesBusquedas/servlets/ImageServlet?accion=41&txt_ id_imagen=17&txt_rotar=0&txt_contraste=0&txt_ zoom=10&appOrigen=&cabecera=N

13 Barrington, 1911, p.185.

14 Third letter of Pérignon. Reference number ESTADO, 37, N.32B. Spain – General Archives of the Indias; http://pares. mcu.es/ParesBusquedas/servlets/ImageServlet?accion=41&txt_ id_imagen=21&txt_rotar=0&txt_contraste=0&txt_ zoom=10&appOrigen=&cabecera=N

15 French newspaper founded in 1789 by Charles-Joseph Panckouke. *Le Moniteur Universel* was at first known as the *Gazette Nationale*. It was a real propaganda showcase and was for a long time the official body of the French government. This newspaper announced the decisions of the government, gave news on the politics of other countries, the various conflicts and the transcription of parliamentary debates.

16 Mercey, 1837, p.351.

17 https://archive.org/stream/gazettenationale1797panc#page/310/ mode/1up

18 Michel, 1862. p.482.

19 Barrington, 1911, p.167.

20 'Brumaire', starting in late October and ending in late November, was the second month of the autumn quarter in the new revolutionary calendar; year 6 refers to the calculation of years in the calendar used between 1793 and 1805.Years are counted from the establishment of the first French Republic on 22 September 1792. Year '6' under this arrangement began on 22 September 1797.

21 Michel, 1862, p.482.

22 Nouvelle Biographie générale, Volume 13, sous la direction de Jean-Chrétien-Ferdinand Hœfer, Firmin Didot frères et Cie. Paris. 1866.

https://archive.org/stream/nouvellebiograph13hoef#page/n126/mode/1up

23 https://archive.org/stream/gazettenationale1797panc#page/289/mode/1up
https://archive.org/stream/gazettenationale1797panc#page/290/mode/1up

24 https://archive.org/stream/gazettenationale1797panc#page/309/mode/1up

25 Directory's minutes and Directory's worksheet of 14 frimaire year VI (December 4th, 1797). National Archives. Pierrefitte-sur-Seine. Reference number: AF/III/8 N°3 (pages 53-5).

26 Directory's minutes and Directory's worksheet of 8 pluviôse year VI (January 21th, 1798). National Archives. Pierrefitte-sur-Seine. Reference number: AF/III/9 N°2 (pages 27-30).

27 Lettre signée de Talleyrand datée 26 mars 1798, collection privée: http://www.osenat.fr/html/fiche.jsp?id=2681534&np=1&lng=fr&npp=10000&ordre=&aff=1&r=&gsessionid=1566BACD2BC9CA51125BFE8E4BB1CE5E

28 https://archive.org/stream/gazettenationale1798panc#page/421/mode/1up
https://archive.org/stream/gazettenationale1798panc#page/422/mode/1up

29 https://archive.org/stream/gazettenationale1798panc#page/582/mode/1up

30 Anon, 1798. Link: https://archive.org/stream/gazettenationale1798panc#page/612/mode/1up

31 Anon, 1798, p.17.

32 Anon, 1798, p.19.

33 Anon, 1798, p.19.

34 Between 1798 and 1800, the 'Quasi-War' was a period of latent conflict between the French Republic and the United States, not regarded as true naval warfare. In the United States, the conflict is sometimes called the non-declared war with France.

35 https://archive.org/stream/gazettenationale1797panc#page/289/mode/1up
https://archive.org/stream/gazettenationale1797panc#page/290/mode/1up

36 Bewley, 1981, p.168.

37 MacMillan, 2005, pp.256-63.

38 Bewley, 1981, p.165.

39 Bewley, 1981, p.177.

40 http://gallica.bnf.fr/ark:/12148/bpt6k49333r/f125.item.langFR.zoom

Muir's 'Good Cause' 1820

TJ Dowds

The threat of a French invasion, coupled with the government crack-down on any demand for change, which led to the trial and transportation of Thomas Muir in 1793 for sedition, also resulted in a reduction in radical activity by the end of the eighteenth century. In the eyes of the establishment, any suggestion of change was regarded as a threat to the constitution and led to the middle classes, who had been the backbone of the earlier movement to extend the suffrage, distancing themselves from groups seeking reform and falling in behind the government,[1] believing that without their leadership the movements would collapse. But, rather than cease to function, radical groups came under the control of the literate artisan class. As Michael Donnelly has pointed out, the reform movement 'had found in Muir their first martyr, and instead of disintegrating, actually stiffened their resistance to Government coercion',[2] albeit under new leadership.

The emergence of a working class-led radical movement can be dated to this period, as the history of James 'Purlie' Wilson, the radical weaver executed in 1820, illustrates. Wilson's political activism began around 1792, when some Whigs formed the 'Friends of the People' advocating an extension of the right to vote. The Strathaven branch was made up of local landowners; Wilson and other tradesmen were allowed to attend meetings, but not take part. When the Duke of Hamilton expressed hostility to reform, most of the middle class members withdrew. As a result, Wilson, along with some weavers and mechanics took over, organizing meetings and publishing new resolutions.[3] The weavers were revolutionary and at meetings read aloud from Cobbett's *Register*, *The Black Dwarf*, and other radical pamphlets, including the writings of George Mealmaker, who had helped set up the Society of United Scotsman in 1793.[4] Meetings were held from 1792 in Wilson's house or under his direction elsewhere.

James Wilson, the Strathaven radical, c.1810.

These meetings discussed issues that affected the members – poor wages, long hours of work, and a means of improving their situation. Political events in America and France were discussed and literate weavers read aloud about movements elsewhere, where change was being sought. Some had links with the Society of United Scotsmen and its Irish equivalent, with the result that the concept of creating a separate Scottish parliament was mentioned. In 1793, when Thomas Muir and Thomas Fyshe Palmer were sent to await transportation to New South Wales, Wilson wrote to William Skirving, the secretary of the Friends of the People, expressing his regret at the loss of these men to the organization.

He attended the Convention of the Friends of the People on 19 November 1793, where the delegates discussed universal suffrage and annual parliaments, as well as plans to spread radical literature in the Highlands.[5] Two representatives of the Society of United Irishmen attended the meeting.[6] After the failure of the United Irishmen's rising in June 1798 and the associated, briefly successful, invasion by French troops in August,[7] it was natural that the government should regard any proposed political change by associates of the United Irishmen as treasonable and find it easy to convince the public of the threat of 'Jacobinism'.

By the end of 1793, with Muir and his associates out of the way and Robert Watt sent to the gallows for possessing arms in Edinburgh, the government was convinced that 'the threat from radicals was well and truly vanquished'.[8] The reality, however, was that there were a few left who would continue to seek the opportunity to advance the radical cause, but were prepared to keep their heads down until the time was right.

A Changing Situation

Rapid industrialisation led to a growth in the combinations of working people to protect their rights. The government, concerned at links between unions and radicals, made it an offence to strike, organize strikes or support strikers, under pain of imprisonment. Shoemakers in Edinburgh struck for higher wages in 1798, but were tried for 'combination'. This legislation forced the United Scotsmen even further underground and, given their procedure to destroy all documentation, it is difficult to find hard evidence of their activities. Many were arrested and charged with all manner of 'crimes', and there were several deportations to Australia.[9] In 1802 the last trial of a United Scotsman took place when a Fife weaver, Thomas Wilson from Strathmiglo and a delegate to the National Committee, was banished from Scotland for two years for spreading sedition amongst farm labourers.[10] In England republicans were arrested in connection with the Despard Conspiracy when it was alleged that they planned to kill the King and spark an uprising;[11] and in 1803 the Irish were again in a short-lived rebellion under Robert Emmet[12] – clear warning signs that radicalism was not dead. Napoleon's appointment as 'First Consul for Life' and then 'Emperor of France', however, destroyed faith in revolutionary

France. The democratic ideals were gone, and with it any hope of establishing a Scottish Republic assisted by French arms. When war was restarted with France in 1803 the government found it easier to whip up patriotism against a France which was no longer interested in expanding democracy but instead upon expanding a continental empire.

The Militia riots of 1799 raised awareness of class divisions within Scottish society. At Tranent, the Conscription Officer was warned that the conscripts could not be depended upon 'if ever we are called upon to disperse our fellow countrymen or to oppose a foreign foe'.[13] In riots in the town nine men, two women and a boy were killed when dragoons attacked the protesters.[14] There were disturbances throughout central Scotland, but with no further loss of life. One factor differentiating radicalism in Scotland from that elsewhere was the defection of the middle classes and the recantation of some radicals when faced with the threat of a French invasion. Establishing regiments, officered by landowners and merchants with the rank and file coming from shopkeepers, tradesmen, clerks, teachers and farmers, was encouraged. By 1803 of the 103 regiments in the United Kingdom, Scotland provided 51, with 52,000 volunteers enlisted.

It is unlikely that the United Scotsmen ever posed any real threat, and it has been estimated that 'at their height probably never attracted more than a few thousand, active and nominal'[15] or about the same as the number of voters in Scotland. There was a greater degree of stability in the Lowlands as landowners felt a duty towards their employees that prevented disputes escalating too far. During years of scarcity they bought grain and sold it to their tenants at subsidised prices, paid rates for poor relief, which was flexibly applied up to 1834, and provided a safety net in the crisis years of 1782-3, 1792-3 and 1799-1800.[16] As Justices of the Peace the landed class played a major role in preventing industrial disputes by arbitrating on wages, and protecting some groups from the impact of rising grain prices.[17]

Industrialisation destroyed the old relationships, denying apprentices the prospect of progressing to be masters and leaving them as wage earners at a time when manufacturers set wages according to demand, abandoning traditional standards. This was the factor behind the Glasgow weavers' strike of 1787, during which six people were killed when the authorities used troops to suppress strikers.[18] The free market economy embraced by employers by the end of the century forced workers to unionise to protect themselves against unscrupulous employers, fluctuating wages, and the flood of migrant workers from Ireland and the Highlands that was depressing living standards. At the same time, the two groups drifted apart as employers formed associations to ensure their right to hire and fire as the market dictated, and to strengthen their position against workers.

The growth of towns as a result of immigration placed strains on the Poor Law, and led many to suggest change. Dr Thomas Chalmers of St John's parish argued that poor relief should be based on charitable contributions rather than taxation, as the latter destroyed the bond between receiver and giver that held society together. Many agreed with Thomas Malthus's theory that the Poor Law encouraged early marriage, increased the labour force and thus depressed wages causing more poverty.[19] Many towns now applied more rigorous standards for relief just as a recession was throwing more people out of work, persuading Glasgow cotton spinners to unionize in 1809 and resulting in strikes by calico printers in 1810-11.[20]

In 1812 weavers petitioned for a minimum wage 'with fair hours and proper application, to feed, clothe and accommodate himself and his family', but, although the magistrates, the Sheriff, and Lanarkshire Justices of the Peace accepted their case, the manufacturers refused to implement the new wage structure, and the Court of Session declined to force them to do so. With 30,000 looms idle, Lanarkshire and Renfrewshire sheriffs, alarmed at the scale of the strike, arrested the organisers, sending them to prison for combination – the first such case in Scots law.[21] Cotton merchants and manufacturers claimed that 'antiquated laws' were hampering economic progress, quoting Adam Smith to back their case. The legal establishment agreed and repealed the 1661 statute allowing JPs to regulate wages. As a result the only course open to workers was to change the way the state was governed and turn to political radicalism.

Revival of Radicalism

Weavers were at the forefront of the new wave of radicalism. They had been prominent in the Friends of the People and the

United Scotsmen, and in places like Paisley there was a culture of political debate and discussion. An influx of labour destroyed their standard of living, as the number of weavers grew from 25,000 then to 78,000 by 1820, but the law had crushed weaving trade unions, causing anger that was exacerbated when wages fell by one-third after the Napoleonic Wars, leaving the workers powerless.[22] The same period was marked by meal riots as the price of food rose, and there were strikes by colliers and shoemakers. The Commissioner of Police in Glasgow reported an increase in the number of 'Thieves, Rogues, Vagabonds and Defendators of every description' in the city.[23]

The Scottish revival was encouraged by English reformers. William Cobbett's *Political Register* argued that parliamentary reform was essential to end the misery of poverty, and was widely read in Scotland. Major John Cartwright, author of *Take Your Choice*,[24] toured Scotland giving speeches demanding annual parliaments, the vote by ballot, equal electoral districts and payment of MPs to allow the working class to stand for parliament. He believed that bad government was the cause of economic difficulties and that widening the representation would solve the problem. He attracted huge crowds in Paisley and Glasgow in 1816, during a time of depression and high prices; the Glasgow meeting at Thrushgrove was attended by 40,000 people, some of whom wore 'caps of liberty'. Like Muir he advocated the use of moderate petitions that appealed to the middle class, which sought a reduction in taxation and the abolition of sinecures.[25]

When government ignored the reformers' constitutional and moral approach, secret societies were set up in many cities, particularly Glasgow, Paisley, Perth and Dundee. Each had a central committee to maintain contact with English radicals, and some of the leaders were from Ulster and had United Irish backgrounds. There were rumours that they planned to overthrow the government and had stocks of weapons, with demobilised soldiers ready to train the rebels. In early 1817 Glasgow magistrates arrested the leadership and twenty-six people were sent to prison for being part of secret societies, with the threat of insurrection used to frighten off middle class support.[26]

It was not until 1819 that truly radical activity resumed, and again the impetus came from England. Joseph Brayshaw proposed the creation of 'union societies' and refusal to buy goods on which excise was levied, with a view to reducing revenue and bringing down the government. He also advocated annual parliaments and universal suffrage and addressed meetings on the subject. The government decision to crack down on demands for reform in England culminated in the Peterloo Massacres, and the passing of the Six Acts to outlaw meetings of over fifty people.[27] When cavalry charged a largely peaceful reform meeting in St Peter's Fields, Manchester, in 1819, killing nineteen people and injuring many more, including women and children, there were riots throughout Scotland protesting at the 'Peterloo Massacre'. Large protest meetings were held in Stirling, Airdrie, Ayrshire and Fife, and a meeting of 5,000 people at Paisley was broken up by the use of cavalry.[28]

In Scotland union societies became insurrectionary cells, with a co-ordinating committee and possession of arms, mostly pikes; drilling took place in several areas. A network of associations connected the groups and maintained contact with unions in the north of England. The authorities responded by recruiting volunteer regiments throughout the Lowlands and Borders to deal with any rising and defend the Union. Government believed strikes were a sign that seditious elements were planning armed insurrection, and their suspicions seemed confirmed when spies reported secret drilling, the presence of arms and printing presses turning out posters calling on workers to take up arms. It is difficult to be certain about the strength of revolutionary activity as members tended to keep a low profile and government agents had much to gain from exaggerating their 'findings'. There was growing discontent with the continuing depression and government refusing to act on the suffering of the people while defending the Corn Laws which kept the price of bread high to appease landowners.

A Committee for Organising a Provisional Government was formed early in 1820, made up of twenty-eight men appointed by various radical committees, to organise an armed uprising. In Glasgow, Dougald Smith was elected 'Commandant' of the Glasgow area, and orders were sent to other areas to appoint their own commanders: Daniel Bell in Paisley, Robert Hamilton in Strathaven and John Baird in Condorrat.[29] Some of these men were ex-soldiers who had served in the French wars and were able to provide training in arms to the inexperienced recruits.

The Insurrection of 1820

In February 1820 the Cato Street Conspiracy to murder the Cabinet and set up a French-style Republic, although a government ploy, gave authorities the excuse to brand all opponents as assassins and to take the offensive against reformers. Spies infiltrated local unions and reported to the authorities. With the cooperation of the local authorities in Glasgow, the Organising Committee was infiltrated and reports about their activities passed on. The alleged government spy, Alexander Richmond, had persuaded a group of men to take an oath in January 1817, and a copy was immediately sent by the Glasgow MP, Kirkman Finlay, to Lord Sidmouth.[30]

When the committee of twenty-eight met in a Glasgow tavern on 21 March, Glasgow's police chief, James Mitchell, was able to arrest the organising committee, but kept the arrests secret to encourage others to show themselves, while the government agents who were members of the committee were encouraged to go ahead with the plan to ensnare others.[31] Mitchell may well have concocted the plan to issue a Proclamation calling for a strike to change the law to win support for action.

It is clear from correspondence received by Major William Murray of Polmaise, the Vice-Lieutenant of Stirlingshire and second-in-command of the Stirlingshire Yeomanry,[32] that the military authorities were aware that there was likely to be a rising and that they were preparing to put it down. As early as 21 December 1819 the Duke of Montrose, the Lord Lieutenant, had expressed concern about distributing arms to units in Kilsyth and Denny, fearing they might fall into the hands of radicals.[33] Toward the end of February, Murray was told of rumours about a rising to overthrow the government 'in our 3 kingdoms'.[34]

The chief spy, John King, urged workers to arm themselves and organised a proclamation of the Provisional Government. It has been argued that the proclamation was drafted by agents-provocateurs to bring radicals into open rebellion and allow the authorities to arrest them.[35] It has been pointed out that the 'Address to the inhabitants of great Britain and Ireland', to give it its full title, makes reference to English historical events like Magna Carta and the Bill of Rights, rather than to Scottish events such as the Declaration of Arbroath or the Claim of Rights, suggesting the author was not familiar with Scottish history.[36] However, since most of the history taught in Scottish schools then, and indeed well into the last half of the twentieth century was essentially English history with little or no reference to Scotland, the author could well have been a Scot – although that does not negate the possibility that he was in the employ of the authorities.

Despite the Address later being used to accuse the radicals of inciting armed rebellion, there is no overt reference to the use of arms.[37] It advocated equality of rights (not of property), stressing that the protection of these rights was of benefit to both rich and poor. Its appeal to soldiers to desist from attacking their fellow countrymen could be interpreted as an incitement for troops to refuse to obey orders, but just as readily, in light of previous incidents, an invitation for the military authorities to exercise discretion when dealing with public assemblies: an interpretation reinforced by the appeal to Justices of the Peace to 'suppress outrage of every description', and in the last paragraph where it stated that anyone guilty of pillage or plunder should receive 'the severest Punishment'. It is the penultimate paragraph however, that is the real point of the Address. It asks that all should 'desist from their Labour' from 1 April and stay on strike until they attain the 'Rights which distinguishes the Freeman from the Slave'. This is clearly a call for a general strike, albeit for political rather than industrial reasons, and perhaps the first such call in British history;[38] what it is not, is a call for armed insurrection.

That the Address was issued in the name of the 'Committee of Reformation for Forming a Provisional Government' has led to the suggestion that the 1820 Radicals were nationalists intent on creating a separate Scottish Parliament. This has been rejected by later writers who have pointed out that similar statements were associated with English radicals when disturbances took place in Huddersfield, Sheffield, Carlisle and elsewhere.[39] Equally, the proclamation is addressed to 'Britons' rather than Scots, indicating that this was a 'shared struggle for rights and liberties' of the working class in England as well as Scotland.[40] Yet it is agreed that there was specific reference to Scottish figures like Wallace and Bruce, and radical marchers often sung 'Scots Wha Hae' during their demonstrations,[41] which raises reasonable doubt about their 'unionist' tendencies.

On 1 April John King, who had been at the meeting in Glasgow but had left just before the police raid, together with the tinsmith Duncan Turner, a weaver John Craig and 'an Englishman' named Robert (or Thomas) Lees, was active in distributing the proclamation and encouraging workers to prepare to use arms in defence of their rights.[42] This clearly goes far beyond what was requested in the Address, and indicates an escalation from civil action to armed revolt, exemplified by pikes being made at St Ninians, Stirling.[43] It is this action that has been seized upon by proponents of the 'government spies' theory to prove their case, by raising questions about the motives of these leaders. Radicals were informed that there was to be a general rising in England and that Scots were to rise in support of their southern colleagues, despite a report from one of their delegates to England, John Porter, that there were no preparations for a rising there.[44] The failure of English radicals to rise[45] meant that the Scottish rising was doomed to failure.

On Monday 3 April an estimated 60,000 stopped work, with the government receiving reports from Glasgow and Paisley that the mills had been brought to a standstill.[46] Weapons were found at Kilbarchan and troops dispersed groups that had assembled in Balfron and Stewarton.[47] Paisley, always a hotbed of radicalism, was put under curfew as rumour spread that an English army of radicals was on the way and that a force of French troops under Marshal MacDonald was stationed at Cathkin Braes.[48] Later in the day John Craig, who was leading a group of men out of Glasgow, was arrested by police – to the annoyance of the Hussars who were waiting in ambush at Port Dundas Toll. Most escaped but Craig was taken prisoner. He was fined five shillings and the magistrate, the mill owner Mr Houldsworth, paid this and released him.[49]

Next day, Andrew Hardie left Glasgow with two men whose names he would later decline to disclose, having been informed that 'the whole city would be in arms in the course of an hour [...] and that England was all in arms'.[50] He led a group of thirty men from Glasgow towards Carron where he had been told the workers would supply arms for the rising, and was given half a torn card by Turner and told that the matching half was held by supporters at Condorrat.[51] There, John Baird had been given the other half of the card by John King, who told him to take command of the 'army' coming from Glasgow, and when Baird expressed concern at the small number of men with Hardie, reassured him that more help would be forthcoming when they reached Falkirk. Craig left with a Condorrat man, Kean,[52] to rally support at Camelon. Meanwhile, the authorities had taken action to thwart the 'rebellion'. On 2 April, orders were sent for the yeomanry to assemble at Falkirk and Kilsyth, and Major General Sir Thomas Bradford was informed of the move.[53] Two days later, Major Murray was informed that the strike was strong in Camelon, and asked that 'each man of the Yeomanry might receive six guineas' (three times the normal rate for their service).[54] Significantly, most military effort was directed to the road from Glasgow to Falkirk, rather than the areas where arms had previously been discovered.

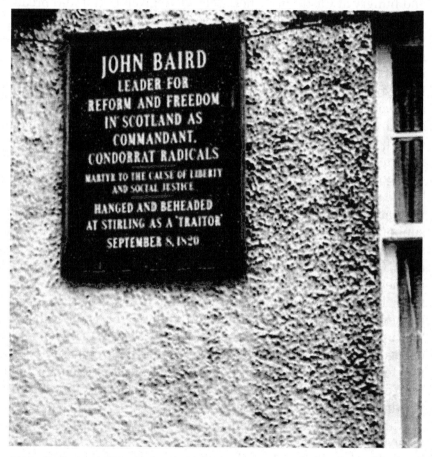

Site of John Baird's residence, Condorrat.

In addition to the Volunteers, who only served locally, regular troops were to be deployed, and Lieutenant Ellis Hodgson and a troop of 10th Hussars left Perth to defend Carron Ironworks, where an attack was expected on 5 April. After a 'forced march' from Stirling,[55] his sixteen men arrived at Kilsyth where they were joined by Lieutenant Davidson and sixteen men from the Stirlingshire Yeomanry.[56] Clearly the authorities were not only well aware of the rising, but also its planned target and route, information that could only have come from spies, and thus giving credence to the conspiracy theory.

Early on 5 April Baird, Hardie and their men arrived soaked and hungry at Castlecary where they were given porter and bread at the inn, for which Baird paid seven shillings and six pence and was given a receipt by the proprietor, Archibald Buchanan, before moving off in two groups to avoid detection.[57] But their presence was noted by a traveller who told the authorities and Lieutenant Hodgson left Kilsyth with sixteen Hussars and sixteen Yeomanry and went to Bonnybridge. A trooper from the Yeomanry and a sergeant of the Hussars also encountered Hardie's group, one of whom, Henderson, gave the sergeant copies of the address;[58] both reported their presence to the officers at Kilsyth.

At 9.00am King met the Radicals, who had reunited beyond 'Radical Pend' at Bonnybridge, and told them to wait off the road at Bonnymuir while he went on ahead to Camelon to gather support; there was no trace of Kean, who King claimed had become separated from him earlier.[59] Hardie recorded that as they rested on a hill, Hodgson's troops arrived and seemed to know their location as they made straight for the radicals, who engaged them in a fight. The 'battle' was short, but, according to Hodgson's evidence at the later trial and Hardie's account, quite fierce as the radicals 'put up a stout defence'.[60] When Hodgson cleared the dyke and engaged Baird, the radicals surrendered and the troops captured nineteen of them. Hodgson protected the radical prisoners when the Yeomany attempted to attack them.[61] The captives were taken to Stirling Castle to await trial.[62]

Meanwhile, Lees persuaded James Shields, a weaver, to deliver a message to the veteran radical James Wilson at Strathaven, informing him that a French army was at Cathkin and urging him to bring men there.[63] On 6 April a group of twenty-five men carrying a banner 'Scotland Free or a Desart'[64] set out for Glasgow, with Wilson marching in the rear,[65] but warned of an ambush at East Kilbride Wilson sensed treachery and returned home. The others skirted the troops and arrived at Cathkin to find no army, and Rutherglen radicals persuaded them to disperse.[66] Ten of them were later identified and taken to Hamilton jail.

Memorial on site of battle at Bonnymuir, erected by the 1820 Society.

By 5 April, Glasgow was an armed camp: the 1st Rifle Brigade and Ayrshire Yeomanry were stationed in Gallowgate and the 7th and 10th Hussars in Eglinton Street, with Yeomanry in St Enoch's Square and guns sited at the Glasgow bridges. Four other regiments were on their way to the city, but despite minor disturbances at Bridgeton, Tradeston, Dalmarnock and Pollokshaws, there was no further trouble. Prisoners from Paisley were taken to Greenock on 8 April by Port Glasgow Militia, who were attacked along the way but delivered the prisoners. On their way back they were again attacked and fired into the crowd killing eight people, including an eight-year old boy, and wounding ten others. The Greenock mob attacked the prison and freed only the radical prisoners, although all were later recaptured.[67]

The Trials

While the strike had widespread working class support in industrial areas, there was less enthusiasm outside the central belt. For the middle classes who aspired to the vote, the insurrection was seen as a setback that could threaten the prospect of the franchise being extended. In this light, some came to demand the severest punishment for the 'rebels'. Robert Rennie, the Minister of Kilsyth wrote to Murray demanding that the trial of 'those taken at Bonny Muir' should be conducted with solemnity and their execution 'be a display of military force'.[68] Like many middle class people, the minister saw the actions of the Radicals as a threat to society and the established order and wanted an example made of the prisoners, even before evidence of guilt was presented in court. The Bonnymuir prisoners were interrogated at Stirling and Edinburgh, where they stated their aim was 'annual Parliaments, and Election by Ballot'.[69]

Government arranged for trials at Stirling, Glasgow, Dumbarton, Paisley and Ayr under a Commission of Oyer and Terminer ('to hear and to determine') as it was more likely to secure guilty verdicts, for as Lord President Hope informed the Grand Jury, Scots Law was not equipped to deal with such offences.[70] The decision to try the insurgents under English Law caused concern, as did the presence in court of two leading members of the English legal establishment, Sir Samuel Shepherd, the Lord Chief Baron, as advisor on English Law to Sir William Rae,[71] the Lord Advocate, and Mr Sergeant John Hullock to conduct the prosecution. Even the Clerk to the Commission was English, Thomas George Knapp of Haberdashers Row, London.[72]

Writs were issued for the detention of suspects not already in custody, a number of whom were recorded as having left the country.[73] At each grand jury, Hope announced that there were to be no reports made until 'all the trials in the country' had been completed, 'otherwise the severest punishments that this court can inflict will be pronounced against them'.[74] The accused faced four main charges, two under the 1351 Treason Act (25 Ed III):

compassing or imagining the death of the king;
levying war

and two under the treasonable and Seditious Practices Act of 1795 (36 Geo III):

compassing and intending to depose the King from the
style, honour and kingly name of the Imperial Crown of the
realm;
compassing to levy war against the King in order to compel
him to change his measures.

Each of the above was made up of nineteen different offences, such as 'reading the Proclamation', 'withdrawing from work' or 'persuading others to strike', any one of which could be regarded as proving the main charge.[75]

James Wilson was the first to be tried, on 20 July, with Lord Pitmilly presiding and troops stationed around the High Court in Glasgow to prevent any rescue bid. The Lord Advocate, Sir William Rae, opened the case, by referring to the proclamation, 'this abominable production' that brought about strikes and disturbances. Several witnesses identified Wilson as the leader of the Strathaven radicals although some pointed out that he had been reluctant to take up arms. JA Murray for the defence argued that his client had not been properly informed of the charges as Scots Law required. At this point Mr Hullock launched an attack on Murray claiming it was not necessary 'to make a dictionary of charges'.[76] Murray rejected the idea that because Wilson had read radical publications this was proof of treason, and stressed that no evidence had been advanced to show treasonable activities. After two days of evidence the jury retired for two hours and brought in a verdict of Not Guilty on three of the charges but Guilty of 'comprising to levy war against the King in order to compel him to change his measures'. James Ewing, the foreman, added that the jury unanimously recommended mercy.[77] Pitmilly ignored the jury's plea and Wilson was condemned to death. When five other Strathaven prisoners were tried they were found Not Guilty, despite judicial abuse. On 30 August, James Wilson was hanged and beheaded at Glasgow before a crowd of twenty thousand, amid cries of 'Murder, Murder, Murder', while troops stood guard against any trouble. His body was later recovered by relatives and buried at Strathaven.

Before the Grand Jury at Stirling on 13 July, Francis Jeffrey questioned Hullock's right to plead in a Scottish court.[78] Sergeant Hullock's response[79] was so slighting about Scots and Scotland that the high Tory Sheriff of Stirling, Sir Ranald MacDonald of Staffa sent Jeffrey a note offering to second him if he challenged Hullock to a duel. Lord President Hope realised what was happening and persuaded Hullock to apologise to Jeffrey to allow the trial to continue. On 4 August, the trial began at Stirling of the Glasgow detachment of Andrew Hardie, together with the Condorrat men, John Baird, John Barr, William Smith and Thomas MacFarlane, all weavers, who had been captured at Bonnymuir. Each of the accused was to be tried separately and Lord Hope again ordered that there be no press reports to avoid 'popular excitement'.

Although Hardie, the first to be tried, mentioned the men who had advised him that the country had risen, no attempt was made to identify these men, so furthering the suspicion that they were in fact government spies. Indeed, he ridiculed the evidence of Hugh Nicol Baird of the Kilsyth Yeoman Cavalry who testified he had confronted the radicals and threatened them, despite Hardie and the others never having seen him.[80] For the defence, Francis Jeffrey argued, to no avail, that 'persons unknown' had led the Radicals into a trap.[81] After Hardie was found guilty, Jeffrey advised the others to plead guilty and hope for clemency. Lord President Hope wanted mercy, but felt an example had to be made of the leaders, Baird and Hardie, who were sentenced to death by hanging, beheading and quartering,[82] while the others were transported. It is perhaps significant that the leaders who were executed had been soldiers and had seen active service during the Napoleonic Wars,[83] which may explain why they were shown no mercy. While awaiting execution, Hardie wrote an account of the rising which was smuggled out by 'Grannie Duncan', who fed the prisoners.[84] On 8 September 1820 Baird and Hardie were hanged and beheaded at Broad Street, Stirling, before a large crowd.

Broad Street Stirling, where Baird and Hardie were hanged and beheaded.

Several of the other rebels, including the fifteen-year old Alexander Johnstone, were transported to New South Wales.[85] Despite a campaign by the Glasgow journalist Peter Mackenzie, who later published a biography of Thomas Muir, the government refused to pardon them or reduce their sentences. On 1 August two weavers, James Spiers of Johnstone and John Lang of Kilbarchan were tried for treason before a jury of local merchants and businessmen, chaired by the landed magnate Sir Michael Shaw Stewart, in George Street Church, Paisley.[86] The jury found them guilty only of striking, and despite pressure from the judge and Sir Samuel Shepherd refused to condemn them of treason. When Shepherd insisted they bring in a guilty verdict, some of the jurors argued with him,[87] before finally pronouncing them 'Not Guilty'.[88]

George Street Church Paisley, where James Spiers and John Lang were tried.

This signalled the end of the show trials as it was clear that juries resented the influence of English legal advisors and were not prepared to be brow-beaten into verdicts they did not find. At the same time, it was becoming clear that the prolonged legal process was giving huge publicity to the radical movement. As a result it was announced that the authorities had agreed to abandon all other outstanding cases.[89] On 4 August, Andrew Dawson and John McMillan of Camelon pleaded guilty and another six were discharged.

Aftermath

The events of 1820 caused serious alarm in government circles, partly because it was seen as an attempted rising, but more so because it was not confined to weavers. What is striking is that a number of other occupations were represented, including labourers, shoemakers, blacksmiths, a tailor, a cabinet-maker and a bookbinder, all of whom had taken part in the general strike in the first few days of April. This was seen as a serious challenge and more serious than the earlier and larger confrontations in England, in particular that at Peterloo in August 1819. The immediate effect of the failure was that working class energies were diverted into trade unions rather than political action, with a movement away from violence.[90] Yet the lesson of working class solidarity was not lost and it was realised that, despite occupational and religious differences, members of the working class could work together to attack the corrupt political system.

The 1820s saw a number of reforms by the Tory government designed to remove some of the oppressive legislation affecting the working class. In 1824 the Combination Acts that had prevented public meetings and given magistrates the power to use the military to break up meetings deemed seditious, were repealed. Two Scots, Joseph Hume, the wealthy Radical who later led the campaign for a monument to Thomas Muir and the other political radicals on Edinburgh's Calton Hill, and John McCulloch, editor of *The Scotsman*, were prominent supporters of Francis Place during agitation against these acts. Further changes affecting Scots Law that had been advocated by the radical *Edinburgh Review* were enacted by parliament, allowing jurors to be chosen by ballot, giving the accused the right to challenge the choice of juror, and reducing the penalty for sedition. Sir Robert Peel was persuaded to abolish capital punishment for many trivial offences.

In an effort to distract the public and offer them a spectacle, Lord Melville, Lord Liverpool's chief Scottish minister supported Sir Walter Scott's plan to have George IV visit Scotland. His visit in 1822 began the Lowland love-affair with tartanry and led to the creation of 'Highland Societies' while Scott arranged for unemployed weavers from the west of Scotland to pave a path round Salisbury Crags in Edinburgh for the event; it became known as 'Radical Road'. More effective in destroying the radical movement was fear of government and legal repression. An upturn in trade within a few months of the defeat of the radicals at Bonnymuir helped to ensure that as employment rose and wages increased many of the grievances that had been at the heart of the trouble disappeared. In late 1820 there was recovery in trade and this resulted in increased employment. The boom lasted for nearly five years and this, rather than government action, was the reason that radicalism was not prominent in the aftermath of the Radical war. Encouraged by the Church society came to accept that respectability and restraint were required and that change could only come gradually and through the existing system; it was the enlightened thing to do.

The chief difference between the Scottish Rising of 1820 and similar abortive attempts in England was in the reaction of government to the situation in the two countries. Whereas the Scots leaders Baird, Hardie and Wilson were executed no Englishman suffered the death penalty. Scottish transportees were sent to New South Wales and were later pardoned by the king. Of the Scots it has been claimed that 'most returned to Scotland',[91] but this was not the case: of the nineteen Bonnymuir men sentenced to transportation, only two, Andrew White and Thomas MacFarlane, are known to have returned home. White lived in Glasgow until his death in 1872, and is buried at Sighthill, near the monument to Baird and Hardie, and MacFarlane is recorded as being resident in Condorrat in the 1841 census and died around 1850, when he was buried in Cumbernauld churchyard.[92]

It is perhaps fitting to conclude with the last words of the three Radicals condemned to death, firstly from James Wilson's speech from the scaffold in Glasgow, 30 August 1820:

> I commit my sacred cause, which is that of Freedom, to the vindication of posterity [...] I appeal to posterity for the justice which has in all ages, and in all countries been accorded to them who have suffered martyrdom in the glorious cause of truth and liberty.[93]

John Baird's speech from the scaffold at Stirling on 8 September 1820 included the words:

> I do not mean to say much, only that what I have hitherto done, and which has brought me here, was for the cause of Truth and Justice.[94]

Andrew Hardie's speech, also at Stirling on 8 September 1820, included the following:

> Friends, I declare before God, I believe to die a martyr in the cause of Truth and Justice. Please, after this is over, go quietly home and read the Bible, remembering the fate of Baird and Hardie.[95]

Of the three only Wilson was a contemporary of Thomas Muir, and may have met him at the Convention of 1792. The others were young children when Muir's trial took place, yet all of them echo his famous speech from the dock:

> What then has been my crime? [...] having dared to be, according to the measure of my feeble abilities, a strenuous and active advocate for an equal representation of the People – in the House of the People [...] I have devoted myself to the cause of the People. It is a good cause. – It shall ultimately prevail. – It shall finally triumph.[96]

Appendix

ADDRESS TO The Inhabitants of Great Britain & Ireland;

FRIENDS AND COUNTRYMEN:
Roused from that torpid state in which We have been sunk for so many years, We are, at length, compelled, from the extremity of our sufferings, and the contempt heaped upon our Petitions for redress, to assert our Rights, at the hazard of our lives and proclaim to the world the real motives, which (if not misrepresented by designing men, would have United all ranks) have reduced us to take up Arms for the redress of our Common Grievances.

The numerous Public Meetings held throughout the Country have demonstrated to you that the interests of all Classes are the same. That the protection of Life and Property of the Rich Man, is the interest of the Poor Man, and in return, it is in the interest of the Rich to protect the Poor from the iron grasp of Despotism; for when its victims are exhausted in the lower circles there are no assurance but that its ravages will be continued in the upper; For once set in motion, it will continue to move until a succession of Victims fall.

Our principles are few, and founded on the basis of our Constitution which was purchased with the Dearest Blood of our Ancestors, and which we swear to transmit to posterity unsullied, or Perish in the Attempt. Equality of Rights (not of Property) is the object for which we contend, and which we consider as the only security for our Liberties and Lives.

Let us show to the world that We are not that Lawless Sanguinary Rabble which Our Oppressors would persuade the higher circles we are — but a Brave and Generous People, determined to be Free. Liberty or Death is our Motto, and we have sworn to return home in triumph - or return no more!

SOLDIERS:

Shall You, Countrymen, bound by the sacred obligation of an oath, to defend your Country and your King from enemies, whether foreign or domestic, plunge your Bayonets into the Bosoms of Fathers and Brothers at the unrelenting Orders of a Cruel Faction and sacrifice those feelings which hold in common with the rest of mankind? Soldiers, turn your eyes towards Spain, and there behold the happy effects resulting from the Union of Soldiers and Citizens. Look to that quarter, and there behold the yoke of hated Despotism, broke by the Unanimous wish of the People and Soldiery, happily accomplished without Bloodshed. And shall You, who taught those Soldiers the principles of Liberty, refuse to spread them in your own Country? Forbid it Heaven! Come forward then at once, and Free your Country and your King~ from the influence of those base maxims that have ruined our Country.

FRIENDS AND COUNTRYMEN:

The eventful period has now arrived, where the Services of all will be required, for the forwarding of an object so universally wished, as just and equal Laws. Come forward, then, and countenance those who have begun the completion of so arduous a task, and support the laudable efforts which we are making to give to Britons those rights consecrated to them by the Magna Carta and the Bill of Rights and Sweep from our Shores that Corruption which has degraded us below the dignity of Man.

Owing to the misrepresentations which have gone abroad with regard to our intentions, we think it indispensably necessary to Declare inviolable all Public and Private Property. And, we hereby call upon all Justices of the Peace, and all others, to suppress Outrage of every description; and to endeavour to secure those Guilty of such offences, that they may receive that Punishment which such violation of Justice demand.

In the present state of affairs, and during the continuation of so momentous a struggle, we earnestly request all to desist from their Labour from and after this day, the First of April, and attend wholly to the recovery of their Rights and consider it as the duty of every man not to recommence until he is in possession of those Rights which distinguishes the Freeman from the Slaves, viz. That of giving consent to the laws by which he is governed. We, therefore, recommend to the Proprietors of Public Works, and all others, to Stop the one, and Shut up the other, until order is restored, as We will be accountable for no damages which may be sustained; and which after this Public Intimation, they can have no claim to.

And We hereby give notice to all those who shall be found guilty of Pillage or Plunder that they shall meet with the severest Punishment, as we are determined by every means in our power, to prevent those evils of which we have ourselves so just reason to complain.

By order of the Committee of Reformation for Forming a Provisional Government,

Glasgow 1st April, 1820.

Britons – God – Justice – The wishes of all good Men are with us. – Join together and make it one Cause and the Nations of the Earth shall hail the day when the Principles of Liberty shall be those of our Native Soil.

Notes and References

1 Devine, 1999, p.227.
2 Donnelly, 1975, p.10.
3 Berresford Ellis and Mac a'Ghobhainn, 1989, p.183.
4 Halliday, 1993, pp.15-16; Devine, 1999, pp.209-10; Berresford Ellis and Mac a'Ghobhainn, 1989, pp.72-3.
5 Young, 1996, p.39; Donnelly, 1995, p.11.
6 Berresford Ellis and Mac a'Ghobhainn, 1989, p.66.
7 Dowds, 2000; Dowds, 2001, pp.8-15.
8 Devine, 1999, p.209.
9 Devine, 1999, pp.211-2.
10 Berresford Ellis and Mac a'Ghobhainn, 1989, pp.84-5.
11 Elliott, 1977, pp.45-61.
12 Moody and Martin, 1994, p.247.
13 Berresford Ellis & Mac a'Ghobhainn, 1989, p.77.
14 Devine, 1999, p.211.
15 McFarland, 1994; Young, 1996, pp.47-50.
16 Lynch, 1992, p.390.
17 Devine, 1999, pp.217-8.
18 Devine, 1999, pp.219-20.
19 Malthus, 1803.
20 Devine, 1999, p.220.
21 Berresford Ellis and Mac a'Ghobhainn, 1989, pp.93-4.
22 Berresford Ellis and Mac a'Ghobhainn, 1989, p.94; Halliday, 1993, pp.16-17.
23 Report, dated 3 February 1820, in Glasgow City Archives, E1/1/10.
24 Berresford Ellis and Mac a'Ghobhainn, 1989, p.91.
25 Devine, 1999, p.224.
26 Berresford Ellis and Mac a'Ghobhainn, 1989, pp.107-109.
27 Devine, 1999, p.226.
28 Berresford Ellis and Mac a'Ghobhainn, 1989, pp.118-9.
29 Berresford Ellis and Mac a'Ghobhainn, 1989, p.138.
30 [Mackenzie], 1832, p.14.
31 Berresford Ellis and Mac a'Ghobhainn, 1989, p.139.
32 Mileham, [nd]. p.3.
33 National Records of Scotland (NRS), RH4/187, *Murray of Polmaise Papers*, 1/41 Letter of Duke of Montrose, 21 December 1819.
34 NRS, *Murray of Polmaise Papers*, 1/42, Letter of Alexander Junkin, Nail-maker at St Ninians, 26 February 1820.
35 [Mackenzie], 1832, pp.9-12.
36 Bayne, 1995, p.16: Donnelly, 1976, pp.27-8.
37 See Appendix, p.286 above.
38 Bayne, 1995, p.17.
39 Donnelly, 1976, p.28.

40 Devine, 1999, pp.227-8.
41 Halliday, 1993, pp.19-20.
42 Halliday, 1993, p.23; Berresford Ellis and Mac a'Ghobhainn, 1989, pp.144-5.
43 NRS, RH4/187, *Murray of Polmaise Papers*, 1/44, Letter of John Fraser, 2 April 1820.
44 Clark, 1993, p.7.
45 The *Glasgow Chronicle* carried an article on 18 April indicating that there were disturbances in Yorkshire in the first days of 1820, and these may have been an attempt to co-ordinate a rising with the Scots.
46 Donnelly, 1976, p.29; Clark, 1993, pp.7-8.
47 Bayne, 1995, pp.16-19; Donnelly, 1976, p.32; Dowds, 2013, p.11.
48 Halliday, 1993, p.26; Berresford Ellis and Mac a'Ghobhainn, 1989, pp.181-2.
49 Berresford Ellis and Mac a'Ghobhainn, 1989, pp.151-152.
50 A Hardie, *The Radical Revolt*: written in prison and published by P Walsh, Rutherglen 1820, p.3. Letters and the notes for this account of the rising were smuggled out of the prison by Grannie Duncan who, with her daughter, was responsible for feeding the prisoners. The documents were hidden in the porridge pot she brought with her. Delivered to John Fallon in Stirling they were sent on to Robert Goodwin in Glasgow, as the letter indicated.
51 Dowds, 2013, p.11.
52 Kean was never seen again. King claimed they became separated while hiding from cavalry. Dowds, 2013, p.12.
53 NRS RH4/187, *Murray of Polmaise Papers*, 1/45, Murray to Sir Thomas Bradford, 1/46, Michael Shaw Nicolson to Murray, 1/48, James Davidson to Murray.
54 NRS, *Murray of Polmaise Papers*, 1/52 Two Letters of Captain MS Nicolson to Murray, 4 April 1820.
55 Green, 1825, vol.1, p.320. Evidence of Lieutenant Hodgson.
56 Green, 1825, vol.1, p.135.
57 Hardie, 1820, p.4; Green, 1825, vol.1, pp.132-3; Berresford Ellis and Mac a'Ghobhainn, 1989, pp.167- 8; Halliday, 1993, p.29; Dowds, 2013, p.12.
58 Hardie, 1820, p.4; Green, 1825, vol.1, pp.133-4.
59 Dowds, 2013, p.12.
60 Green, 1825, vol.1, pp.135-6; Hardie, 1820, p.5; with reference to Lieutenant Hodgson, Hardie wrote, 'Although my enemy, I do him nothing but justice by saying that he is a brave and generous man; he came up in front of his men, and I am truly happy (but surprised) that he was not killed, as I know there were several shots fired at him'.
61 Hardie, 1820, p.3.
62 Green, 1825, vol.1, p.327.
63 Berresford Ellis and Mac a'Ghobhainn, 1989, pp.182-4; Halliday (1993), pp.32-3.

64 Devine (1999), p.227; Berresford Ellis and Mac a'Ghobhainn, 1989, p.187; Halliday, 1993, p.33.
65 Berresford Ellis and Mac a'Ghobhainn, 1989, p.187.
66 Halliday (1993), p.33; Berresford Ellis and Mac a'Ghobhainn, 1989, pp.188-190.
67 Berresford Ellis and Mac a'Ghobhainn, 1989, pp.191-203; Halliday, 1993, pp.333-4.
68 NRS, RH4/187, *Murray of Polmaise Papers*, 11/81, letter of Reverend Robert Rennie, 26 April 1820.
69 Hardie, 1820, p.6.
70 Green, 1825, vol.1, pp.14-17.
71 Sir William Rae's background serves as an example of the political system the radicals sought to change; he was chosen at different times as MP for the rotten boroughs of Anstruther, Hawick and Bute in Scotland and Portarlington in Ireland.
72 NRS, JC21/1. Treason Trials. Commission of Oyer and Terminer.
73 NRS, JC21/7. Treason Trials. Writs of Capias Against Persons Not Brought to Trial.
74 CJ Green, 1825, vol.3, p.8.
75 NAS, JC21/1. Treason Trials 1820-21. Commission of Oyer and Terminer.
76 Berresford Ellis and Mac a'Ghobhainn, 1989, p.249.
77 Berresford Ellis and Mac a'Ghobhainn, 1989, p.251.
78 Macfarlane, 1981, pp.11-12.
79 Green, 1825, vol.1, pp.81-9.
80 Hardie, 1820, p.7.
81 *Stirling Journal*, 15 July 1820; and *Glasgow Herald*, 19 July 1820.
82 Dowds, 2013, p.14.
83 Hardie had served with the Berwickshire Militia, and Baird with the 2nd Battalion, 95th Regiment (Rifle Brigade) during the French Wars.
84 Berresford Ellis and Mac a'Ghobhainn, 1989, p.241.
85 Macfarlane, 1981, gives brief biographical details of all the Scottish Radical convicts of 1820 who were sent to New South Wales.
86 Clark, 1993, pp.8-10; Dowds, 2014-15, pp.10-11.
87 Green, 1825, vol.3, pp.469-71; Dowds, 2014-15, p.15.
88 Green, 1825, vol.3, pp.473-4; Dowds, 2014-15, pp.14-15.
89 Green, 1825, vol.3, p.474.
90 Pentland, 2008, pp.141-2.
91 Donnelly, 1976, p.33.
92 Macfarlane, 1981, pp.57-60 and pp.37-40.
93 Sherry, 1968, p.34.
94 Sherry, 1968, p.50.
95 Sherry, 1968, p.52.
96 Robertson, 1793, p.130.

James Muir, Hop Merchant, Glasgow
and his family connection with the Parish of Campsie

Alex Watson

The involvement of Thomas Muir, younger of Huntershill, in the movement for political reform in Britain catapulted him on to the world stage of the 1790s. Without doubt he was politically enlightened and his unswaying determination to stand up for universal suffrage is to be highly commended. However, his treatment by the establishment of the day was harsh to say the least and he paid the ultimate price for his convictions, and ultimately this led to his early death at the age of 33 in Chantilly, France.

Thomas was the only son of James Muir, a prosperous hop merchant in Glasgow, and his wife Margaret Smith; they also had one daughter, Janet. Much has been written about Thomas and his short but significant life. The purpose of this essay is to use this material, and some other less well-known sources, to trace the parentage of his father, James Muir and connect him with the Muir brothers that settled in the parish of Campsie about 1650.[1] Today there is an unparalleled interest in genealogy and the internet has made access to family trees, public records and archive material available to computer users all over the world. People can now make contact with other researchers and share information in a way previously unimagined. The down side of this is that a great deal of information that is unsourced and has no tangible evidence to back it up is being linked together and accepted by others as factual; this information is being repeatedly published on websites and blogs. Many people across the world are driven to trace their family history in this way, often with a concentration on tales of lost family fortunes or a relationship to someone of note. Thomas Muir is a typical case; there are no known descendants of Thomas, and so any connection has to be through his sister Janet's descendants or from a sibling of one of his parents, James and Margaret. There are many people who claim to be descended from the brothers of James Muir. The source of these claims has been based on oral history which has been passed down over several generations, without a paper trail to confirm the family connection. Unfortunately, no one has so far been able to confirm their stories, because of the lack of records, and also the poor condition of the parish records that do exist.

A further problem relates to the fact that Muir is a very common surname in Scotland, found all over the country and further afield. George Black's reference work, *The Surnames of Scotland*, states that it derives from 'residence beside a moor or heath', one of the earliest records of the name being Thomas de la More who was the executor of the will of Devorguilla de Balliol in 1291.[2]

An excellent record of the history of the Parish of Campsie was collected by John Cameron. In 1876 Cameron became involved in the annual Campsie Re-union that was held at that time. In February 1885 he was offered the chair and wishing to impart some freshness to his speech as Chairman, he 'referred to some matters connected with the early history of the parish'.[3] The speech that Cameron gave was widely enjoyed and he recalls that

[...] this led to my receiving an invitation from the committee of the Campsie Mechanics' Institution to deliver one or two lectures in the Town Hall, Lennoxtown, in connection with their following winter course. I accepted this invitation, and gave two lectures – one on 'The Ecclesiastical History of the Parish' and another on 'The Parish of Campsie: its Physical Features and Geology, its Landed Families, and the Rise of its Manufactures'.[4]

Cameron was to accumulate a large amount of local history over the next few years from people in the Parish. His information regarding the Birdston feuars came from Dr DP Stewart, who in turn had received it from Mr Alexander Galloway, a resident of Birdston in the period 1836-44 when he was the resident factor to Mr JLK Lennox of Woodhead. The documents are entitled 'Notes for Dr Stewart as to the lands of Birdston, and the families of the Muirs, portioners thereof. 4th December, 1860'.[5] These notes were presumably recorded by Mr Galloway from oral history passed on to him by members of the Muir families. A great deal of

Cameron's research has been preserved and is deposited with East Dunbartonshire Archives in Kirkintilloch. The information that he gathered was diligently recorded, after which he gave lectures on his research. Eventually the material was compiled and printed in a single volume in 1892, as *The Parish of Campsie*.

Cameron tells us that 'The brothers Muir were said to have come from the neighbourhood of Rowallan Castle, between Kilmarnock and Stewarton, in Ayrshire, and were connected by lineal descent from the Mures, Barons of Rowallan. A member of this family, Elizabeth Mure, was first wife of King Robert II'.[6] This may be true, but unfortunately no further information was given about this connection by Cameron; it is possible that he was adding a bit of spin to his lectures. The novels of Sir Walter Scott inspired many tourists to visit Scotland and Queen Victoria's love of Balmoral, which was purchased in 1852 by Prince Albert, helped to perpetuate the romantic image of the country in the public imagination. Queen Victoria is known to have been deeply interested in her Stewart ancestry. It may be that further research into the Muir brothers will establish whether their link to the Mures of Rowallan was founded in fact. If possible a DNA project could help to make this connection.

There is a testament dated 28th August 1622 for a Robert Muir,[7] in Beirzairdis (Bearyards) at Bishop Briggs, Parish of Calder. This document is very difficult to read, but there are two names that are legible: William Muir and Robert Muir. The author has been unable to confirm a relationship, but it could be that the Muir brothers that went to Birdston are connected to Robert Muir of Beirzairdis. Cameron goes on to summarise the writs for William Muir of Birdston:

William Muir, Ellishaugh, 21st October, 1653. Birdston, ⅛th part. Crooked ridge possle by said William Muir and his son Robert. In 1752, by contract of excambion, John Muir, then owner, and Malcolm Brown, Kirkintilloch, some small portions of land are interchanged for mutual convenience, probably in consequence of a change in the bed of the Kelvin. The lands of Wester Aulton were acquired by one of these Muirs, Another of the Muirs went to Glasgow, from whom sprang the famous Thomas Muir of Huntershill.[8]

Because of this last statement the author feels justified in attaching James Muir to the family tree of William Muir of Ellishaugh. William of Ellishaugh had at least one son, Robert (mentioned in the above writs). In his testament[9] dated Burdstone 1 July 1678, his spouse and executrix is named as Jonet Rankon [sic]. Two daughters are mentioned: Joanna and Barbara. The testament is witnessed by James Muir in Burdstone [sic], Robert Muir, David Muir coupar in Kirkintilloch and William Muir. William died shortly afterwards. His testament testamentar was recorded at Hamilton & Campsie Commissary Court of 18 September 1678.

There are several publications about Thomas Muir that mention his relations and the family connection to the parish of Campsie; unfortunately there are no primary sources given for most of this information. The present author's objective is to establish the primary sources where possible and attempt to establish James Muir's link to the parish of Campsie. This would then enable others to make a connection to this branch of the Muir of Birdston family tree. The Parish records for Campsie are in very poor condition and many pages are incomplete. It may be that the records were stored at the manse and were damaged during the fire that took place there on 22 August 1797, as recounted by Cameron: '[...] when Mr. and Mrs. Lapslie were absent, the outbuildings at the manse were deliberately set on fire and burned to the ground, and but for the prompt assistance rendered by the people in the Clachan, the manse itself would have shared the same fate'.[10] Whether the records were damaged during this event or not, they appear to have suffered from fire damage; in many entries only names can be partially made out, rendering the information of little or no use to the researcher. There are also large gaps where the records just don't exist, sometimes for several years at a time. This leaves you with links missing from the chain of a family tree.

The Muirs of Campsie

One way round this is to look for other sources of information. Cameron provides a chapter on the history of Birdston, a small hamlet in the parish of Campsie (county of Stirling). He tells us that the Muir family in question appeared in Birdston about 1653. Birdston had been part of the Kincaid lands, which were subsequently possessed by the Hamiltons of Bardowie. Between 1653 and 1658 the lands of Birdston were divided and feued off in eight parts. James Donaldson feued one half of the lands, while David Calder and three Muir brothers, William, John and James, feued ⅛th each.[11] William Muir, feued his ⅛th part of Birdston on 21 October 1653; he was recorded as, 'then in Bogqhuharrage'.[12] The lands of Bogqhuharrage were like Birdston historically possessed by the Hamiltons of Bardowie; archives for the title to these lands can be found in the Lennox of Woodhead archives deposited in Glasgow City Archives. A search of the name record cards in the archives produced a reference for 'Muir, William of Balqharrage, par of Campsie, Stirlingshire. title to lands of Balglass, 1648'.[13]

Birdston village in the nineteenth century.

The Parish records for Campsie are 'available' for the periods:
Births 1646 – 1854
Marriages 1663 – 1854
Deaths 1732 – 1854

However, these runs are not complete. On inspection it is evident that a great deal of fire damage has affected them, rendering many passages unreadable, while large sections are missing or are in such poor condition that only parts of the recorded information is legible.

So what do we learn about Thomas Muir's parents?

James Muir[14] died on 24 April 1801, aged 67 years, cause of death recorded as 'Aged'.

Margaret Smith[15] died on 14 October 1803, aged 65 yrs, cause of death again given as 'Aged'.

James Muir and Margaret Smith were married in 1764. There was a proclamation of the forthcoming marriage in Bo'ness on 5 October 1764.[16] Margaret, we are told in the proclamation is from the parish of Bo'ness. The marriage took place in Glasgow on 7 October 1764.[17]

Their first child, Thomas, was born on 24 August 1765. As Christina Bewley notes this was most likely above his father's shop on the east side of the High Street of Glasgow. The birth was witnessed by Thomas Wright and David Muir, merchants.

A daughter, Janet followed, born on 30 May 1767, in Glasgow. The birth was witnessed by Thomas & John Wright.

A description and location for James Muir's premises in the High St can be found on the Sasine for the purchase of the property, dated 13 December 1771, in favour of James Muir merchant in Glasgow:

All and Whole these the said William Allan his two shops on the ground story of the fore tenement of land aftermentioned lying within the Burgh of Glasgow on the East side of the street Leeding from the mercate cross to the Blackfriars wynd Item the Little cellar at the back of the said shops and which cellar is now taken into and possessed as a part of one of the said shops, as the said Shops are now possessed by John Craig Cordiner, and the said James Muir himself [...] William Allan merchant in Glasgow with consent of Marrion Calder his Spouse and she for herself with consent of her husband for all Liferent or other right and title whatever she had or could claim for the fore shops & cellars aftermentioned. And they both with and consent & assent and also with consent of David Calder white iron smith in Glasgow Son procreate between the deceased David Calder farmer in Inchbreak and Helen Graham his spouse.[18]

The Calders were one of the original feuing[19] families along with the Muirs and Calder's of Birdston from the 1650s. There is also a connection through marriage: Agnes Calder[20] relict of the deceased James Muir portioner of Birdstone and last spouse of David Findlay of Boogside [sic]. From James's death record we are told that he was 67 years at the time of his decease, suggesting that he was born about 1734, but a search on the ScotlandsPeople website for births in Campsie provides no records for a James Muir born 1715-1741. A full search covering the whole of Scotland returns only twenty births for the period 1733-1735, none of which are for the Parish of Campsie. So if James was born in Campsie, the record of his birth must have been in one of the years that suffered most from the fire.

Christina Bewley[21] tells us that 'My grandfather was a descendant of one of Muir's uncles, and was only eight when his parents and sisters were lost at sea' and that 'His father, James was a younger son of the 'bonnet laird' (roughly equivalent to a tenant farmer) of Hayston and Birdston farms near Kirkintilloch'.[22] She gives no source for this information, neither does she give a name for her grandfather or the uncle of Thomas Muir's that he was descended from. However, we know from Annie Fisher's testimony during Thomas's trial in 1793 that he had an uncle by the name of Alexander Muir:

She depones that she has bought, at two different times, for my uncle Alexander Muir, at my desire, a copy of the first part, and a copy of the second part of the Rights of Man. Can you suppose, that if my intentions had been felonious, I would have introduced such writings to my own family? Can you imagine that I could have wished to involve, in the conflagration of my country, my nearest relations to whose property I may eventually succeed. Why is not Alexander Muir brought forward as a witness? Certain it is, that he was closely interrogated, before the inquisition held by Mr. Sheriff Honeyman. But the Lord Advocate says, that his feelings would not permit him to examine the uncle against the nephew.[23]

There is no death record for Alexander Muir; however there is a Testament Dative and inventory for 'Alexander Muir late Portioner of Haystoun',[24] dated 25 April 1797, with his brother, James Muir Grocer in Glasgow, named as Cautioner. James Muir placed an advertisement in the *Glasgow Courier* on 15 December 1798:[25] 'To be let or sold' Huntershill with forty five acres of Arable land and thirty acres of moss and also 'A small farm in Hayston, in the parish of Campsie'.

Muir of Hayston

The Sasine for the sale of the above land at Hayston is dated 27 March 1800. It recounts 'that the now deceased Alexander Muir Farmer at Huntershill and portioner of Hayston Brother of the said James Muir [...] that the said James Muir is immediate elder Brother and nearest lawful heir of conquest of the deceased Alexander Muir'. The lands are more fully described in the following way:

[...] the subjects are a part of the just and equal fourth part of the lands of Hayston sometime purchased by David Muir of Springfield from Mathew Drew of Westquarter with the teinds parsonage and vicarage of the same all now known by the name of Springfield lying within the parish of Campsie and Sheriffdom of Stirling and contained in a charter of Confirmation thereof granted by the now deceased Archibald Stirling of Keir Esquire to the also deceased William Jaffray sometime Keeper of his Majesty's stores at Halifax thereafter residing in Stirling dated the twenty third day of December seventeen hundred and seventy six.[26]

When James Muir purchased Huntershill on 17 April 1782, Alexander Muir Portioner of *Braehead of Kirkintilloch* is one of the witnesses to the Disposition.

A search of the Dumbarton Sasines abridgements for Alexander Muir returns the following:

Alexander Muir in Braehead dated Jan 1st 1783; Seised, Nov 30. 1782, in a Tenement called BRAEHEAD, and a piece of in the territory of Kirkintilloch; part of Easter mains of Kirkintilloch called Adamshaugh, & a piece of ground on the north side of the water of Kelvin, and Teinds, par. Wester Lenzie; in security of £130; on Bond by John Winning, tenant, Easter Calder, Nov. 9. 1782.[27]

The full Sasine recalls that the property being disposed of was formerly the property of William Muir Portioner of Kirkintilloch, it was sold to Alexander Cuthill who appears to have defaulted on payments when he was proprietor of the land, an inhibition was raised against Cuthill and Alexander Muir subsequently sold it to John Winning, on payment of the heritable bond.

A further search of the Sasine register shows that the disposition by 'William Muir portioner of Kirkintilloch heretable proprietor of the lands and oyrs' to Alexander Cuthill Dyster in Kirkintilloch, took place on 5 November 1743 and was recorded on 6 August 1751.[28]

A Sasine recorded 11 May 1752[29] recalls a disposition of an 'Eight part of the Easter mains of Kirkintilloch' dated 11 November 1748 to 'William Muir lawfull son of the deceased John Muir portioner of Birdstoun'. It may be that these lands are part of the lands subject to the 1752 disposition, but unfortunately there is not a full description. It may be that this is another Muir altogether, as so many of the Muir cousins share the same Christian name. We also know from John Cameron's book that by a contract of excambion in 1752 some small portions of land are exchanged for mutual convenience, probably in consequence of a change in the course of the Kelvin; this exchange of lands took place several times again including the 1760s and 1770s.[30]

A disposition by David Muir late Portioner of Hayston then of Springfield, dated 14th December 1769, recorded 29th December 1795, to John Watt Surgeon in Kirkintilloch, for an annual rent of twelve pounds ten shillings sterling... 'All and Whole these the said Robert Muir his four acres or thereby of the lands of Easter mains of Kirkintilloch'.[31]

There appears to be some relationship between Alexander Muir, David Muir of Hayston of Springfield, and William Muir, Portioner of Kirkintilloch.

At some point prior to 1782, Alexander Muir acquired the land at Braehead which was formerly possessed by William Muir, portioner of Kirkintilloch. In 1787, Alexander Muir, Farmer at Huntershill is seized of several parcels of land; at Hayston, Easterhaugh and Well acre in a disposition dated 3 March and recorded 14 May 1787,[32] part of the land included in this disposal was formerly possessed by 'David Muir late Portioner of Hayston then of Springfield'. David Muir disposed of part of his lands to William Jaffray in 1776[33]. The Sasine register prior to 1782 is not indexed and would require being searched page by page to locate Sasines to confirm how and when David Muir was seised in this land and how it ultimately transferred to Alexander Muir. There are no birth records for an Alexander Muir born in this parish at the appropriate period; it would appear that like James's record this has been lost.

James Muir, Merchant

We know from the marriage record of James Muir and Margaret Smith that at the time of the marriage James was a 'merchant'. To be a merchant he would need to have been a Burgess and Guild Brother; this would have allowed him to carry out business within the boundary of the Burgh. The author has not been able to identify him as an apprentice from *Burgesses and Guild Brethren of Glasgow, 1751-1846*.[34] However, it is possible that he could have served an apprenticeship in either Stirlingshire or Dunbartonshire. We do not know anything about his early work/life before he moved to Glasgow but he is mentioned in 1795, when his son in law David Blair becomes a Burgess and Guild Brother through James:

Blair, David, merchant, B. And G.B., as mar. Janet, dau to James Muir, merchant, B. and G.B. 15 Jan

Glasgow City Archives have the original 'List of the Matriculated members of the Merchants' House of Glasgow',[35] a volume dating from 1768. The pages are set out in columns with headings to record information about the 'Intrant': Membership number, Year of Matriculation, Intrant's name, designation and parent's name and designation. The information in the matriculation book is recorded by the member in their own hand writing, and when compared to a letter known to be written by James Muir, it would appear to be the same:[36]

No.	Year of Matriculation	Intrant's name	Designation	Parents name and Designation
184	1789 Sept, 3	James Muir	Home & Foreign Trader	Son of William Muir farmer in Campsie Shire of Stirling & Agins [sic] Young his Spouse

This would appear to be the only record of James Muir's parentage; it also confirms his connection to Campsie, which we have not been able to establish by means of the parish records.

With this information a new search of the OPR records is possible in the hope that although the records condition is poor there may a record of marriage and possibly other children born to James's parents other than Alexander.

The following records are available:

01/02/1721 William Muir in this paroch ... Young in Kilsyth Gave up ... For proclamation in order to ... [37]
25/12/1721 William Muir and his ... Agnes Young in Haystoun ... their child baptized called Jo[38]
12/01/1724 William Muir and his Spouse Agnes Young in Haystoun had ye child baptized called William Wittnesses Thomas Reid and Robert ...[39]
07/07/1726 William Muir and his spouse A ... Young in Haystoun had ye child ... Called David Wittness John Muir & ... William Henderson [40]

No other relevant OPR records appear to exist; however there may have been more children as there is a gap between David's birth in 1726 and James c.1734, with Alexander's birth still later.

It would seem likely that the David Muir merchant, who was a witness to the birth of Thomas in 1765 was the third son born to William Muir and Agnes Young on 7 July 1726 in Haystoun[41] and therefore elder brother to James and Alexander, the same David from whom Alexander acquired the land in Hayston. The author has not found any links to show what became of the other two children of William and Agnes for which there are birth records. It may be that they are simply hard to identify amongst the numerous

Muirs in the Parish of Campsie or they may have pre-deceased David who may then have come into possession of the land that was tenanted or feued by his father at Haystoun. David appears to have passed ownership to Alexander who we know was a farmer. It may be that Alexander actually farmed the land and that is why it came to him when David moved to Leith.

It is also difficult to know if the first child born to William & Agnes was male or female as the only letters decipherable of the Christian name are 'Jo', which could be for Jonet(t) or John. We know that William and Agnes were living in Haystoun and they had at least three children whilst living there. James Stirling of Keir feued the land of Haystoune [sic] in four parts:

> 9th Nov 1710,[42] One fourth part of Haystoune ... thereof as the Samen are possessed by John, Patrick & Robert Reid, Wm Henderson & John Muir, to Malcolm Willsone, in Kilwannatt
> 9th Nov 1710,[43] One fourth part of Haystoune ... thereof as the Samen are possessed by John, Patrick & Robert Reid, Wm Henderson & John Muir to Thomas Reid in Carlestoun
> 9th Nov 1710,[44] One fourth part of Haystoune ... thereof as the Samen are possessed by John, Patrick & Robert Reid, Wm Henderson & John Muir to William & Patrick Drews, lawfull sons of William Drews of Auchenloch.
> 22nd May 1712,[45] One fourth part of Haystoune ... thereof as the Samen are possessed by John Muir & Jonet Henderson his spouse, to William Grahame, merchant in Campsie. [sic]

It may be coincidental that David Muir's birth was witnessed by John Muir and William Henderson, but the author believes that it is more likely that William Henderson, who like John Muir was a tenant in Haystoun, was a relative of Jonet Henderson (possibly her father or brother). There is no marriage record for John Muir and Jonet Henderson. There are two OPR birth records for children to a William Muir and Jonet Henderson in Campsie: Elizabeth Muir[46] on 6 November 1693 (in very poor condition and impossible to make out if there is a place name); and a second child named William[47] on 12 July 1696 in Hayston [sic].

We do not know what happened to John & Jonet Muir after

William Grahame purchased the land at Hayston. It may be that they are the parents of William Muir who was seised in one eighth part of Easter Mains in Kirkintilloch in 1752, described as 'William Muir Lawfull son of the deceased John Muir portioner of Birdstoun'.

The author can find no records for John Muir that would confirm this theory, but it is possible that William Muir of Ellishaugh and Jonet Rankein (Rankon) had more than one son. We know that they had a son named Robert because he is mentioned by John Cameron as acquiring land with his father in 1658.[48] There are no records for Robert Muir, either for marriage or birth of children. Cameron's phrase that 'In 1752, by contract of excambion, John Muir, then owner, and Malcolm Brown, Kirkintilloch' implies that John Muir is descended from William of Ellishaugh, which would mean that there is a link missing between William and Jonet Rankein and the owner of their land in 1752.

The author can find no record of David Muir as a Burgess and Guild Brother in Glasgow, neither is he listed as a Member of the Merchants House. We know from the Sasines registry that he was described as a Portioner of Springfield of Hayston. There is no mention of him as a merchant in the Sasines.

However there are several OPR records for David Muir of Haystoun:

10/08/1769 (Baptism) David Muir & Christian Parlane, Haystoun – Had a daughter named Margaret Wittnesses William Muir Robert ... [49] [sic]
18/08/1771 David Muir of Springfield – And Christian Parlane his spouse – Had a daughter Bapt named Margaret Witnesses William & Alexander Muir [50] [sic]
19/08/1773 David Muir & Christ ... Parlane of Springfie .. Had their daughter bap .. At Calder called Christi .. Witnesses John Forsyt.. And James Henderson [51] [sic]

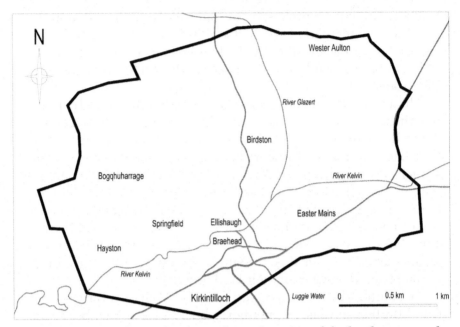

The above map shows the approximate location of the lands possessed by this branch of the Muir family, in the Parish of Campsie and Kirkintilloch in the 17th/18th century.

The Leith Connection

There are no other records for David Muir and Christian Parlane in Campsie; they appear to have moved to Leith, possibly about 1776. A Sasine registered on 11 August 1792 recalls a disposition and assignation by Robert Galloway in favour of David Muir of Springfield of Hayston and further records a disposition by David Muir to William Jaffray on 19 August 1776.[52]

Post Office Directories for Edinburgh and Leith[53] were printed annually for the years 1773-76, then again for 1784 onwards. There is no listing for David Muir in the 1773-76 Leith directories; however he does appear later, as follows:

June 1784 - June 1785, p.103. Muir David, hop merchant, on the Shore.
June 1785 - June 1786, p.107. Muir David, hop merchant, on the Shore.
June 1788 - June 1790, p.118. Muir David, hoop [sic] merchant, on the Shore.

It appears that David followed his brother James into the
hop business and established premises at Leith, moving from
Haystoun at some point after 1776, and before 1787. This is only
a supposition as we do not know exactly when Alexander Muir
came into possession of the land at Haystoun that had formerly
belonged to David Muir of Springfield, but it was prior to David's
death, which was reported the *Scots Magazine* in 1789.[54]

Were James and David Muir in a partnership, running separate
businesses, or had James expanded his business to Edinburgh,
with his brother employed by him? Christina Bewley tells us
that 'James had relations who were prosperous hop growers at
Maidstone in Kent, so, as he was unlikely to inherit his father's
property, he went into the hop trade'.[55] Again Bewley does not give
a source for this information; but from an advert in the *Glasgow
Mercury* dated 18 October 1781, we can see that James Muir is
selling produce from Kent:

JAMES MUIR – Has brought from Kent, a large parcel of
Kentish Hops, which he sells as low as any merchant in
London.
Also Kentish apples – Golden pippens, Nonpareils, Golden
Remets, Lemon pippens, Long Lasters, Grey Rustins,
Polonia, Peermains & etc.
Also – Sun-raisins, currants, Jordan & Valencia Almonds,
Carvey seed, Orange Peel, Poland starch. 94th door above
the Cross-well.

The death of David's wife Christian was recorded in 1803:
Christian Parling relict of David Muir late Merchant in
Leith aged 64 years died the 9th buried the 12th October
1803 in the Traffickers ground 4 paces East from the No
side of Wm Campbell's headstone [sic].[56]

There is no headstone visible for Christian Parlane's grave
today, but just a short distance from the area that is described in
the death record as her burial spot, on the surrounding wall of
South Leith Parish Churchyard, there is a large memorial to several
members of the Muir family. The first name on the gravestone is to
the memory of:

Janet Cowan, Relict of, William Muir, Merchant in
Hamburgh, Died 17th April 1852, Aged 78 years.

This would appear to be the wife of Thomas Muir's cousin,
William Muir, referred to by James Muir in a letter written in
1793: 'William Muir formerly of Leith is lying at Philadelphia his
ship is an american Bottom'.[57] Thomas wrote to William on more
than one occasion. Christina Bewley records that 'On 1 May Muir
had written, this time from Maison d'Espagne, rue Colombière,
to a cousin William Muir, a merchant at Hamburg'.[58] William and
Janet (Cowan) Muir appear to have had at least two sons: William,
born about 1801, a merchant in Leith (who married Mary Campbell
Howland and established the William Muir (Bond 9) Ltd. Whisky
distillery in Leith, in 1823);[59] and David, a banker in Leith, who
was born about 1791; also a daughter, Elizabeth, born about 1793.

Muir family graves in South Leith Parish Churchyard.

Janet Muir, and the Family Skeleton

Thomas Muir had one sister, Janet. She married David Blair, a naval officer, who later became a manufacturer in Glasgow; they had several children: David, Thomas, Janet, Robert, James, William and Louisa. Louisa married the Reverend Laurence Lockhart, DD, minister at Inchinnan, Renfrewshire. In 1857 he inherited the property of his half brother Captain William Lockhart of Milton Lockhart, Lanarkshire and Germiston, near Glasgow.[60] They had nine children: John Somerville, Janet Margaret, David Blair, Laurence William Maxwell, Elizabeth Catharine, Louisa Matilda, Violet Sophia, Mary Veronica, and William Stephen Alexander. After Louisa Blair died in 1847, Laurence Lockhart married Marion Maxwell daughter of William Maxwell of Dargavel, in 1849.[61] The latter couple had three children: James Somerville, Alexander Francis Maxwell, and Walter Somerville.

John Gilbert Lockhart, the son of Alexander Francis Maxwell Lockhart, was fascinated by the family stories of Thomas Muir. He published an article in *Blackwood's Magazine* entitled 'A Skeleton in the Cupboard', of which the following is an extract:[62]

There was a time when Thomas Muir was a skeleton in my family's cupboard; when if the story is true, a small bust of him as a boy was taken from the place of honour it had occupied in my grandfather's house and relegated to the kitchen, where its influence was evidently judged likely to be less corrupting. No doubt the removal solved the parents' problem of what should be answered when the children asked what had become of Uncle Tom. Should father swiftly change the subject, or should he mumble with shame that Uncle Tom was no longer a topic, that he was – well, he was – but surely it was bedtime. Today no such grounds for concealment or apology remain, and the truth can be told with sympathy, even pride.

The mention of a bust of Thomas is very interesting, as when Thomas was on the *Surprize* at Portsmouth awaiting transportation to Botany Bay, Thomas Banks, a sculptor took a cast of Muir's face from which he afterwards made a bust. The whereabouts of this bust is unknown. as an engraving was made of the bust we know what it looks like, and this has become the iconic image of Thomas Muir:

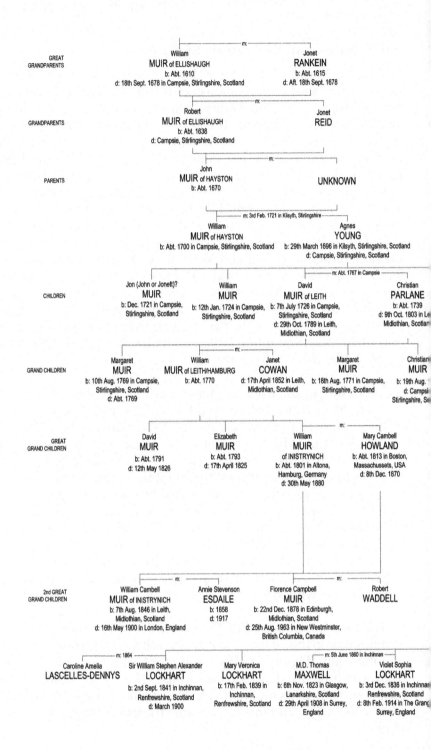

m:

William
MUIR of ELLISHAUGH
b: Abt. 1610
d: 18th Sept. 1678 in Campsie, Stirlingshire, Scotland

Jonet
RANKEIN
b: Abt. 1615
d: Aft. 18th Sept. 1678

m:

Robert
MUIR of ELLISHAUGH
b: Abt. 1638
d: Campsie, Stirlingshire, Scotland

Jonet
REID

m:

John
MUIR of HAYSTON
b: Abt. 1670

UNKNOWN

m: 3rd Feb. 1721 in Kilsyth, Stirlingshire

William
MUIR of HAYSTON
b: Abt. 1700 in Campsie, Stirlingshire, Scotland

Agnes
YOUNG
b: 29th March 1696 in Kilsyth, Stirlingshire, Scotland
d: Campsie, Stirlingshire, Scotland

m: Abt. 1767 in Campsie

Jon (John or Jonett)?
MUIR
b: Dec. 1721 in Campsie, Stirlingshire, Scotland

William
MUIR
b: 12th Jan. 1724 in Campsie, Stirlingshire, Scotland

David
MUIR of LEITH
b: 7th July 1726 in Campsie, Stirlingshire, Scotland
d: 29th Oct. 1789 in Leith, Midlothian, Scotland

Christian
PARLANE
b: Abt. 1739
d: 9th Oct. 1803 in Lei Midlothian, Scotlan

m:

Margaret
MUIR
b: 10th Aug. 1769 in Campsie, Stirlingshire, Scotland
d: Abt. 1769

William
MUIR of LEITH/HAMBURG
b: Abt. 1770

Janet
COWAN
d: 17th April 1852 in Leith, Midlothian, Scotland

Margaret
MUIR
b: 18th Aug. 1771 in Campsie, Stirlingshire, Scotland

Christian
MUIR
b: 19th Aug.
d: Campsi Stirlingshire, Se

m:

David
MUIR
b: Abt. 1791
d: 12th May 1826

Elizabeth
MUIR
b: Abt. 1793
d: 17th April 1825

William
MUIR
of INISTRYNICH
b: Abt. 1801 in Altona, Hamburg, Germany
d: 30th May 1880

Mary Cambell
HOWLAND
b: Abt. 1813 in Boston, Massachussets, USA
d: 8th Dec. 1870

m:

William Cambell
MUIR of INISTRYNICH
b: 7th Aug. 1846 in Leith, Midlothian, Scotland
d: 16th May 1900 in London, England

Annie Stevenson
ESDAILE
b: 1858
d: 1917

Florence Campbell
MUIR
b: 22nd Dec. 1878 in Edinburgh, Midlothian, Scotland
d: 25th Aug. 1963 in New Westminster, British Columbia, Canada

m:

Robert
WADDELL

m: 1864

Caroline Amelia
LASCELLES-DENNYS

Sir William Stephen Alexander
LOCKHART
b: 2nd Sept. 1841 in Inchinnan, Renfrewshire, Scotland
d: March 1900

Mary Veronica
LOCKHART
b: 17th Feb. 1839 in Inchinnan, Renfrewshire, Scotland

m: 5th June 1860 in Inchinnan

M.D. Thomas
MAXWELL
b: 6th Nov. 1823 in Glasgow, Lanarkshire, Scotland
d: 29th April 1908 in Surrey, England

Violet Sophia
LOCKHART
b: 3rd Dec. 1836 in Inchinnan Renfrewshire, Scotland
d: 8th Feb. 1914 in The Grang Surrey, England

WILLIAM MUIR FAMILY TREE

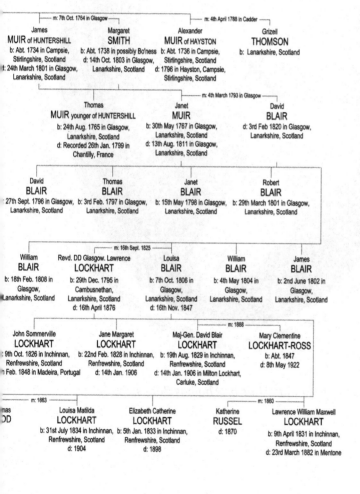

— m: 7th Oct. 1764 in Glasgow —

James
MUIR of HUNTERSHILL
b: Abt. 1734 in Campsie,
Stirlingshire, Scotland
d: 24th March 1801 in Glasgow,
Lanarkshire, Scotland

Margaret
SMITH
b: Abt. 1738 in possibly Bo'ness
d: 14th Oct. 1803 in Glasgow,
Lanarkshire, Scotland

— m: 4th April 1788 in Cadder —

Alexander
MUIR of HAYSTON
b: Abt. 1736 in Campsie,
Stirlingshire, Scotland
d: 1796 in Hayston, Campsie,
Stirlingshire, Scotland

Grizell
THOMSON
b: Lanarkshire, Scotland

— m: 4th March 1793 in Glasgow —

Thomas
MUIR younger of HUNTERSHILL
b: 24th Aug. 1765 in Glasgow,
Lanarkshire, Scotland
d: Recorded 26th Jan. 1799 in
Chantilly, France

Janet
MUIR
b: 30th May 1767 in Glasgow,
Lanarkshire, Scotland
d: 13th Aug. 1811 in Glasgow,
Lanarkshire, Scotland

David
BLAIR
d: 3rd Feb 1820 in Glasgow,
Lanarkshire, Scotland

David
BLAIR
27th Sept. 1796 in Glasgow,
Lanarkshire, Scotland

Thomas
BLAIR
b: 3rd Feb. 1797 in Glasgow,
Lanarkshire, Scotland

Janet
BLAIR
b: 15th May 1798 in Glasgow,
Lanarkshire, Scotland

Robert
BLAIR
b: 29th March 1801 in Glasgow,
Lanarkshire, Scotland

— m: 16th Sept. 1825 —

William
BLAIR
b: 18th Feb. 1808 in
Glasgow,
Lanarkshire, Scotland

Revd. DD Glasgow. Lawrence
LOCKHART
b: 29th Dec. 1795 in
Cambusnethan,
Lanarkshire, Scotland
d: 16th April 1876

Louisa
BLAIR
b: 7th Oct. 1806 in
Glasgow,
Lanarkshire, Scotland
d: 16th Nov. 1847

William
BLAIR
b: 4th May 1804 in
Glasgow,
Lanarkshire, Scotland

James
BLAIR
b: 2nd June 1802 in
Glasgow,
Lanarkshire, Scotland

— m: 1868 —

John Sommerville
LOCKHART
9th Oct. 1826 in Inchinnan,
Renfrewshire, Scotland
Feb. 1848 in Madeira, Portugal

Jane Margaret
LOCKHART
b: 22nd Feb. 1828 in Inchinnan,
Renfrewshire, Scotland
d: 14th Jan. 1906

Maj-Gen. David Blair
LOCKHART
b: 19th Aug. 1829 in Inchinnan,
Renfrewshire, Scotland
d: 14th Jan. 1906 in Milton Lockhart,
Carluke, Scotland

Mary Clementine
LOCKHART-ROSS
b: Abt. 1847
d: 8th May 1922

— m: 1863 —

mas
DD

Louisa Matilda
LOCKHART
b: 31st July 1834 in Inchinnan,
Renfrewshire, Scotland
d: 1904

Elizabeth Catherine
LOCKHART
b: 5th Jan. 1833 in Inchinnan,
Renfrewshire, Scotland
d: 1898

Katherine
RUSSEL
d: 1870

— m: 1860 —

Lawrence William Maxwell
LOCKHART
b: 9th April 1831 in Inchinnan,
Renfrewshire, Scotland
d: 23rd March 1882 in Mentone

Engraving of bust of Thomas Muir by Thomas Banks.

A start was made with a local movement to honour Thomas Muir on 17 January 1838:

PUBLIC DINNER IN HONOUR OF
THOMAS MUIR, ESQ., ADVOCATE,
Martyred to Freedom in 1793.

This splendid festival in honour of departed worth and patriotism, was held in the elegant new mansion of James Duncan, Esq. of Mosesfield. Near Glasgow, on Tuesday se'ennight. Thomas Davidson, Esq., in the absence of C. J. Tennant, Esq. of St Rollox, by indisposition, in the chair James Turner, Esq. of Thrushgrove, Bailie of the River and Frith [sic] of Clyde, and William Lang, Esq., acted as croupiers.
The room was decorated with two busts of Mr Muir, one of them in marble by Mossman; also with portraits of his father and mother, and other interesting ornaments. The dinner was excellent and abundant, and nearly 100 gentlemen were present. The Kirkintilloch band attended and played many delightful and spirited stirring pieces.[63]

The Mossman bust was produced in 1831.[64] The author believes that the other bust mentioned in the above newspaper article above is most likely the missing bust by Thomas Banks, probably commissioned or paid for by Thomas's parents and sent to them at Huntershill on completion. It then passed to Janet Blair's family where it remained. Thomas's nephew, James Blair, was a guest at the dinner and evidently took the family portraits and bust to the event. The Muir heirlooms would have later passed down Louisa Blair's family, namely the Lockhart's of Milton Lockhart, Lanarkshire. The author has been in contact with David Cranstoun of that Ilk and Corehouse, formerly Lockhart,[65] who is not a blood relative of the Muirs because he is descended from Laurence Lockhart's second wife Marion Maxwell. David's father, John Gilbert Lockhart, was the author of 'The Skeleton in the Cupboard', mentioned above, originally prepared as a family history record for his children but re-written in 1950 for publication in *Blackwood's Magazine*.

It is interesting that no portrait is mentioned in the article. We are told by Christina Bewley[66] that Muir's father died in 1801. A year later when Huntershill was sold, his mother, who died in 1803, asked that a portrait should be kept in the house, but the house subsequently changed hands and the portrait was removed. Under it was an inscription:

Doomed from this mansion to a foreign land
To waste his days of gay and sprightly youth,
And all for sowing with a liberal hand,
The seeds of that seditious libel truth.

Christina Bewley's source, Dr JA Russell, tells us that 'We have at least a picture of Muir, and it was, in fact, the wish of his mother that his picture would always remain in the house. However, a later occupier seems to have removed the one she had in mind and the original may be the portrait to be seen now in the Lord Provost's room in Glasgow City Chambers'.[67]

Possibly the Gallaway family who had purchased Huntershill had disposed of the portrait, or would not allow the festival to take place in their home. This may be an explanation as to why the Huntershill festival was held in Mosesfield and not at Huntershill. David Martin produced a chalk on paper sketch of Thomas Muir, which can be seen at the Scottish National Portrait Gallery.[68] The author believes that this is an artist sketch from which an oil portrait would have been painted. David Martin held a reputation as a portrait artist; he had re-settled in Edinburgh in 1780.[69]

It is very likely that when Muir was called to the bar in 1787 he would have had his portrait painted by a well-known artist as this would have been beneficial to both his social standing and his career. He is depicted by the artist in a relaxed, confident pose, with the whole world at his feet. This portrait, if it was commissioned from the artist sketch, has disappeared, and may be in a private collection with its provenance long forgotten; however we do have the chalk sketch which gives us a true glimpse of Thomas at that time.

Stephen Alexander Lockhart,[70] 5th of Milton Lockhart, 3 x great-grandson of James Muir and Margaret Smith, sold Milton Lockhart in 1951. Prior to the sale of the house the contents were sold at auction. It may be that the Muir heirlooms were disposed of at this time or they could be lying in an attic somewhere still waiting to be discovered.

Notes and References

1 Cameron, 1892, p.215.
2 Black, 1946, p.617.
3 Cameron, 1892, p.iii.
4 Cameron, 1892, p.iii.
5 Cameron, 1892, p.214.
6 Cameron, 1892. p.215.
7 National Records of Scotland (NRS), 1622 Muir, Robert (Hamilton & Campsie Commissary Court CC10/5/4).
8 Cameron, 1892, p.217.
9 NRS, 1678 Muir, William (Hamilton & Campsie Commissary Court CC10/5/9.)
10 Cameron, 1892, p.12.
11 Cameron, 1892, pp.213-8.
12 Cameron, 1892, p.215.
13 Glasgow City Archives (GCA), T-LX 1/8/21,22,23. Lennox family of Woodhead.
14 NRS, Muir, James_OPR_Deaths_644/01_0001_Glasgow.
15 NRS, Smith, Margaret (Muir)_OPR_Deaths_644/01_ 0092_ Glasgow.
16 NRS, Muir, James & Smith, Margaret_OPR_ Marriages_663/00_0038_Bo'ness.
17 NRS, Muir, James & Smith, Margaret_OPR_ Marriages_644/001_0250_0365_ Glasgow.
18 GCA, Register of Sasines, B10/2/48.
19 Cameron, 1892, pp.215-21.
20 NRS, 1744 Calder, Agnes (Glasgow Commissary Court CC9/7/58).
21 Bewley, 1981, pp.IX, X.
22 Bewley, 1981, p.1.
23 Robertson, 1793, pp.117-118.
24 NRS, 1797 Muir, Alexander (Hamilton & Campsie Commissary Court CC10/5/12).
25 East Dunbartonshire Archives, P9467; *Glasgow Courier*, 15 December 1798.
26 NRS, RS59/35/508, Sasine, James Muir. Stirling 27 March 1800.
27 GCA, T-SA 4/1/1. Sasine abridgements for Dunbartonshire 1781-1820.
28 NRS, RD2_170, Disposition, Muir to Cuthill, Braehead. 6 August 1751.
29 NRS, RS10/8/301, Sasine, William Muir, ⅛th part of the Easter Mains of Kirkintilloch. 11 May 1752.
30 NRS, RS/10/35/280, Sasine, Mr Galloway, Lands of the Easter Mains of Kirkintilloch. Dumbarton, 10 April 1819.
31 NRS, RS/10/14/395, Sasine in favour of John Watt. Dumbarton, 29 December 1795.

32 NRS, RS/3/443/82, Sasine in favour of Alexander Muir, 14 May 1787.

33 NRS, RS/10/13/477, Sasine in favour of Andrew Freeland, 11 August 1792.

34 Anderson, 1935, *p.195*.

35 GCA, *List of the Matriculated members of the Merchants' House of Glasgow*, T-MH17/1. 12-13.

36 NRS, JC26-276-6, Letter from James Muir to the Master of Hope, Belfast.

37 NRS, OPR Marriages_ 475/00_0010_ 0317_ Campsie.

38 NRS, Muir, J_OPR_Births_475/00_ 0010_ 0349_ Campsie.

39 NRS, Muir, William_OPR_Births_475/00_ 0010_ 0355_ Campsie.

40 NRS, Muir, David_OPR_Births_475/00_ 0010_ 0365_ Campsie.

41 NRS, Muir, David_OPR_Births_475/00_0010_ 0365_ Campsie.

42 GCA, T-SK6 Vol.45 No.8.

43 GCA, T-SK6 Vol.45 No.9.

44 GCA, T-SK6 Vol.45 No.10.

45 GCA, T-SK6 Vol.45 No.13.

46 Muir, Elizabeth_OPR_Births_475/00_0010_0252_Campsie.

47 Muir, William_OPR_Births_475/00_0010_0262_Campsie.

48 Cameron, 1892, p.215.

49 Muir, Margaret_OPR_Births_475/00_0020_ 0097_ Campsie.

50 Muir, Margaret_OPR_Births_475/00_ 0020_ 0105_ Campsie.

51 Muir, Christian_OPR_Births_475/00_ 0020_ 0115_ Campsie.

52 NRS, RS10/13/477, Sasine in favour of Andrew Freeland.

53 *National Library of Scotland, http://digital.nls.uk/directories/*

54 *Scots Magazine*, Vol.51, p.510, November 1789.

55 Bewley, 1981, p.1.

56 NRS, Parling, Christian_Deaths_692/02_ 0160_ 0208_ Leith.

57 NRS, JC26-276-6, Letter from James Muir to the Master of Hope, Belfast.

58 Bewley, 1981, p.175.

59 The Ultimate Cigar Party, http://ultimatecigarparty.com/syndicate-586-scotch-whisky/ [accessed 28 June 2016].

60 http://www.lockharts.com/2010/01/09/lockharts-of-waygateshaw/ [accessed 29 June 2016].

61 http://www.lockharts.com/2010/01/09/lockharts-of-waygateshaw/ [accessed 29 June 2016].

62 *Blackwood's Magazine* (1950), Vol.267. January-June 1950, pp.36-49.

63 British Newspaper Archives *The Fife Herald, and Kinross, Strathearn, and Clackmannanshire Advertiser*. No. 832. http://www.britishnewspaperarchive.co.uk/viewer/bl/0000447/18380215/025/0004 [accessed 4 July 2016].

64 http://www.glasgowsculpture.com/pg_biography.
php?sub=mossman_w [accessed 5 July 2016].
65 http://thepeerage.com/p28345.htm#i283444 [accessed 7 July
2016].
66 Bewley, 1981, p.183.
67 *Bishopbriggs News*, 12 March 1971.
68 https://www.nationalgalleries.org/collection/artists-a-z/m/artist/
david-martin/object/thomas-muir-1765-1799-parliamentary-
reformer-pg-1668 [accessed 23 September 2016].
69 https://en.wikipedia.org/wiki/David_Martin_(artist) [accessed 23
September 2016].
70 http://www.lockharts.com/2010/01/09/lockharts-of-waygateshaw/
[accessed 7 July 2016].

John McFarlan – an Honest Man

David McVey

One great advantage in going to school in the 1970s in what is
now East Dunbartonshire was that we actually got to learn about
Thomas Muir of Huntershill. I don't think he was specified in the
Scottish History option in the Ordinary Grade History syllabus, but
he was a local hero and our teachers at Kirkintilloch High School
shoehorned him into their lessons anyway – somewhere amongst
those improving landlords and innovations in the iron industry.
Muir's character and achievements were interesting enough –
and History at the school was well-taught enough – for me to
remain curious. When I came to study History at the University of
Strathclyde, I looked in the library for books that might mention
Muir and routinely consulted the indexes of likely volumes. In
my second year I took a Scottish History class (our lecturer was
one TM Devine) and, of course, the main text was TC Smout's
magisterial *A History of the Scottish People 1560-1830*. Smout
gave a succinct summary of what we knew and believed:

> Thomas Muir, a Glasgow advocate of very great eloquence
> and power [...] was sentenced by Lord Braxfield (after a
> travesty of a trial in 1793) to fourteen years at the Australia
> convict settlement in Botany Bay.[1]

Some years later I picked up a copy of Christina Bewley's 1981
biography, *Muir of Huntershill* in a bargain bookshop; I have
the same copy in front of me now, oft-thumbed but still in good
condition. Bewley's book has been criticised by some since then
– 'the content of her work', wrote Hector MacMillan, 'leaves a
very great deal to be desired'[2] – but it was ground-breaking in its
way, remains a gripping read and was an important landmark in
reviving Muir's fame. It certainly cemented *my* interest in Muir. I
also read Robert Louis Stevenson's *Weir of Hermiston* and learned

that the demonic yet compelling title character was based on Lord Braxfield; in the novel it was Lord Hermiston who was responsible for 'that furious onslaught of his upon the Liberals, which sent Muir and Palmer into exile...'[3]

In the 1980s, Strathkelvin District Council and the Fort Theatre in Bishopbriggs organised a competition for a play based on Muir's life. I started out with high hopes but never completed the project; writing was hard work in those pre-laptop days. Only two entries were received for the competition, and while they both must have been streets ahead of anything I could have produced, I now rather regret missing out on coming a distant third. What struck me at the time, and remains with me now, is what a colourful, action-packed, moving and involving *film* could be made of Muir's life and work.

Not every writer is as impressed with Muir and the Scottish Radicals of the 1790s. For example, Michael Fry disposes of the movement in a single page, concluding that '[...] it cannot be said that Scotland was seething with barely repressed revolutionary fervour' and doesn't mention Muir at all.[4] It is difficult, though, at a distance of more than 200 years, to make a definitive judgement about the level of support for reform in Scotland in the 1790s. More was going on than conventions of the Friends of the People or trials of its leading figures. And so we turn to a legal contemporary of Muir's, also from East Dunbartonshire, whose contribution to progress and reform was quieter and more cerebral, perhaps, and who in the 1790s was rather off the radar.

My interest in John McFarlan (sometimes rendered as 'MacFarlan' or even 'MacFarlane') of Ballencleroch was just as slow-burning in its development as my enthusiasm for Muir. I first encountered him in his memorial – a slender obelisk in pink granite that stands at the western end of Clachan of Campsie kirkyard. It bears a moving and powerful tribute which is worth quoting in full:

IN MEMORY
OF
JOHN MCFARLAN ESQ
OF BALLENCLEROCH
BORN 12 JANUARY 1767: DIED 18 DECEMBER 1846
THE PRIME OF HIS LIFE
WAS PASSED IN THE PRACTICE OF THE LAW

AND IN THE ARDENT PROMOTION OF THE CAUSE
OF CIVIL AND RELIGIOUS LIBERTY.
IN HIS LATER YEARS
BUT IN THE VIGOUR OF HIS INTELLECTUAL POWERS
HE RETIRED FROM THE BAR
WITHOUT WEALTH OR WORLDLY ADVANCEMENT
TO SPEND HIS LIFE IN DOING GOOD
BY HIS WRITINGS, HIS COUNSEL AND HIS EXAMPLE
HE LOVED MERCY AND WALKED HUMBLY WITH HIS GOD.
FINALLY
POSSESSING THE ESTEEM OF ALL THE GOOD WHO KNEW HIM
THE LOVE OF HIS NEIGHBOURS
AND
THE AFFECTION AND VENERATION OF HIS NUMEROUS
DESCENDANTS
HE PASSED FROM THE WORLD
REJOICING IN THE BLESSED HOPE OF EVERLASTING LIFE
THROUGH OUR LORD JESUS CHRIST

There's no direct hint there of any link to Thomas Muir, but given McFarlan's location, profession and date of birth, combined with the reference to 'civil and religious liberty', any Muir scholar's antennae would start to twitch. At first, though, it was the mysterious reference to 'writings' that attracted me. What did McFarlan write about? Where were these works published? Were any of them still extant and accessible? – but the phrase 'civil and religious liberty' did ring a bell, and I shall return to it later.

It should be obvious by now that I'm a writer rather than a historian – I don't doggedly pursue research, digging deeper and deeper, producing a synthesis and seeking to embed it with published work. Rather, people and their stories excite my curiosity and I'm compelled to find out more and write about them. I decided to seek out McFarlan's forgotten writings, if I could. Once I'd tracked them down – and the four pamphlets I'll refer to are all in the National Library of Scotland – they helped me to place McFarlan as someone who kept the light of democracy and liberty alive after Muir had departed the scene, albeit in a more literary, donnish manner. McFarlan was a contemporary of Muir, two years younger, in fact, but who was able, unlike Muir, to live out his allotted Biblical span and more. As we'll see, he did not have death-defying adventures on three continents as Muir did; there are many roads to being a pioneer of democratic reform.

Obelisk in memory of John McFarlan in the churchyard at Clachan of Campsie.

John McFarlan was the eldest son of John Warden (1740-1788), a Church of Scotland minister who took the additional name McFarlan after marrying Anne, daughter of Hugh Macfarlan of

Ballencleroch.[5] Warden was the author of a then-famous work of practical theology, *Inquiries Concerning the Poor*.[6] 'Ballencleroch', incidentally, was a variously-spelled Gaelicised version of 'Kirkton' and the building was the McFarlan family home dating back to the early seventeenth century, situated by the Glazert Burn just where it issues from Campsie Glen. It is sometimes referred to as 'Ballencleroch Castle' in the records but was only ever a basic laird's house, added to over time, not least during John McFarlan's tenure.

Campsie Glen in bygone times.

Born in 1767, John McFarlan became the Laird of Ballencleroch in 1788 on his father's death, but much of his early life was spent in Edinburgh, where he was a scholar at the High School of Edinburgh and studied law at the University. He was admitted to the practice of the law in 1789 when he entered the Faculty of Advocates. In heady Enlightenment Edinburgh, he mixed with luminaries such as Dugald Stewart and Sir Henry Moncrieff. He and Sir Walter Scott studied German together in Edinburgh in 1785. Scott is another character who intrigues me, although his politics, and in particular his well-known distaste for reform and reformers, are less appealing. Such views surfaced early in his career when during his legal studies he dedicated his thesis to Lord Braxfield.[7] John Sutherland in his biography of Scott has suggested that 'excessive and bloodthirsty reaction to any sign of popular uprising was to be a regular feature of Scott's politics'.[8] So with the likes of Scott, Braxfield, McFarlan and Muir the legal world of Edinburgh during the late eighteenth century must have been a small and incestuous one.

Back in the Parish of Campsie, McFarlan is still remembered as the man who opened the lands of Ballencleroch, effectively the entire glen and hillside to the west of the Glazert Burn, to the public, anticipating the spirit of the Scottish Access Concordat by 200 years. His only stipulation was that access to the glen should be prohibited on Sundays during times of church service. The Glen began to become quite a resort for people for miles around and in 1833 McFarlan was presented with a petition from a number of locals claiming to be upset by the number of people abusing the amenity and getting drunk during their visit; the petitioners asked that the Glen be closed on Sundays. By 1833 the Clachan Kirk had been replaced by a new facility in Lennoxtown. McFarlan responded in writing; he himself had seen little sign of the boorish behaviour the petitioners objected to, and, in particular, he noticed that most of the petitioners were well-to-do farmers and landowners, well-used to the open air life. He refused to close Campsie Glen on the one day that ordinary working people were free to go there and benefit from it.[9] This theme of representing the interests of the working classes is a recurrent one in records of McFarlan. He retired from the bar in 1830 and from 1832 spent most of his time on his estate as a genial local laird. Much of his effort went into writing on religious and political issues.

In politics, McFarlan was a Whig; in religion, his *Scotsman* obituary[10] described him as 'decidedly Calvinistic', following on from his father, '[...] one of the leading men in his time of the Evangelical or popular party in the church'. This can surprise modern observers used to stereotypical portrayals of heroic Enlightenment free-thinkers, supported by genial 'Moderates' in the Kirk and opposed by stern, bigoted Evangelicals. Hector MacMillan, in his otherwise canny and insightful study of Muir, struggled with this dichotomy in the context of Muir himself: 'It may be that the progressive young man in politics was reactionary in his faith [...]'[11] This shouldn't actually be surprising, though 'reactionary' is a misleading term.

There are a couple of misunderstandings here. Firstly, while questioning and inventive, Enlightenment men were often far from being radical or liberal. Some supported slavery or opposed electoral reform and many had little real interest in alleviating poverty. The agricultural 'improvers' who mercilessly cleared estates in both Highlands and Lowlands were Enlightenment men, applying rational, scientific thinking to estate management. Some writers are perhaps inclined to discuss the Enlightenment as it if were unquestionably, with a whiff of *1066 and All That*, 'A Good Thing'.[12]

Evangelicals in the Kirk, like Muir and McFarlan, were more inclined to support political reform and oppose the patronage of wealthy landowners in the church than Moderates; indeed, patronage was one of the key issues behind the Disruption and the formation of the Free Kirk of Scotland in 1843. McFarlan stayed loyal to the established Kirk but had a great deal of sympathy with those who broke away; his younger brother Patrick was a leading light in the Disruption, and held the unusual distinction of being the Moderator of the General Assembly of the Church of Scotland (in 1834) and of the Free Kirk (in 1845). Patrick McFarlan was also involved in the discussions that led to the formation of the Evangelical Alliance in 1846.[13]

John McFarlan, like Thomas Muir, would have observed the iniquities of patronage at first hand. In the eighteenth century, the patronage of the Parish of Campsie was in the hands of the Crown. The minister of Campsie, the Reverend William Bell, was a generally respected and long-serving pastor when he died in 1783. The Reverend James Lapslie was a local boy who had made good and was serving as a tutor in the family of a wealthy man called Mr Suttie. He seems to have used Mr Suttie's high connections to influence the Government which exercised its right of patronage by announcing Lapslie as the new Campsie minister, even though the congregation had expressed a preference for the man who had been Mr Bell's assistant.[14] Lapslie would go on to become a colourful and controversial figure, one who worked hard to secure the conviction of Thomas Muir.

It is instructive that the inscription on McFarlan's memorial should suggest that 'civil and religious liberty' is a single cause, not two separate causes. It recalls the words of Archibald Bruce, Auld Licht minister and supporter of the Friends of the People:

Civil and religious liberty are but two great branches of
the same expanded tree. They have ever been found most
intimately allied. They have both had the same common
enemies [...][15]

McFarlan's religious and political opinions come out clearly
in his published writings, all shortish pamphlets of around thirty
pages. Four of them survive in the National Library. I have written
about them before[16] and here I will try to expand on them, perhaps
relating them to Muir and his legacy.

A Letter to the Electors of Stirlingshire[17] is a piece of election
literature from 1837 in which McFarlan delivers some acerbic one-
liners that modern Liberal, Labour or SNP campaigners could still
easily hijack: 'The grand problem with a Tory always is, not how
much liberty a people is qualified to possess and to enjoy, but how
much servitude they may be made to endure'.[18] He shows a talent
for a skilfully delivered punch-line:

[...] the honest Tory has no desire but to do what he
believes is best for the community, and you will find him
well-disposed, kindly and beneficent to all around about
him; provided always you are willing to do his bidding.[19]

As he nears the end of his closely-argued 34-page pamphlet (how
different from today's slick, shallow, glossy election leaflets) he
offers a loaded but powerful challenge: 'Are you willing to bear
a helping-hand in the destruction of your own rights, your own
liberty, your own laws? Then choose a Tory for your member'.[20] He
then concludes with words that few politicians today would dare
use: 'That God may be your guide in all your ways, is the prayer of
your affectionate friend, JOHN McFARLAN'.

A Letter to the Electors of Stirlingshire was a rejoinder,
like McFarlan's next work, *Who are the Friends of Religion
and the Church?* (1838)[21] to comments made by Sir Archibald
Edmonstone of Duntreath, a fellow-landowner/grandee from
nearby Strathblane. The two men were probably friendly enough,
but McFarlan clearly had little time for Edmonstone's politics.
Edmonstone had written six letters to the electors of Stirlingshire.
Here, we are only a few years on from the first Reform Bill of 1832,
and McFarlan frames the entire text of *Who are the Friends* [...]

as a letter to Edmonstone. The tone is courteous but McFarlan certainly doesn't hold back and employs a nice line in sarcasm;

> The tribunal before whom we stand – the Electors – is modern. It is the workmanship of Lord Grey, and it is most delightful to see you address it in terms so affectionate and respectful; for the time is not long gone by, since you Tories told us 'that the Reform Bill is the greatest curse that ever was inflicted on Scotland, and fraught with every mischief under the sun'.[22]

McFarlan drew parallels between historic attempts to foist unpopular forms of worship on to the Church of Scotland, and what he saw as Tory attempts to stifle the cause of reform, justice and change. In particular, Edmonstone seems to have opposed spending on education in Ireland and India, on the grounds that the people of neither country were likely to benefit from it and, in any case, widespread literacy would lead to a contagion of dangerous ideas among the lower classes. McFarlan condemns this attitude to the poor and advocates literacy and education for its own sake. He also cites a number of examples from the Empire of how missionaries saw a great response of faith from local people as a result of their being educated and thus able to read the Bible for themselves: 'What is the use of any church?' he asks Edmonstone, himself a writer of devotional works from a high church perspective, 'I know of none but to maintain the worship of the true God, and to bring religion home to the consciences and lives of men. And how can that be done, unless the men can read their Bible; that is, unless you begin with education?'[23]

Thomas Muir also, of course, had been accused of trying pointlessly to inform and educate working-class people about politics and justice. Both Muir and McFarlan recognised that democracy was about more than just the right to vote; people also needed education so that they could participate in an informed way. A shorter pamphlet, though with a much longer title, *An Honest Man's Creed with the grounds thereof and some hints for Clergymen of all denominations,*[24] appeared in 1840. It picks up some of the themes of his previous work, but in the form of a wide-ranging confession of faith, which appeals to philosophy and metaphysics to challenge the religious sceptics of the time. To

McFarlan, the confusion of doubt stirred up by the Enlightenment was already starting to settle: '[...] a considerable change has been going forward in the minds of the learned since the days of David Hume. Men of science are now satisfied that there are more things in heaven and earth than impressions and ideas [...]'[25]

The last work of McFarlan that we have is *The Presbyterian Empire, Its Origin, Decline and Fall*[26] that appeared in 1842. As we have seen, McFarlan stayed loyal to the established Church of Scotland, but he was well aware of its flaws and certainly did not keep quiet about them. In this sober assessment of his chosen denomination, McFarlan criticised the incoherent response of the leading Evangelical ministers to the challenges of the Enlightenment:

The clergy did not attempt to meet [David Hume's] argument. They did not honour it with attention enough to enable them to understand it. But they reviled the man, and held him up as a just object of public vengeance. This made no impression on the people; but it disgusted men of liberal habits, and went far to recommend the sceptic and his principles. Scoffing at religion became the tone of good company...[27]

McFarlan clearly saw the challenges by Hume and others as an opportunity for the church to strengthen its beliefs and the quality of its apologetics by responding intelligently; but this opportunity, he felt, had been squandered by simplistic denunciations. He repudiated the spiritual arrogance of certain ministers (both Moderates and his fellow-Evangelicals) and blamed the failure of their attempts to convert Roman Catholics on their own lofty view of themselves. Like most Evangelical Presbyterians of the time, McFarlan viewed Roman Catholicism as a flawed, lesser, tainted faith, but he also recognised many of its positive qualities, particularly in the simple faith of Roman Catholic believers and the dedicated work of many of their priests.

He also criticised patronage in the Kirk, tellingly so in a publication that appeared the year before the Disruption. As a fearless, intelligent, passionate layman who remained with the national Kirk, McFarlan must have been viewed with no little suspicion by some of the haughtier Moderate clergy who also remained. It is also surely possible to picture some full and frank exchanges of views in his early years with his then parish minister, the Reverend James Lapslie.

McFarlan died at Ballencleroch House on 19 December 1846. His *Scotsman* obituary records another published work of McFarlan's that I've so far been unable to trace: *Letters on Education*, 'a work containing principles and rules for the education of children'. 'He was not a man who could be bought,' continues the *Scotsman* obituarist, 'or whose continued support needed to be secured by preferment or money'. The obituary also mentions that once McFarlan left the bar he carried out '[...] unwearied endeavours to improve the welfare of the people in his immediate neighbourhood'. This hints at traditions that McFarlan practised a kind of early legal aid, offering free advice to poorer people in the neighbourhood of Ballencleroch: '[...] at a certain hour, on stated days of the week,' writes John Cameron,[28] 'he took his seat on the balcony of Ballencleroch, to give the benefit of his legal lore, gratuitously, to all who chose to consult him'. Thomas Muir was also, of course, said to provide legal advice to the poor for free.

Ballencleroch House before it was burned down in the 1980s.
Photograph courtesy East Dunbartonshire Archives & Local Studies.

Ballencleroch House remained in the McFarlan family until 1921 and became, after the Second World War, the luxury Campsie Glen Hotel. This was a favoured resort of entertainers who were performing in Glasgow; Bob Hope and The Beatles both enjoyed its comforts. Tragically, in the 1980s it was burned down, but part of the shell of the ruin has been restored in a new Ballencleroch House by the Schoenstatt Sisters of Mary who run it as a shrine and retreat centre; the tolerant Presbyterian John McFarlan would be quite happy with this, and with the fact that the grounds can still be enjoyed by all respectful visitors. Only two of the four pamphlets I have reviewed are mentioned in McFarlan's *Oxford Dictionary of National Biography* entry, so it is safe to assume that they are little-known and little-read. Yet they reveal someone who was a well-read, deep-thinking individual, and an excellent, fluent writer with a ready wit. It is a pity he was never persuaded to write a longer work.

The Schoenstatt Centre that was built on the site of Ballencleroch House in the early 1990s.

Clearly, McFarlan regarded the 1832 Reform Bill as a great consummation. It's difficult to see Thomas Muir, the advocate of universal suffrage, being as satisfied with the minimal enfranchisement it enacted. Perhaps McFarlan, the comfortable, landed lawyer was a more moderate reformer. Nonetheless, he discernibly embraced and continued the kind of views that Muir lived and died for; he was still a radical, particularly in the context of his times, and his lively and readable writings testify to this. I hope this paper encourages others to seek them out.

A mere two minutes' walk from Ballencleroch is the old Kirkyard at the Clachan of Campsie. Here McFarlan was laid, within sound of the burn, and the slender granite obelisk still recalls him today. But his writings are also worthy if rather hidden memorials.

Notes and References

1 Smout, 1998, p.415.
2 MacMillan, 2005, p.280.
3 Stevenson, 1974, p.261.
4 Fry, 2014, pp.297-8.
5 McFarlan's family background and biography are briefly and helpfully outlined in WAJ Archbold's biography in the *Oxford Dictionary of National Biography*, http://www.oxforddnb.com/view/article/17487 [Accessed 20 June 2016].
6 McFarlan, 1782.
7 Sutherland, 1995, p.49.
8 Sutherland, 1995, p.50.
9 The story is told in Cameron, 1892, pp.88-91.
10 *The Scotsman*, 20 January 1847.
11 MacMillan, 2005, p.18.
12 Arthur Herman's, *The Scottish Enlightenment* (Herman, 2003), for example, is subtitled 'The Scots' invention of the modern world'.
13 See LA Ritchie's biography of Patrick McFarlan in the *Oxford Dictionary of National Biography* http://www.oxforddnb.com/view/article/17488 [Accessed 20 June, 2016].
14 Cameron, 1892, pp.4-5.
15 From 'Reflections on Freedom of Writing', quoted in Brims, 1989, p.56.
16 McVey, 2011.
17 McFarlan, 1837.
18 McFarlan, 1837, p.10.
19 McFarlan, 1837, p.2.
20 McFarlan, 1837 p.34.
21 McFarlan, 1838.
22 McFarlan, 1838, p.1.
23 McFarlan, 1838, p.14.
24 McFarlan, 1840.
25 McFarlan, 1840, p.1.
26 McFarlan, 1842.
27 McFarlan, 1842, p.4.
28 Cameron, 1892, p.69.

Appendix

Rogues and Vagabonds

In every century men o' destiny
wi thoughts beyond thir time
hae been the guiding lights in the darkness
though few forever shine

Even though they fade away
its the legacy they lea that will endure
and the world is a better place
through the hardship and suffering o' Thomas Muir

Rogues and Vagabonds hae seen thir day
the seeds o' bitterness are blawn away
but the seed he planted will bloom forever
and flourish in the cauldest clay

A revolution o' constitutional change
was a' he planned
ne'er a wild uprising or bloody battle
he'd stomach for the rights o' man

Mair an education in quiet persuation
and a voice for silent men
but an agitator tae men o' title
a thorn within thir rosy den

Rogues and Vagabonds hae seen thir day....

Frae the ferms and cotton mills
O'er the Campsie hills – the bleaching fields and a'
tae a tryst o' working men
intermingled wi sleekit yins wha'd see him fa'

Weel paid infiltrators these mischief makers
oot tae justify thir fees
and thir accusations brought ruination
tae martyrs banished o'er the seas

Rogues and Vagabonds hae seen thir day...

This song was offered for inclusion in the volume by the author/composer Iain Ingram, who provided the following note to go with it:

The inspiration for this song came from the book Handful of Rogues *by Hector MacMillan.*
Although I knew of Thomas Muir, this was the first detailed account I'd read of his story. My introduction to the man came on an early morning walk with an old friend and mentor, back in 2003. He painted such a vivid picture of Thomas Muir's life, that I felt compelled to write about him. This resulted in my first song about Thomas Muir 'Awa frae Huntershill'. However, I feel 'Rogues and Vagabonds' has far more depth and detail.

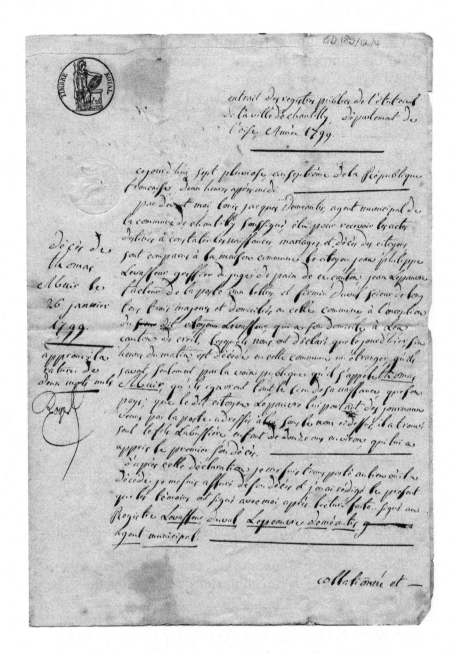

Copy of Thomas Muir's death certificate. From Peter Mackenzie Papers, East Dunbartonshire Archives, William Patrick Library, Kirkintilloch, Reference GD185/12/4.

Bibliography

Addison, WI, 1898. *A roll of the graduates of the University of Glasgow, 1727-1897*. Glasgow: John Maclehose and Sons.

Addison, WI, 1902. *Prize lists of the University of Glasgow from Session 1777-78 to 1832-33*. Glasgow: Carter and Pratt.

Addison, WI, 1913. *The matriculation albums of the University of Glasgow from 1728 to 1858*. Glasgow: James Maclehose and Sons.

Allan, D, 2002. *Scotland in the eighteenth century: Union and Enlightenment*. Harlow: Pearson Education.

Anderson, JR, ed, 1935. *The burgesses and guild brethren of Glasgow, 1751-1846*. Edinburgh: Scottish Record Society.

Anderson, R, 1901. *A history of Kilsyth and a memorial of two lives*. Edinburgh and Glasgow: John Menzies and Co.

Angus, D, 1993. 'Robert Louis Stevenson: the secret sources'. *Studies in Scottish Literature*, 28:1, pp.81-91.

Anon, 1780-96. *The parliamentary register of history of the proceedings and debates of the House of Commons*. 45 vols. London: J Almon and J Debrett.

Anon, 1790. *The Group, a letter containing articles exhibited against Dr William McGill*. n.p.

Anon, 1792. *The trial of Thomas Paine, for a libel, contained in the second part of the Rights of Man*. London: C and G Kearsley.

Anon, 1792a. *The procedure of our church courts in the case of Dr William M'Gill of Ayr, with a complaint lately exhibited against him; and a narrative of the rise, progress and termination of a prosecution carried on against him before our church judicatories, by the laity of Scotland; to which is added a conclusion containing reflections on the defection of our church courts, &c &c, by the Friends of Truth*. n.p.

Anon, 1792b. *A memorial and remonstrance concerning the proceedings of the Synod of Glasgow and Ayr and of the General Assembly in the case of Dr William McGill*. n.p.

Anon, 1798. *Histoire de la tyrannie du gouvernement anglais exercée envers le célèbre Thomas Muir, écossais, sa déportation à Botany Bay, son séjour dans cette isle, son évasion, son arrivée à Paris, avec une description de Botany Bay, et des renseignements sur la fin tragique de Lapeyrouse*. Paris: Chez Prudhommes.

Anon, 1842. *The altar of liberty, or songs for the people.* n.p.

Anon, 1946. *Thomas Muir of Huntershill.* Glasgow: Wm C McDougall.

[Arbuckle, J], 1722. *A short account of the late treatment of the students of the University of G[lasgo]w.* Dublin: n.p.

Armstrong, M, 2014. *The liberty tree: the stirring story of Thomas Muir and Scotland's first fight for democracy.* Edinburgh: Word Power Books.

Barrell, J, 2000. *Imagining the king's death: figurative treason, fantasies of regicide 1793-1796.* Oxford: Oxford University Press.

Barrington, G, 1911. *Débuts de Botany Bay: souvenirs de Georges Barrington, annotés d'après les documents d'archives et les mémoires.* Paris: Collection Historique Illustrée.

Baylen, JO and NJ Gossman, eds, 1979. *Biographical dictionary of modern British radicals.* Vol.1: 1770-1830. Hassocks: Harvester Press.

Bayne, I, 1995. 'The 1820 radical rising'. *Scottish Local History,* 35, pp.16-21.

Beaumont, J, 1990. *Cadder Parish Church, Bishopbriggs.* Bishopbriggs: Cadder Parish Church.

Beckett, JV and M Turner, 1990. 'Taxation and economic growth in eighteenth-century England'. *Economic History Review,* 43:3, pp.377-407.

Benchimol, A, R Brown and D Shuttleton, eds, 2015. *Before Blackwood's: Scottish journalism in the Age of Enlightenment.* Oxford: Routledge.

Bennett, S, 1865. *History of Australian discovery and colonisation.* Sydney: Hanson & Bennett.

Berresford Ellis, P and S Mac a'Ghobhainn, 1989. *The Scottish insurrection of 1820.* London: Pluto Press.

Bewley, C, 1981. *Muir of Huntershill.* Oxford: Oxford University Press.

Black, GF, 1946. *The surnames of Scotland: their origin, meaning and history.* New York: New York Public Library.

[Blackburn, F], 1780. *Memoirs of Thomas Hollis, Esq.* 2 vols. London.

Blackstone, W, 1765-9. *Commentaries on the laws of England.* 4 vols. Oxford: Clarendon Press.

Blair, D, 1879. *The history of Australasia.* Glasgow, Melbourne & Dunedin: McGready, Thompson & Niven.

Bond, WH, 1990. *Thomas Hollis of Lincoln's Inn: a Whig and his books.* Cambridge: Cambridge University Press.

Brewer, J, 1976. *Party ideology and popular politics at the accession of George III.* Reprinted Cambridge: Cambridge University Press, 1981.

Brims, J, 1987. 'The Scottish "Jacobins", Scottish nationalism and the British union'. In: RA Mason, ed, *Scotland and England 1286-1815.* Edinburgh: John Donald.

Brims, J, 1989. 'The Covenanting tradition and Scottish radicalism'. In: T Brotherstone, ed, *Covenant, charter, and party: traditions of revolt and protest in modern Scottish history*. Aberdeen: Aberdeen University Press.

Broadie, A, ed, 1997. *The Scottish Enlightenment: an anthology*. Edinburgh: Canongate Classics.

Broadie, A, ed, 2003. *The Cambridge companion to the Scottish Enlightenment*. Cambridge: Cambridge University Press.

Broadie, A, 2007. *The Scottish Enlightenment*. Edinburgh: Birlinn.

Brown, M, 2007. 'Dugald Stewart and the problem of teaching politics in the 1790s'. *Journal of Irish and Scottish Studies*, 1:1, pp.87-126.

Brown, SW, 2009. 'The market for murder and Edinburgh's eighteenth-century book trade'. In: J Hinks, C Armstrong and M Day, eds, *Periodicals and publishers: the newspaper and journal trade 1750-1914*. New Castle, DE: Oak Knoll Press and London: The British Library.

Brown, SW, 2015. 'Advertising and the *Edinburgh Evening Courant*'. In: A Benchimol, R Brown and D Shuttleton, eds, *Before Blackwood's: Scottish journalism in the Age of Enlightenment*.

Brown, SW and W McDougall, 2012. 'The Encyclopaedia Britannica'. In: *The Edinburgh History of the Book in Scotland, Volume 2: Enlightenment and expansion 1707-1800*. Edinburgh: Edinburgh University Press.

[Bruce, A], 1794. *Reflections on the freedom of writing; and the impropriety of attempting to suppress it by penal laws*. Edinburgh: n.p.

Burns, R, 1968. *The poems and songs of Robert Burns*, ed J Kinsley. 3 vols. Oxford: Clarendon Press.

Cairns, JW, 1995. '"Famous as a school for law, as Edinburgh [...] for medicine": legal education in Glasgow, 1761-1801'. In: A Hook and RB Sher, eds, *The Glasgow Enlightenment*. East Linton: Tuckwell Press.

Callender, JT, 1792. *The political progress of Britain*. Edinburgh: printed for Robertson & Berry.

Cameron, J, 1892. *The Parish of Campsie*. Kirkintilloch: D Macleod.

Camic, C, 1983. *Experience and enlightenment: socialization for cultural change in eighteenth century Scotland*. Edinburgh: Edinburgh University Press.

Carlyle, A, 1860. *Autobiography*. Edinburgh and London: William Blackwood and Sons.

Chancellor, V, 1986. *The political life of Joseph Hume, 1777-1855*. London: n.p.

Claeys, G, 1989. *Thomas Paine: social and political thought*. London: Unwin Hyman Ltd.

Claeys, G, ed, 1995. *The politics of English Jacobinism: writings of John Thelwall*. University Park: Pennsylvania State University Press.

Claeys, G, 2007. *The French Revolution debate in Britain: the origins of modern politics*. Basingstoke: Palgrave Macmillan.

Clark, JCD, 2000. *English society 1660-1832: religion, ideology and politics during the Ancien Regime*. Cambridge: Cambridge University Press.

Clark, S, 1993. 'The crime of rebellion'. *Scottish Local History*, 29, pp.5-10.

Clune, F, 1969. *The Scottish martyrs: their trials and transportation to Botany Bay*. Sydney: Angus and Robertson.

Cockburn, H, 1856. *Memorials of his time*. Edinburgh: Adam & Charles Black.

Cockburn, H, 1874. *Journal of Henry Cockburn, being a continuation of Memorials of his time, 1831-1854*. 2 vols. Edinburgh: Edmonston and Douglas.

Cockburn, H, 1888. *An examination of the trials for sedition which have hitherto occurred in Scotland*. 2 vols. Edinburgh: David Douglas.

Cockburn, H, 2004. *Life of Lord Jeffrey*. 3rd ed. 2 vols. Colchester: Lexden.

Coleridge, ST, 1971. 'A moral and political lecture' [1795]. In: L Paton and P Mann, eds, *Lectures 1795 on politics and religion*. London and Princeton, NJ: Routledge Kegan Paul and Princeton University Press.

Collins, D, 1798. *An account of the English colony in New South Wales*. London; reprinted in facsimile, Adelaide: Libraries Board of South Australia, 1971.

Coutts, JA, 1909. *A history of the University of Glasgow*. Glasgow: James Maclehose and Sons.

Cowley, S, 2015. *Rational piety and social reform in Glasgow: the life, philosophy, and political economy of James Mylne (1757-1839)*. Eugene, Oregon: WIPF and Stock.

Craig, J, 1806. 'Account of the life and writings of John Millar, Esq'. In: J Millar, *The origin of the distinction of ranks*. 4th ed. Edinburgh: William Blackwood.

*[Creech, W], 1793. *An account of the trial of Thomas Muir, younger of Huntershill, before the high court of justiciary at Edinburgh*. Edinburgh: William Creech.

Cumpston, JS, 1964. *Shipping arrivals and departures Sydney 1788-1825*. Parts I, II and III. Canberra: Roebuck Society.

Davis, MT, 2005. 'Prosecution and radical discourse during the 1790s: the case of the Scottish sedition trials'. *International Journal of the Sociology of Law*, 33:3, pp.148-58.

deLolme, JL, 1784. *The constitution of England: or an account of the English government.* 4th ed. London: G Robinson and J Murray.

Devine, TM, 1999. *The Scottish nation 1700-2000.* London: Allen Lane the Penguin Press.

Devine, TM, 2006. *The Scottish nation 1700-2007.* London: Penguin.

Donnelly, M, 1975. *Thomas Muir of Huntershill.* Bishopbriggs: Burgh of Bishopbriggs.

Donnelly, T, 1976. 'The Scottish rising of 1820: a re-interpretation'. *International Review of Scottish Studies,* VI.

Dowds, TJ, 2000. *The French invasion of Ireland 1798.* Dublin: IHR Publishing.

Dowds, TJ, 2001. 'General Humbert's gamble'. *Military Illustrated,* 156, pp.8-15.

Dowds, TJ, 2013. 'The Condorrat Radicals of 1820'. *Scottish Local History,* 85, pp.11-16.

Dowds, TJ, 2014-15. 'The Paisley Radical Trial of 1820'. *Scottish Local History,* 90, pp.9-16.

Drummond, AL and J Bulloch, 1973. *The Scottish church, 1688-1843.* Edinburgh: Saint Andrew Press.

Durey, M, 1990. *'With the hammer of truth': James Thomson Callender and America's early national heroes.* Charlottesville and London: University Press of Virginia.

Earnshaw, J, 1959. *Thomas Muir Scottish martyr.* Cremorne NSW: Stone Copying Company.

Elliott, E, 1840, *The poetical works.* Edinburgh: Tait.

Elliott, M, 1977. 'The "Despard Conspiracy" reconsidered'. *Past & Present,* 75, pp.45-61.

Emerson, RL, 1993. 'Politics and the Glasgow professors 1690-1800'. In: A Hook and RB Sher, eds, *The Glasgow Enlightenment.* East Linton: Tuckwell Press.

Epstein, JA, 1994. *Radical expression: political language, ritual, and symbol in England, 1790-1850.* Oxford: Oxford University Press.

Epstein, JA, 1996. '"Our real constitution": trial defence and radical memory in the age of revolution'. In: J Vernon, ed, *Re-reading the constitution: new narratives in the political history of England's long nineteenth century.* Cambridge: Cambridge University Press.

Eyre-Todd, G, 1934. *History of Glasgow, Vol. III: From the Revolution to the passing of the Reform Acts.* Glasgow: Jackson, Wylie & Co.

Ferguson, A, 1773. *An essay on the history of civil society.* 4th ed. London: printed for T Caddel.

Ferguson, W, 1968. *Scotland: 1689 to the present.* Edinburgh: Oliver & Boyd.

Fleischacker, S, 2003. 'The impact on America'. In: A Broadie, ed, *The Cambridge Companion to the Scottish Enlightenment*. Cambridge: Cambridge University Press.

Fry, M, 2004. *The Dundas despotism*. Edinburgh: John Donald.

Fry, M, 2014. *A higher world – Scotland 1707-1815*. Edinburgh: Birlinn.

Galt, J, 2015. *Annals of the Parish* [1821], ed I Campbell. In: *Four Galt Novels*. Edinburgh: Kennedy & Boyd, p.73.

Gerrald, J, 1794. *The address of the British convention assembled at Edinburgh, November 19th 1793, to the people of Great Britain*. London: DI Eaton.

Goodwin, A, 1979. *The friends of liberty: the English democratic movement in the age of the French Revolution*. London: Hutchinson & Co.

Green, CJ, 1825. *Trials for High Treason in Scotland, under a Special Commission, held at Stirling, Glasgow, Dumbarton, Paisley and Ayr in the year 1820*. 3 vols. Edinburgh: Manners and Miller.

Habermas, J, 1962. *The structural transformation of the Public Sphere: an inquiry into a category of bourgeois society*, translated by Thomas Berger. Reprinted Oxford: Polity, 1989.

Halliday, J, 1993. *The 1820 rising*. Glasgow: The 1820 Society.

[Hamilton, G], 1796. *The Telegraph: a consolatory epistle from Thomas Muir Esq. of Botany Bay to the Hon. Henry Erskine, late Dean of Faculty*. Edinburgh: n.p.

Hardie, A, 1820. *The radical revolt*. Rutherglen: P Walsh.

Harris, B, 1996. *Politics and the rise of the press*. London: Routledge.

Harris, B, 2005. 'Scotland's newspapers, the French Revolution and domestic radicalism (c.1789-1794)'. *Scottish Historical Review*, 84:217, pp.38-62.

Harris, B, 2005a. 'Scottish-English connections in British radicalism in the 1790s'. In: TC Smout, ed, *Anglo-Scottish relations from 1603 to 1900*. Oxford: Oxford University Press.

Harris, B, 2008. *The Scottish people and the French Revolution*. London: Pickering & Chatto.

Hellmuth, E, 1990. '"The palladium of all other English liberties": reflections on the liberty of the press in England during the 1760s and 1770s'. In: E Hellmuth, ed, *The transformation of political culture: England and Germany in the late eighteenth century*. Oxford: Oxford University Press.

Hellmuth, E, 2007. 'After Fox's libel act: or, how to talk about the liberty of the press in the 1790s'. In: U Broich, HT Dickinson and M Schmidt, eds, *Reactions to revolutions: the 1790s and their aftermath*. Münster: LIT.

Henry, R, 1771-93. *The history of Great Britain, from the first invasion of it by the Romans under Julius Caesar*. 6 vols. London: T Cadell and A Strahan.

Herman, A, 2003. *The Scottish Enlightenment*. London: Fourth Estate.

Heron, R, 1799. *Observations made in a journey through the western counties of Scotland, in the autumn of 1792*. Perth: W Morrison.

Herron, A, 1985. *Kirk by divine right, church and state: peaceful co-existence*. Edinburgh: Saint Andrew Press.

Hill, C, 1954. 'The Norman yoke'. In: J Saville, ed, *Democracy in the labour movement: essays in honour of Dona Torr*. London: Lawrence &Wishart.

Honeyman, V, 2009. '"A very dangerous place?": radicalism in Perth in the 1790s'. *Scottish Historical Review*, 87:2, pp.278-305.

Hook, A and RB Sher, eds, 1995. *The Glasgow Enlightenment*. East Linton: Tuckwell Press.

Howell, TJ, ed, 1809-28. *A complete collection of state trials and proceedings for high treason and other crimes and misdemeanours from the earliest period to the present time*. 34 vols. London: Longman, Hurst, Rees, Orme and Brown.

Howell, TJ and W Cobbett, 1817. *Cobbett's complete collection of state trials and proceedings for high treason and other crimes and misdemeanours from the earliest period to the present time*, vol.23. London: Hansard.

Huch, RK and PR Ziegler, 1985. *Joseph Hume: the people's MP*. Philadelphia.

Hughes, R, 1987. *The fatal shore: a history of the transportation of convicts to Australia, 1787-1868*. London: Collins Harvill.

Irvine, R, 2016. 'Burns's politics "in another view": late 1792/early 1793'. *Studies in Scottish Literature*, 41:1.

Kay, J, 1877. *A series of original portraits and caricature etchings*. 2 vols. Edinburgh: Adam & Charles Black.

Kennedy, TD, 1995. 'William Leechman: pulpit eloquence and the Glasgow Enlightenment'. In: A Hook and RB Sher, eds, *The Glasgow Enlightenment*. East Linton: Tuckwell Press.

Kidd, C, 1993. *Subverting Scotland's past: Scottish Whig historians and the creation of an Anglo-British identity, 1689-c.1830*. Cambridge: Cambridge University Press.

Kidd, C, 1996. 'North Britishness and the nature of eighteenth-century British patriotisms'. *Historical Journal*, 39:2, pp.361-82.

Kidd, N, 1996a. *The story of Chryston Parish Church*. Chryston: Chryston Parish Church.

Leask, N, 2007. 'Thomas Muir and *The Telegraph*: radical cosmopolitanism in 1790s Scotland'. *History Workshop Journal*, 63, pp.48-69.

Leask, N, 2015. "'The pith o' sense, and pride o' worth": Robert Burns and *The Glasgow Magazine*'. In: A Benchimol, R Brown and D Shuttleton, eds, *Before Blackwood's: Scottish journalism in the Age of Enlightenment*. Oxford: Routledge.

Lehmann, WC, 1960. *John Millar of Glasgow 1735-1801*. Cambridge: Cambridge University Press.

[London Corresponding Society], 1794. *At a general meeting of the London Corresponding Society, held at the Globe tavern Strand, on Monday the 20th day of January, 1794*. London: n.p.

Lynch, M, 1992. *Scotland: a new history*. London: Pimlico.

McCormick, T and others, 1987. *First views of Australia 1788–1825: a history of early Sydney*. Chippendale NSW: David Ell Press.

McElroy, DD, 1969. *Scotland's Age of Improvement: a survey of eighteenth-century literary clubs and societies*. Washington: Washington State University Press.

McFarlan, J, 1782. *Inquiries concerning the poor*. Edinburgh: J Dickson and London: T Longman.

McFarlan, J, 1837. *A letter to the electors of Stirlingshire*. 2nd ed. Edinburgh: Adam & Charles Black.

McFarlan, J, 1838. *Who are the friends of religion and the Church?* Edinburgh: Adam & Charles Black.

McFarlan, J, 1840. *An honest man's creed*. Edinburgh: Adam & Charles Black.

McFarlan, J, 1842. *The presbyterian empire*. 2nd ed. Edinburgh: Adam & Charles Black.

McFarland, EW, 1994. *Ireland and Scotland in the age of revolution: planting the green bough*. Edinburgh: Edinburgh University Press.

Macfarlane, M and A, 1981. *The Scottish radicals tried and transported to Australia for treason in 1820*. Stevenage: Spa Books.

McGill, W, 1786. *A practical essay on the death of Jesus Christ*. Edinburgh: Mundell & Wilson.

[Mackenzie, CP] 'A Ten-Pounder', 1832. *Exposure of the spy system pursued in Glasgow during the Years 1816-17-18-19 and 20, with the original letters of Andrew Hardie*. Glasgow: Muir, Gowans & Co.

Mackenzie, P, 1831. *The life of Thomas Muir, Esq, Advocate*. Glasgow: WR McPhun.

Mackie, JD, 1954. *The University of Glasgow 1451-1951: a short history*. Glasgow: Jackson, Son & Co.

MacMillan, H, 2005. *Handful of rogues: Thomas Muir's enemies of the people*. Glendaruel: Argyll Publishing.

McVey, D, 2011. 'A man who couldn't be bought: John McFarlan of Ballencleroch'. *Scottish Local History*, 81, pp.37-9.

Malthus, TR, 1803. *Essay on the principle of population*. London: printed for J Johnson.

Marshall, W, 1795. 'Memoirs of Mr Thomas Muir'. *The Glasgow Magazine*, July 1795.

Martin, D, 2011. 'Thomas Muir and the Scottish Enlightenment'. *Scottish Local History*, 81, pp.14-7.

Mee, J, 2015. 'The buzz about the *Bee*: policing the conversation of culture in the 1790s'. In: A Benchimol, R Brown and D Shuttleton, eds, *Before Blackwood's: Scottish journalism in the Age of Enlightenment*. London: Pickering & Chatto.

Meikle, HW, 1912. *Scotland and the French Revolution*. Glasgow: James Maclehose & Sons.

Mercey, F, 1837. *Les premiers réformistes écossais*, Revue des Deux Mondes, 4ᵉ série, Tome XII. n.p.

Michel, F, 1862. *Les Ecossais en France, les Français en Ecosse, Tome 2*. Paris: A. Franck.

Mileham, PJR, n.d. *The Stirlingshire Yeomanry Cavalry and the Scottish radical disturbances of April 1820*. Balfron: Balfron Heritage Group.

Millar, AH, 1886. 'Thomas Muir of Glasgow'. *Aberdeen People's Journal*, 24 July 1886.

Millar, J, 1796. *Letters of Crito, on the causes, objects, and consequences, of the present war*. 2nd ed. Edinburgh: Office of the Scots Chronicle.

Millar, J, 1803. *An historical view of the English government from the settlement of the Saxons in Britain to the Revolution in 1688*. London: J Mawman.

Millar, J, 1806. *The origin of the distinction of ranks*, 4th ed. 2 vols. Edinburgh: William Blackwood.

Millar, J, 2006. *An historical view of the English government*, ed MS Phillips and DR Smith. Indianapolis: Liberty Fund.

Milton, J, 2007. *Paradise lost*, ed BK Lewalski. Oxford: Blackwell.

Moody, TW and FX Martin, 1994. *The course of Irish history*. Dublin: Mercier Press.

Moore, T, 2010. *Death or liberty: rebels and radicals transported to Australia 1788-1868*. Millers Point NSW: Murdoch Books.

Muir, J, 1950. *John Anderson pioneer of technical education and the college he founded*. Glasgow: John Smith & Son.

Murray, D, 1927. *Memories of the Old College of Glasgow*. Glasgow: Jackson, Wylie.

Nyquist, M, 2014. 'Equiano, satanism, and slavery'. In: C Gray and E Murphy, eds, *Milton now: alternative approaches and contexts*. New York: Palgrave Macmillan.

Parssinen, TM, 1973. 'Association, convention and anti-parliament in British radical politics, 1771-1848'. *English Historical Review*, 88:348, pp.504-33.

Patterson, A, 1997. *Early modern liberalism*. Cambridge: Cambridge University Press.

Peebles, W, 1788. *The great things which the Lord hath done for this nation: illustrated and improved; in two sermons preached on the 5th November, 1788, the day appointed by the General Assembly of the Church of Scotland, for a national thanksgiving, in commemoration of the Revolution, 1688*. Kilmarnock: John Wilson.

[Peebles, W], 1811. *Burnomania: The celebrity of Robert Burns considered in a discourse addressed to all real Christians of every denomination*. Edinburgh: by G Caw for J Ogle and M Ogle, Glasgow, and R Ogle and T Hamilton, London.

Pentland, G, 2004. 'Patriotism, universalism and the Scottish conventions, 1792-1794'. *History*, 89:295, pp.340-60.

Pentland, G, 2008. '"Betrayed by Infamous Spies"? The commemoration of Scotland's "Radical War" of 1820'. *Past & Present*, 201:1.

Pentland, G, 2016. 'The posthumous lives of Thomas Muir'. In: G Pentland and M Davis, eds, *Liberty, property and popular politics: England and Scotland, 1688-1815. Essays in honour of HT Dickinson*. Edinburgh: Edinburgh University Press.

Philp, M, ed, 1995. *Thomas Paine: Rights of Man, Common Sense and other political writings*. Oxford: Oxford University Press.

Philp, M, 2013. *Reforming ideas in Britain: politics and language in the shadow of the French Revolution, 1789-1815*. Cambridge: Cambridge University Press.

Pittock, M, 2003. 'Historiography'. In: A Broadie, ed, *The Cambridge companion to the Scottish Enlightenment*. Cambridge: Cambridge University Press.

Poole, S, 2000. *The politics of regicide in England 1760-1850: troublesome subjects*. Manchester: Manchester University Press.

Robertson, J, 1792. *Overture concerning Dr McGill's errors and process*. Paisley: printed by John Neilson.

*[Robertson, J.], 1793. *An account of the trial of Thomas Muir, esq. younger, of Huntershill, before the high court of justiciary, at Edinburgh. On the 30th and 31st days of August, 1793, for sedition*. Edinburgh: James Robertson.

Roy, GR, ed, 1985. *The letters of Robert Burns*. Vol.1, 1780-1789. Oxford: Clarendon Press.

Salmond, A, 2015. *The dream shall never die: 100 days that changed Scotland forever*. London: HarperCollins.

*[Scott, A.], 1793. *The trial of Thomas Muir, esq., younger of Huntershill; before the high court of justiciary, upon Friday and Saturday the 30th and 31st days of August 1793*. Edinburgh: Alexander Scott.

Scott, A, 1794. *Reasons justifying the departure of A Scott*. Edinburgh: n.p.

Scott, J, 1960. 'The Scottish martyrs' farms'. *Journal of the Royal Australian Historical Society*, 46:3, pp.161-8.

Scott, WR, 1900. *Francis Hutcheson*. Cambridge: Cambridge University Press.

Scott, WR, 1937. *Adam Smith as student and professor*. Glasgow: Jackson, Son and Company.

'Senex' [R Reid], 1856. *Glasgow: past and present*. Vol.3. Glasgow: David Robertson.

Sher, R, 1985 [2015]. *Church and university in the Scottish Enlightenment*. Edinburgh: Edinburgh University Press.

Sher, R, 1995-96. 'Commerce, religion and enlightenment in eighteenth-century Glasgow'. In: TM Devine and G Jackson, *Glasgow, Volume I: Beginnings to 1830*. Manchester: Manchester University Press, 1995-96.

Sherry, B, 1989. *Hunter's Hill: Australia's oldest garden suburb*. Balmain NSW: David Ell Press.

Sherry, B, 2009. 'Thomas Muir and the naming of Hunter's Hill'. *Hunters Hill Trust Journal*, 47.2, pp.3-6.

Sherry, B, 2011. 'A visit to Thomas Muir's Huntershill'. *Hunters Hill Trust Journal*, 49:1, p.1 and pp.4-5.

Sherry, B, 2012. 'Muir, Thomas'. *Dictionary of Sydney* online: http://dictionaryofsydney.org/entry/muir_thomas

Sherry, B, 2015. 'Thomas Muir: an Australian perspective'. *Scottish Local History*, 92, pp.34-40.

Sherry, FA, 1968. *The rising of 1820*. Glasgow: Maclellan.

Smith, A, 1997. 'The origin and development of our property rights'. In: A Broadie, ed, *The Scottish Enlightenment: an anthology*. Edinburgh: Canongate Classics.

Smith, O, 1984. *The politics of language, 1791-1819*. Oxford: Clarendon Press.

Smout, TC, 1972/1998. *A history of the Scottish people 1560-1830*. London: Fontana.

Steer, D, 2009. 'Arminianism amongst protestant dissentors'. In: Th Marius van Leeuwen, Keith D Stauglin and Marijke Tolsma, eds, *Arminius, Arminianism and Europe*. Leiden and Boston: Brill.

Stevenson, RL, 1974. *The Master of Ballantrae/Weir of Hermiston*. London: Collins.

Stewart, D, 1982. 'Account of the life and writings of Adam Smith, LLD'. In: WPD Wightman and JC Bryce, eds, *Adam Smith, essays on philosophical subjects*. Indianapolis: Liberty Fund.

Strain, EH, 1908. *A prophet's reward*. Edinburgh and London: William Blackwood and Sons.

Sutherland, J, 1995. *The life of Walter Scott*. Oxford: Blackwell.

Thompson, EP, 1968. *The making of the English working class*. 2nd ed. London: Pelican.

Tytler, AF, 1807. *Memoirs of the life and writings of the Honourable Henry Home of Kames*. 2 vols. Edinburgh: William Creech.

Vernon, J, 1996. 'Notes towards an introduction'. In: J Vernon, ed, *Re-reading the constitution: new narratives in the political history of England's long nineteenth century*. Cambridge: Cambridge University Press.

Wantrup, J, 1990. *The transportation, exile and escape of Thomas Muir: a Scottish radical's account of Governor Hunter's New South Wales published at Paris in 1798, translated from the French with introduction and notes*. Melbourne: Boroondara Press.

Watt, JBA, 1908. *Cadder: its ecclesiastical history*. Glasgow: printed by Campbell & Tudhope.

Wyatt, O, 2012. *The Democrat*. Edinburgh: Azimuth Books.

Young, JD, 1996. *The very bastards of creation*. Glasgow: Clydeside Press.

*Note. In the interests of clarity, the publishers' names of the different reports of Thomas Muir's trial have been used for purposes of citation.

Contributors to this Volume

Rhona Brown is Senior Lecturer and Head of Scottish Literature at the University of Glasgow. She specialises in the work of eighteenth-century Scottish poets and, in particular, their relationship with the periodical press, cultural and sociable networks. She is author of *Robert Fergusson and the Scottish Periodical Press* (2012) and co-editor of *Before Blackwood's: Scottish Journalism in the Age of Enlightenment* (2015). Rhona is currently working on a digital edition of a radical 1790s newspaper, and on the correspondence of Robert Burns.

Joint Editor **Gerard Carruthers** FRSE is Francis Hutcheson Professor of Scottish Literature at the University of Glasgow. He is also General Editor of the Oxford University Press Edition of the Works of Robert Burns and Co-Editor (with Liam McIlvanney) of *The Cambridge Companion to Scottish Literature* (Cambridge University Press, 2012). He has published several dozen essays and book-chapters on eighteenth-century literature and culture in Scotland.

Sir **Tom Devine** Kt OBE FRSE MRIA FRHistS FBA is Emeritus Professor of History at the University of Edinburgh. He is considered by most people to be the leading historian of Scotland at the present time, with many books to his name. The editors of this volume are grateful to Sir Tom for allowing us to publish the text of the short lecture he gave in Parliament Hall, Edinburgh, on 25 August 2015, on the occasion of the reconstruction of Thomas Muir's trial of 1793 by the Faculty of Advocates.

Tom Dowds was among the first graduates from Strathclyde University and taught history for over thirty years in secondary schools. He is currently Honorary Vice President of the 1820 Society and a tutor in history in the Centre for Lifelong Learning at Strathclyde. He is the author of a number of books and articles.

Iain Ingram began as a musician during the mid-1960s playing bass guitar in a Rhythm & Blues band. After a few years, he drifted towards American folk music – singing and playing acoustic guitar – before becoming involved the traditional Scottish folk music scene. Around this time he starting writing songs – and is still active in this field. Like other Scottish singer/song-writers he believes that Thomas Muir is well worth commemorating in this way.

Satinder Kaur studied History at the University of Strathclyde and completed an MSc in Museum Studies at the University of Glasgow in 2015. Her final project involved the research and curation of an exhibition about Thomas Muir and his time at the University of Glasgow, which was hosted by the Centre for Robert Burns Studies in October 2015. She is currently a volunteer with the National Trust for Scotland.

Thomas Lemoine is a native of Nice in the south of France. He studied history at the Nice Sophia Antipolis University, specializing in the Modern and Contemporary period. Having been inspired by an accidentally discovered article he eventually completed Masters 1 and Masters 2 degree theses on Thomas Muir. He later suspended his doctorate researches to focus on a career as an actor and director. Also involved in the cinema, he has made films about the Landing of Provence on 15 August 1944 and on the French Resistance.

David McVey was educated at Kirkintilloch High School and the University of Strathclyde. He has published hundreds of items, extending both to fiction and a wide range of non-fictional subjects. He is also a lecturer at New College Lanarkshire.

Joint Editor **Don Martin** is a retired librarian who serves as Secretary of the Friends of Thomas Muir. He has published many books and articles on local history subjects and is currently Co-ordinating Editor of the Scottish Local History Forum journal *Scottish Local History*. He is a committee member of several local history societies.

Gordon Pentland is Reader in History at the School of History, Classics and Archaeology, University of Edinburgh. He is a graduate of Oxford and Edinburgh universities. After completing his doctorate in 2004 he worked for some time as a lecturer at the University of York before returning to Edinburgh in 2006 to take up a two-year Leverhulme Early Career fellowship followed by a lectureship in history. He is the author of a range of publications.

As former First Minister, the Right Honourable **Alex Salmond** MP PC is perhaps the most widely recognised Scotsman in the present-day world. He has often made his admiration for Thomas Muir very clear. The editors of this volume are grateful to him for allowing us to publish the text of the Thomas Muir Memorial Lecture he gave in St Mary's Cathedral, Edinburgh on 24 August 2015, the precise 250th anniversary of Muir's birth.

Beverley Sherry has followed a career at the University of Queensland, as a Senior Lecturer in English, the Australian National University, and the University of Sydney, where she is now an Honorary Associate. Her work crosses the disciplines of literature, the visual arts, and history, as evidenced in her books *Australia's Historic Stained Glass* (1991) and *Hunter's Hill: Australia's Oldest Garden Suburb* (1989). She has an international reputation as a Milton scholar and she sees a connection between John Milton and Thomas Muir as champions of liberty.

Alex Watson is from Bishopbriggs. His family lives on the site of the former lodge/gatehouse of Huntershill estate. This has been a major influence in developing his interest in Thomas Muir and the Muir family. He has had a lifelong enthusiasm for history and architecture, especially Scottish and family history.

Jimmy Watson is Chair of the Friends of Thomas Muir. His personality was the driving force behind the establishment of this group in 2010 and he has overseen its development ever since. Every year he organises a Thomas Muir Festival and in 2015 he was the leading organiser of the programme of events for 'Thomas Muir 250' year. Along with his father John (also a Thomas Muir enthusiast) he runs a fleet of haulage vehicles from a yard just opposite the entrance to Thomas Muir's former home at Huntershill House, Bishopbriggs.

Ronnie Young works in Scottish Literature at the University of Glasgow, where he currently convenes a class on the Scottish Enlightenment and online courses on Robert Burns. He has published articles on Burns and James Beattie and is the co-editor with Ralph McLean of a forthcoming volume *The Scottish Enlightenment and Literary Culture* with Bucknell Press. Ronnie is secretary of the Association for Scottish Literary Studies and co-editor of the Scottish Cultural Review of Language and Literature series with Brill/Rodopi.

Index

333

Martyrs (Scottish) of 1793 1, 5, 6, 7, 12, 18, 28, 38, 181, 199, 203, 204, 206, 207, 209, 213, 214, 218-9, 224n, 227n, 228n, 232, 315
Martyrs of 1820 51, 54
Martyrs' Monument
see under Calton Hill
Maxwell, Sir John (Rector, University of Glasgow) 90, 91
Mealmaker, George 249
Mexico 47, 60, 81, 215, 234
Millar, AH 133
Millar, John (1735-1801; Professor) 230
and Glasgow Enlightenment 120
and patronage 71, 73-4, 127
and student reformers 133-4, 136
and Whiggism 127-9
at Glasgow University 93, 105, 113-6, 120-2, 125-6, 133, 136
Muir and 73, 74, 92-3, 96, 105, 112, 113, 120, 122-3, 129, 136, 231
Millar, John (junior) 123, 149, 162
Milton, John (1608-74) 211, 331
Paradise Lost 181, 211
Mitchell, David Scott 226n
Mitchell, James (Glasgow police chief) 256
Mitchell Library, Glasgow 26, 101, 138n
Mitchell Library, Sydney 210
Moffat, WG (printer) 170, 197
Moir, JK (1893-1958) 210
Moncrieff, Henry (Sir) 304
Moniteur Universel, Le 237, 239, 240, 241, 243, 245, 247n
Monterey 215, 227n, 233
Montrose, 1st Duke of and 4th Marquess of (1682-1742; Chancellor of Glasgow University) 90, 100, 105
Montrose, 4th Duke of (1799-1874; Lord Lieutenant of Strilingshire, 1819) 256

Moor, James (c. 1712-79) (Professor of Greek) 96
Moore, John (Dr) 142
More, Thomas 192
Morning Post 213
Mossman bust of Muir 295
Muir, James (1738-1801, father of Thomas) 92, 103, 116, 149, 143, 155, 156, 159, 160, 275-6, 278, 281, 282, 284-5, 289, 290, 296
and Anderson affair 104-5, 109
death 280
marriage 280
see also entries for Cadder Case, Thomas Muir
Muir, Thomas (1765-99)
and Cadder Case
see separate entries for Cadder Case and Cadder Parish
and Democracy – see separate entry for democracy
and Edinburgh University 105, 130
and France/political activities in 219, 230, 232-3, 239-42, 243-5
and Friends of the People xv, 43, 48-9, 77, 78, 112, 123, 129, 175, 176, 178, 179, 204, 231, 250, 301 (see also separate entry for the Friends of the People)
and Ireland/United Irishmen 26, 48-49, 75, 77, 79, 81, 88n, 118, 180, 195, 204, 214, 215, 216, 231, 241, 244
and James Lapslie 63, 64, 67, 68, 85, 146, 306
and John Anderson 92, 96, 102, 104, 105-6, 109, 116, 129, 130, 131-3, 148
see also entry for Anderson
and John Millar 120, 123, 129, 133, 136, 148
and 'McGill Affair' 145, 146, 147, 148

Stuart, William 155, 157, 160
Surprize (ship) 204, 209, 213, 291
Suttie, James (Sir) 64, 86n
Sydney, Australia 17, 203, 209,
210, 215, 216, 218, 220
Sydney Cove 203, 206
Synod of Glasgow and Ayr 63, 69,
144

Tacitus
The Agricola (c. A.D. 98) 198
Tait, Peter 102, 106, 109
Talleyrand, Charles Maurice de
236, 239, 240, 244
Taylor, William (1744-1823)
(Reverend; Moderator, 1798)
99, 101, 102, 104, 105, 133
Tench, Watkin
*Narrative of the Expedition to
Botany Bay* (1789) 216
Thames 141, 204, 238
Thomas Muir Coffee Shop 20, 21,
26, 37
Thomas Muir Festival 18, 24
Thomas Muir Heritage Trail 18, 23
Thomas Muir Trial (staged) 28-9
Thomson, George 34, 48
Todd, Cornelius 156, 157, 158, 160
Tolpuddle Martyrs 203
Tone, Theobald Wolfe 243-4
Trade unions 5, 18, 251, 254, 255,
256, 267
Tradeston 262
Trajan Decius (c.201-251) 146
Treason Act (1351) 263
Tytler, Alexander Fraser (Lord
Woodhouselee) 127
Tytler, James 48, 177

Union of the parliaments (1707)
90, 93, 10, 135, 147, 162, 194,
195, 230, 231, 245
Unitarianism 144

United Scotsmen 231, 246n, 250,
251, 252, 254
trial 251
Universal suffrage xv, 24, 38, 42,
126, 219, 246n, 251, 255, 275,
312
University of Glasgow (Glasgow
College) 89-111 *passim*, 112-40
passim, 142, 147-8, 152-3, 163,
231
*see also separate entries for
John Anderson, John Millar,
Thomas Muir)
Centre for Robert Burns Studies
34
'Moderate' outlook 99
Presbyterian character 90
University of Leyden 90
University of Strathclyde 96, 300

Vancouver Island 47, 215
Volunteers 252, 260

Walker, Una (Provost, East
Dunbartonshire Council) 25,
30, 33, 36
Wallace, William 48, 55
Wantrup, Jonathan 216
Warden, John (1740-88) 303-4
Washington, George 215, 216, 222
Waterston, Davie 20, 26
Watling, Thomas 207
Watson, Alex 18
Watson, Jimmy 4, 18, 27, 37, 65, 66
Watson, John S L 18, 20, 21, 26,
36, 229n, 342
Watt, James 120
Watt, Robert 251
Weavers 1, 8, 118, 249, 250, 252,
254, 264, 265, 267
and radicalism 253-4
Weddel, Robert 195
White, Andrew 268

Lightning Source UK Ltd.
Milton Keynes UK
UKOW05f2353190517
301598UK00006B/420/P